Asylum and Conversion from Islam to Christianity in Europe

Also Available from Bloomsbury:

Evangelical Christian Responses to Islam, Richard McCallum
The Bloomsbury Handbook of Religion and Heritage in Contemporary Europe,
Edited by Todd Weir and Lieke Wijnia
Religious Diversity in Europe, Edited by Riho Altnurme,
Elena Arigita and Patrick Pasture

Asylum and Conversion from Islam to Christianity in Europe

Interdisciplinary Approaches

Edited by Lena Rose and Ebru Öztürk

BLOOMSBURY ACADEMIC
LONDON • NEW YORK • OXFORD • NEW DELHI • SYDNEY

BLOOMSBURY ACADEMIC
Bloomsbury Publishing Plc, 50 Bedford Square, London, WC1B 3DP, UK
Bloomsbury Publishing Inc, 1359 Broadway, New York, NY 10018, USA
Bloomsbury Publishing Ireland, 29 Earlsfort Terrace, Dublin 2, D02 AY28, Ireland

BLOOMSBURY, BLOOMSBURY ACADEMIC and the Diana logo are
trademarks of Bloomsbury Publishing Plc

First published in Great Britain 2024
Paperback edition published 2026

Copyright © Lena Rose, Ebru Öztürk and contributors, 2024

Lena Rose and Ebru Öztürk have asserted their right under the Copyright,
Designs and Patents Act, 1988, to be identified as Editors of this work.

For legal purposes the Acknowledgements on p. vi constitute an
extension of this copyright page.

Cover image © Getty Images

All rights reserved. No part of this publication may be: i) reproduced or transmitted in any form, electronic or mechanical, including photocopying, recording or by means of any information storage or retrieval system without prior permission in writing from the publishers; or ii) used or reproduced in any way for the training, development or operation of artificial intelligence (AI) technologies, including generative AI technologies. The rights holders expressly reserve this publication from the text and data mining exception as per Article 4(3) of the Digital Single Market Directive (EU) 2019/790.

Bloomsbury Publishing Plc does not have any control over, or responsibility for, any third-party websites referred to or in this book. All internet addresses given in this book were correct at the time of going to press. The author and publisher regret any inconvenience caused if addresses have changed or sites have ceased to exist, but can accept no responsibility for any such changes.

A catalogue record for this book is available from the British Library.

A catalog record for this book is available from the Library of Congress.

ISBN: HB: 978-1-3504-0787-9
       PB: 978-1-3504-0791-6
       ePDF: 978-1-3504-0788-6
       eBook: 978-1-3504-0789-3

Typeset by Integra Software Services Pvt. Ltd.

For product safety related questions contact productsafety@bloomsbury.com.

To find out more about our authors and books visit www.bloomsbury.com
and sign up for our newsletters.

Contents

Acknowledgements	vi
Notes on contributors	vii

1 Asylum and conversion to Christianity: An introduction *Lena Rose* 1
2 Definitions of religion as gatekeeping: A discursive approach to asylum and Christian conversion in Finland *Helmi Halonen* 19
3 Credibility assessment in asylum claims based on religious conversion in Germany: A qualitative sociological analysis *Anne K. Schlüter* 39
4 Making the convert speak: The production of truth and the 'apparatus of conversion' in Austria *Markus Elias Ramsauer and Ayşe Çağlar* 61
5 Material conversions: Exploring the materiality of asylum seekers' conversion narratives in Norway *Olav Børreson Fossdal* 81
6 Building belief: Navigating moral tensions through category work while assisting converted asylum seekers in Finland *Valtteri Vähä-Savo and Venla Koivuluhta* 103
7 Tales of transformation: Conversion narratives of unaccompanied refugee minors in the Church of Sweden *Jonathan J. Morgan* 125
8 Becoming Christian, remaining Iranian: The salience of national identity in Iranian evangelical exile churches *Benedikt Römer* 147
9 'She lacks a "male network" in her home country': Gendering the credibility assessment and the discursive space of intersectionality in migration courts in Sweden *Ebru Öztürk* 167

Afterword: In the eye of the inquisitor: The politics of religious asylum *Elizabeth Shakman Hurd* 189

Index 198

Acknowledgements

We are grateful to a number of people and institutions in supporting this book project: firstly, the idea for this book and the workshop it is based on emerged during a Leverhulme Trust Early Career Fellowship held by Dr Lena Rose at the Centre for Socio-Legal Studies at the University of Oxford. We thank the Leverhulme Trust, as well as the Centre for Socio-Legal Studies, for their generous support. Secondly, we are grateful to Dr Marietta van der Tol for spotting Lena Rose's and Ebru Öztürk's joint research interests and for introducing us to each other. Thirdly, we thank everyone who attended the workshop in June 2021 and provided comments, including some who for various reasons were not able to participate in this book project: a particular thanks goes to Nick Gill and Nicole Hoellerer, Jaeeun Kim, Ilona Blumgrund, Hilkka Lydén, Johanna Hiitola, Marie Juul Pettersen, Annelise Reid and Zsofia Windisch. A final thanks to the anonymous reviewers and the excellent team at Bloomsbury Academic!

Lena Rose and Ebru Öztürk

Notes on contributors

Ayşe Çağlar is University Professor in the Department of Social and Cultural Anthropology at the University of Vienna and a permanent fellow at the Institute for Human Sciences (IWM), Vienna. Çağlar has widely published on the processes and interfaces of migration, urban restructuring, dispossession, displacement, confined labour, extractive and cultural industries, as well as on the entanglements between states and transnationalization processes with a special focus on cities. In addition to her co-edited *Locating Migration: Rescaling Cities and Migrants* (2010) and co-authored *Migrants and City-Making: Dispossession, Displacement, and Urban Regeneration* (2018) volumes, she is the editor and the co-editor of *Urbaner Protest. Revolte in der neoliberalen Stadt* (2019) and the Special Issue on 'Displacements and Dispossessions', *Refugee Watch* Vol. 58 (2022) respectively.

Olav Børreson Fossdal is an MA student in religious studies at the Institute for Cultural Studies and Oriental Languages at the University of Oslo, Norway. His research interests are within material culture, religious conversions, vernacular religion and migration studies.

Helmi Halonen is a Doctoral Researcher at the University of Helsinki, Finland. Her research focuses on how religion is discursively defined in the asylum determination of religious persecution claims in Finland. The study examines the case files of claimants representing various religious and non-religious minorities, as well as those persecuted for transgression within their religious group.

Elizabeth Shakman Hurd is Professor of Religious Studies and Political Science at Northwestern University. She studies religion and politics globally. Hurd is the author of *The Politics of Secularism in International Relations* (2008) and *Beyond Religious Freedom: The New Global Politics of Religion* (2015), both published by Princeton, and co-editor of *At Home and Abroad: The Politics of American Religion* (2021), *Theologies of American Exceptionalism* (2020), *Politics of Religious Freedom* (2015) and *Comparative Secularisms in a Global Age* (2010).

Venla Koivuluhta is a doctoral researcher at the Institute of Arab and Islamic Studies, University of Exeter, UK. Her research interests include citizenship, materiality and affect. Her ethnographic PhD thesis is entitled 'Everyday (im)possibility: Women living without identity documents in Cairo'.

Jonathan J. Morgan is a Doctoral Candidate in Ethics at the Center for Theology and Religious Studies, Lund University, Sweden. His research focusses on individual and social change in the context of migration. He has carried out ethnographic work with unaccompanied refugee minors in Sweden and has worked in community development and relief in both South Africa and the Middle East. Among the articles he has published is 'Finding Belonging, Finding Agency: Unaccompanied Refugee Minors Converting to Christianity in the Church of Sweden' (2020).

Ebru Öztürk is Senior Lecturer in Sociology at Mid Sweden University, Sweden. Her research interest focus on the intersection between religious conversion, ontological security, populism and power dynamics concerning religion, ethnicity and gender. Her recent articles include 'Finding a new home through conversion: the ontological security of Iranians converting to Christianity in Sweden' (2022), 'A typology of right-wing populism in Europe: Intersections of gender, religion and secularity' (2023) (co-authored with A. Serdar and K. G. Nygren) and 'The veil as an object of right-wing populist politics: A comparative perspective of Turkey, Sweden, and France' (2022) (co-authored with A. Serdar and K. G. Nygren).

Markus Elias Ramsauer is a Doctoral Researcher in the Department of History at the University of Vienna. He has completed MA degrees in Cultural and Social Anthropology as well as in the History and Philosophy of Science at the University of Vienna. Ramsauer was a non-resident fellow at the Institute for Human Sciences (IWM) as part of the Europe-Asia Research Platform on Forced Migration. His MA thesis at the Department of Cultural and Social Anthropology was entitled 'Who creates what? The apparatus of conversion' (2021).

Benedikt Römer is a Postdoctoral Researcher and Lecturer at Bundeswehr University Munich, Germany. His main research area is the Study of Religions, with a focus on modern Iran and Turkey. His first book is forthcoming with the title *The Iranian Christian Diaspora: Religion and Nationhood in Exile*.

Lena Rose is a Lecturer and Researcher in Anthropology based at the University of Konstanz, Germany. Between 2019 and 2022 she led a research project on asylum processes based on conversion to Christianity and fear of religious persecution at the Centre for Socio-Legal Studies at the University of Oxford. Her work continues to explore the intersections between the Anthropology of Law, the Anthropology of the State and the Anthropology of Religion.

Anne K. Schlüter is a Doctoral Candidate of the Graduate School of Sociology at Münster University, Germany. Her research focuses on credibility assessment in asylum claims based on religious conversion in Germany. In addition to Sociology of Religion and Sociology of Law, her research interests lie in the field of sociological differentiation theory.

Valtteri Vähä-Savo is a post-doctoral researcher and a grant holder at Tampere University, Finland. His research interests include global and transnational sociology, the relationship between power and knowledge, science and technology studies, and sociology of associations. His recent publications include (with Johanna Hiitola) *Reassembling attachments: Place and well-being among Afghan refugees in a small rural town*.

1

Asylum and conversion to Christianity: An introduction

Lena Rose

Increased forced migrations to Europe since 2015 have resulted in an increased number of asylum claims based on conversion to Christianity and fear of religious persecution, typically by ex-Muslim asylum seekers. Conversion to Christianity is not the only ground for asylum based on fear of religious persecution;[1] however, it is the one that has attracted the most attention by the public, media and academics. The claimed belonging to Europe's historical religion and therefore cultural background has provoked reactions from concern, to suspicion, to interest, to delight (e.g. Rose 2021). This introductory chapter describes the legal background to, and state of research on, this phenomenon to help the reader navigate the chapters of this book. I situate our authors' contributions within their wider frameworks and argue that a cross-disciplinary and comparative approach to asylum and conversion is essential to understand the topic in its full impact and complexity. The chapters in this book focus on five European countries (Austria, Finland, Germany, Norway and Sweden), determined by the respective research focus of our authors. The fact that interest and research funding exist in relation to this topic in these jurisdictions suggests a clear geographical focus concerning the themes of asylum and conversion: this will be discussed later in the chapter as well.

It is difficult to provide exact numbers of those who have sought asylum based on fear of religious persecution due to conversion to Christianity in Europe, let alone provide reliable data on the success rate of such claims. Migration offices generally do not publish statistics on specific asylum grounds or their outcomes. However, we can make some general comments regarding typical asylum seekers with this background in the jurisdictions covered in this book. As all authors agree and case law demonstrates, many applicants who have based their asylum claims on conversion to Christianity over the last years come from Iran or Afghanistan. The easiest way to arrive at numerical estimates therefore is to look at applications by Afghan and Iranian applications for asylum in general. Of course, conversion is not the sole reason for seeking protection by these nationals (and applicants from other countries of origin rely on this reason in their applications, too), but as my own research in the German context revealed, about 80 per cent of Iranian applications for asylum in 2020–1 in Germany were based on this reason. Anecdotally speaking, asylum grounds of Afghan applicants are more varied, though still include a relatively high number of conversion-based claims. Thus, for example, between 2015 and 2021, Germany received almost 227,500 applications from Afghans and over 60,000 applications from Iranians (BPB 2023). In contrast, Norway received over 8,000 applications from Afghan nationals and about 1,850 from Iranian applicants in the same time frame (Fossdal, this volume). Estimates from Finland (Halonen, this volume) suggest that around 1,500 out of 50,000 new asylum applications since 2016 have based their claims on conversion. In Germany, the success rate of Iranian claims for asylum has been around 20 per cent in the first instance. Since conversion-based claims make up a high number of these claims, we can arrive at rough estimates regarding success in Germany. Other countries such as the UK have a much higher success rate for Iranian applicants for asylum though, so there is limited insight in looking at these numbers: they must be contextualized within the wider political, societal, geopolitical and religious backgrounds of each jurisdiction, which this volume seeks to achieve. Application rates must be seen in the context of each country's general demography (Germany and Sweden being much more numerous than, say Finland) and specific asylum policies. While application rates based on conversion are particularly high among some nationalities, and these nationalities might try to seek asylum in specific asylum-receiving countries due to varying acceptance rates of conversion-related claims, their general percentage among existing asylum applications is relatively low. However, as several of the authors in this volume highlight, the phenomenon itself seems to have caught the attention of the asylum authorities in the countries in which they conducted research regardless of numbers. Asylum offices have published guidance and discussion pieces specifically on this asylum ground, for example, in Germany and Finland (e.g. see Gräfin Praschma (2019) on Germany and Halonen for such publications on Finland, this volume). The topic is thus of heightened interest among decision-makers and society at large.

How can a person seek refugee protection in Europe? The European asylum system

To situate the discussions of the following chapters, I want to offer a brief overview of how conversion to Christianity and fear of religious persecution can form a ground for asylum in Europe in the first place. How can one seek asylum in European nation-states on the basis of conversion to Christianity? The overarching framework is given by the Refugee Convention of 1951, to which European nation-states are signatories. Its Article 1 stipulates that those who have a 'well-founded fear of being persecuted for reasons of race, religion, nationality, membership of a particular social group or political opinion' and cannot be protected in their country of nationality or return to it due to such fear can apply for protection as refugees. This provision explicitly includes those who have changed their religion or prefer no religious belonging at all (UNHCR 2019). Persecution for religious reasons generally includes discrimination of individuals or religious communities based on their religious belonging, such as limitations to public and private worship or prohibition of religious education.

Almost all asylum applications are processed according to the national legal systems of the EU's member states in which asylum applicants arrive or are distributed to. An exception to the majority of cases discussed in this volume is Norway, which as a non-EU member is not bound by EU directives or the EU tribunal: the specifics of Norway's handling of asylum cases will be discussed in Chapter 5. For all other jurisdictions under consideration here, the Common European Asylum System (CEAS) provides some shared guidelines for how asylum is managed. CEAS has been developed since 1999 in three main stages. The first stage between 1999 and 2005 saw the adoption of six legislative instruments which set minimum standards for the EU's asylum system. They included the Eurodac Regulation, the Temporary Protection Directive, the Reception of Asylum Seekers Directive, the Dublin Regulation, the Asylum Procedures Directive and the Qualification Directive. Of these, the Qualification Directive (Directive 2011/95/EU) is perhaps the most interesting in view of the chapters in this book, given that it provides guidelines for member states regarding who may qualify for asylum and how. Specifically, it envisages international protection in two forms: refugee status, or subsidiary protection for those who do not fully qualify as refugees but may still face severe persecution on return to their countries of origin. The Qualification Directive stipulates the rights of asylum seekers and seeks to harmonize eligibility criteria for asylum seekers.

During the second stage between 2008 and 2013, several of the EU's asylum laws were revised to achieve more cohesive asylum policies across member states and ensure sufficient levels of protection. During this phase, the European Asylum Support Office (EASO) was also established to help member states cooperate and implement EU asylum legislation. In response to much greater numbers of asylum seekers since 2015, further revisions to CEAS have been proposed or adopted during an ongoing third stage. The most central ones for the topic at hand are the replacement of the Qualification Directive with a Qualification Regulation, in the hope to achieve more binding rules for protection rates and processes, and the replacement of EASO with a more wide-ranging EU Asylum Agency (EUAA) which should offer operational support in more unified decision-making.

The EU also provides judicial remedies in the Court of Justice of the European Union (CJEU) and the European Court of Human Rights (ECtHR), which interpret EU asylum law at the highest level and provide clarification on points of dispute. They are generally rarely invoked yet have litigated three important cases on asylum and conversion to Christianity over the last years: *F.G. v. Sweden* (ECtHR, 23 March 2016), *A.A. v. Switzerland* (ECtHR, 5 November 2019) and most recently *M.A.M. v. Switzerland* (ECtHR, 26 April 2022). These judgements concerned applicants from Iran, Afghanistan and Pakistan, respectively. They clarified issues related to the assessment of risk of persecution following a conversion (*F.G. v. Sweden*, *M.A.M. v. Switzerland*) and the tension between public and private faith in seeking to avoid persecution (*A.A. v. Switzerland*; see also Rose and Thebault [2018]). These issues continue to provide difficulty for asylum authorities, as the next part will demonstrate.

While EU guidelines aim to harmonize the member states' asylum systems, they have been translated differently in the different jurisdictions discussed in this book. For example, in some countries, such as Norway, panels decide over asylum appeals, whereas in other countries, such as Germany, decisions are usually taken by individual decision-makers and judges. In complex asylum claims such as those based on fear of religious persecution, decisions by panels may create greater scope for fairness (see Schlüter, this volume). Despite differences in each member states' asylum system, Craig and Zwaan (2019: 45) highlight three correlations between them. Firstly, they point to the correlation between human rights standards which all EU member states have adapted in their national legislation, including their translation of CEAS measures. Secondly, all member states share a concern for security and sovereignty, which impacts their foundational approach to questions of asylum. This has often been argued to be at the roots of restrictive asylum policies or ways of interpreting EU guidance that leads to a lower number of positive refugee decisions (Jubany 2011; Kobelinsky 2019). Thirdly, they also all share an asylum system that is held accountable by numerous actors within and beyond legal authorities. They advocate for those seeking protection particularly when states potentially foreground concerns over security, as some of our contributions highlight (e.g. Vähä-Savo and Koivuluhta, Morgan, this volume).

The complexity of asylum applications based on conversion to Christianity

Religion-based asylum grounds are some of the most complex asylum applications to examine. The reasons for this are manifold: they raise questions about the definition of religion, appropriate means of credibility assessments of religious converts, the assessment and definition of 'persecution', and the interaction between fear of religious persecution with other asylum grounds. Already before the rise in interest in the topic of religious conversion-based asylum claims in the context of the increase in migrant arrivals in Europe since 2015, scholars have highlighted that 'religion' is not conclusively defined in national and international law (Good 2009; Gunn 2003; Musalo 2004). While this has been similar for other human rights protected by the refugee convention[2] it makes the work of decision-makers in religion-based asylum claims exceptionally difficult. Guidance documents have offered attempts at delimiting the term 'religion', though these are not binding. For example, Article 10(1)(b) of the Qualification Directive QD clarifies:

> the concept of religion shall, in particular, include the holding of theistic, non-theistic and atheistic beliefs, the participation in, or abstention from, formal worship in private or in public, either alone or in community with others, other religious acts or expressions of view, or forms of personal or communal conduct based on or mandated by any religious belief.

The guidelines of the UNHCR (2004: 3) specifically on religion-based asylum claims similarly stipulate that 'religion' can mean a set of beliefs, as well as an identity, or 'way of life' or practices.

The difficulty with defining what 'religion', or 'Christianity', is extends into the difficulty of defining what counts as a genuine conversion, particularly in asylum claims based on sur place conversions, i.e. conversions that took place in the country of asylum. As in other asylum processes, decision-makers rely on asylum seekers' own narratives to establish whether they are eligible for international protection (Kagan 2003). They must assess whether their claimed religious identity is genuine and will lead to severe persecution in case of return. In some cases, decision-makers may be assisted by pastors or congregation members; however, this assistance brings its own challenges, as Vähä-Savo and Koivuluhta, Schlüter, as well as Ramsauer and Çağlar, in this volume, discuss. In fact, a recent decision by the Federal Constitutional Court in Germany from April 2020 explicitly states that state authorities are in themselves able to assess the credibility of a conversion to Christianity, without the assistance or input by pastors (BVerfG 2020). These definitional challenges and reliance on the judgement of decision-makers themselves in questions regarding what 'religion', 'Christianity' and 'conversion' are have led to vastly differing acceptance rates of asylum seeking converts to Christianity. As Ramsauer and Çağlar (p. 66) summarize succinctly, 'asylum applications based on conversion often operate outside the secular state's "comfort zone" of objective facts'. Decision-makers have to rely on asylum seekers' narratives and submitted evidence, such as documents, certificates and pictures, to try and 'look into the heart' of the converted appellant and assess the genuineness of their conversion. Schlüter (this volume) argues therefore for a stronger involvement of church personnel in supporting asylum seekers' narratives.

While guidance for decision-makers about how to assess the credibility of a conversion exist, such as an article written by the High Court judges Berlit, Doerig and Storey (2015) or, more recently, the EUAA handbook (European Union Agency for Asylum 2022), these are not binding. Most of these have been aimed at unifying the decision-making process and more comparable results across nation-states. What kinds of questions are asked of applicants, and what kinds of answers are accepted, show clearly the understanding of religion and Christianity that emerges in asylum processes based on conversion. The EUAA guidance suggests to case workers and asylum judges, for example, to explore topics like knowledge of religion, past persecution on the basis of religion and expected future persecution. Over the years of asylum adjudications based on conversion, most jurisdictions have moved from assessing the credibility of a conversion through knowledge questions about the new faith to a combination of testing knowledge and the sincerity of a religious change. Thus, the EUAA guidance specifically cautions that 'the personal interview should never amount to a "quiz" on religion' (European Union Agency for Asylum 2022: 46), and should always be adjusted to the educational level of the applicant. However, as Tuan Samahon (2000) demonstrated, focusing on sincerity does not solve the difficulty of assessing whether a person has truly converted or not. Skilled impersonators could just as easily fool a decision-maker about sincere faith – describing personal meaning of a new religion, for example – as someone who can learn knowledge by heart. Halonen (this volume) demonstrates how asylum officers in the Finnish context effectively produce definitions of religion through credibility assessments. Çağlar and Ramsauer (this volume) theorize the conundrum through the language of 'apparatus' which helps to visualize the different performances and outcomes of the credibility assessment process. It is also important to highlight that there can be significant limitations to achieving clear communication in courts. Issues with correct, nuanced and unbiased translation of the asylum applicants' (and decision-makers') utterances, cross-cultural misunderstandings, incomplete adaption to European legal settings and traumatic experiences of asylum seekers that inhibit memory or communication can all negatively impact the context of asylum hearings (Dahlvik 2019; Gibb and Good 2014; Herlihy and Turner 2007, 2015; Rose and Given-Wilson 2021). This is recognized in guidance documents; however, overcoming these challenges remains very difficult.

Besides the unclear definition of 'religion' and challenges of credibility assessments of converts to Christianity, a third difficulty is to define what counts as religious persecution – or what level of persecution is severe enough to warrant protection as refugee. What can reasonably be expected of a convert to Christianity in order to prevent persecution? Case law (e.g. *F.G. v. Sweden*) has made it very clear that converts – or anyone else fearing religious persecution due to their religious identity for that matter – must not be asked to hide their faith from state or society. Furthermore, particularly in cases in which a person converted after leaving their country of origin, asylum claimants do not have had to face persecution in the past to qualify for refugee protection. It is sufficient to make clear in an asylum process that a prospective return to the country of origin with a changed religious identity could lead to significant persecution. What level of persecution must be expected in case a claimant returned to their country of origin is usually determined by decision-makers by using 'Country of Origin Information'. However, how this information is generated and interpreted varies across jurisdictions (Feneberg et al. 2022). How country of origin information is generated, for example, depends on whether nation-states have direct diplomatic representations in the countries in question, or whether they mainly rely on reports by human rights organizations (Sonntag 2018). This difference also may affect how information is interpreted in light of geopolitical relationships. How country of origin information is presented to decision-makers – for example, as raw data or in annotated, already interpreted form – may also further affect how it is used in asylum adjudications (Aarsheim 2019). Generally speaking, sincerity is still key in country of origin information applications: converted asylum applicants must show that their new religious identity is sufficiently important to them that they would want to live out their faith on return. A recent country guidance case of the Upper Tribunal in the UK in 2020 (PS [Christianity – risk] Iran CG [2020] UKUT 00046 [IAC]) took a more conservative assessment, however. Here, the court found that even if an asylum seeker had not genuinely converted, they might still face persecution if they had previously come to the negative attention of the Iranian state authorities. Due to the relative independence of asylum agencies in different jurisdictions, this case law does not always influence decision-making in other jurisdictions, though.

A last challenge to highlight in this general introduction is that it is sometimes difficult to ascertain how conversion to Christianity and fear of religious persecution might interact with other asylum grounds, which might not always be mentioned by the asylum seekers themselves (e.g. *M.A.M.* v. *Switzerland*). This intersection of asylum grounds could concern gender identities or fear of persecution due to political persecution. As Römer's chapter in this volume demonstrates, for example, for Iranians, conversion to Christianity has deep national and political connotations as well. To reject a dominant religion is therefore not always just a spiritual question, but can be interpreted as political resistance by state authorities and thus also lead to persecution (Enstedt, Larsson, and Mantsinen 2020). These intersections, however, are not always clearly understood by decision-makers.

Why cross-disciplinary and comparative research on asylum and conversion matters

All of these challenges will be addressed in detail in this book. We hope to show in this way that both a cross-disciplinary and a comparative approach to the topic can help both scholars and practitioners to greatly improve their understanding of the asylum/conversion to Christianity complex. Scholars who conducted research on the topic of asylum and conversion are situated in different research fields, pursue different research questions and foreground different actors. Two general research directions can be identified to date. Firstly, given the administrative and legal contexts which determine asylum processes, most research in the asylum-conversion interface to date has foregrounded the analysis of legal documents, as well as asylum hearings and decisions, and guidance documents (Aarsheim 2019; Ganschow 2021; Hoellerer and Gill 2021; Kagan 2010; Karras 2018; McDonald 2016; Pernak 2018; Rose and Given-Wilson 2021; Rose and Thebault 2018; Samahon 2000; Sonntag 2018). Secondly, another prominent angle in this field has explored why asylum seekers convert in the first place, and how they interact with missionaries, churches and religious activists in the process (Akcapar 2006; Carlson 2021; Fine 2017; Hartikainen 2019; Kéri and Sleiman 2017; Kim 2022; Krannich 2020; Leman 2007; Öztürk 2022; Römer 2022; Stadlbauer 2019; Stene 2016; Theißen and Boysen 2020; Wheeler 2021). Researchers' funding opportunities and temporal capacity, as well as methodological and disciplinary restrictions, have meant that while some researchers in these two large sub-fields engage with each other's work, certainly not all do. However, these angles are deeply connected and benefit from sustained cross-referencing to develop meaningful research questions.

In this volume, we advocate for a cross-disciplinary, if not interdisciplinary, and comparative approach to the complex topic of conversion and asylum. Firstly, the topic of asylum and conversion can most beneficially be explored in a cross- and interdisciplinary way because it connects legal challenges with questions in the study of religion and wider sociological, political and anthropological concerns. To ignore one part of this field will lead to limited or distorted answers. For example, as Römer rightly points out in this volume, much existing research on credibility assessments of religious converts has been disconnected from socio-political and socio-cultural contexts in their respective countries of origin. His own work, for example, points to the significance of national identity-formation through Iranian conversions to evangelical Christianity. Very little research exists on the Christianity of those who base their asylum claims on conversion beyond immediate questions for the asylum procedure, or beyond seeing conversion as a strategy to gain refugee protection (e.g. Akcapar 2006). Here, I again point to Römer's and Morgan's chapters this volume, and also Kathryn Spellman-Poots' (2004) slightly more dated work, all of whom take the Christianity of asylum applicants (as well as those who have a different immigration status) seriously. Both Morgan and Römer specifically set out to complicate the received understanding of asylum seekers' conversions in the framework of 'asylum capital' (see Morgan, this volume). Another important cross-disciplinary connection is to explore how legal decisions come to exist. Schlüter's chapter in this volume argues for just such an approach. She uses theories connecting 'law as system' and 'law as practice' and social translation theory to show how the outcomes of challenging hearings are distilled into asylum decisions which often look similar on the surface. She analyses the decisions asylum judges make in this process.

In reverse, many of those working in area or religious studies discuss asylum seeker conversions purely from a point of view of religious and theological interest. Some are openly Christian themselves, leading to a somewhat triumphant, or at least religiously slanted, tone (e.g. Bradley 2014; Miller 2015; Miller and Johnstone 2015). They might miss how the conversion of asylum seekers has been deeply shaped by the necessity to become legible by a Western asylum-granting state. There might also be less understanding of the exclusionary political dynamics and the geopolitical and historical structures that have shaped the contemporary asylum system as a whole, as critical thinkers such as Lucy Mayblin (2017) and Elizabeth Shakman Hurd (2021) have shown. Hurd demonstrated in a powerful political theological intervention how asylum and religious conversion maintain American – and perhaps Western in general – exceptionalism. Cross-fertilization between such perspectives is specifically essential if research aims to inform decision-makers, or those supporting claimants with religion-based applications and asylum seekers themselves, as many of those concerned with the topic hope to do.

Furthermore, from an academic perspective, the topic of asylum and conversion is a highly productive site for theorizing for different research fields. It naturally contributes to research on asylum and migration in Europe as a whole. In this volume, Jonathan Morgan contributes to the vast literature on unaccompanied refugee minors by adding a conversion perspective to this work. Anne Schlüter's research on asylum and conversion makes a strong contribution to translation processes in administrative processes. Markus Ramsauer and Ayse Çağlar develop Foucault's notion of apparatus to discuss how different actors make the voice of asylum seekers audible in hearings – while they discuss this in relation to conversion, this theorization could be made useful for other asylum grounds, too. The topic of conversion and asylum further contributes, for example, to the study of religious conversion, such as Olav Fossdal's chapter in this volume. Fossdal argues that by attending to material religion – i.e. the objects converts relate to during the conversion process – we can nuance understandings of dominant sociological models of religious conversion, which have been concerned predominantly with mental processes. A further area the conversion and asylum field can contribute to is that of area studies. For example, Benedikt Römer's chapter in this volume and his work as a whole is the first sustained qualitative study of Iranian Protestantism among Iranian exiles as such. It has been sparked by the attention Iranian converts have received in media and political discourse. His theorization of Iranian Christianity as contributing to the making of Iranian national identities within and outside of the Iranian diaspora will be of interest to Middle Eastern and Persian studies at large. Asylum and conversion can further serve as site of theorizing for approaches in the discursive study of religion (Helmi Halonen, this volume) if one approaches the phenomenon with an interest regarding what kind of Christianity emerges through credibility assessments of converted asylum seekers. This can further contribute to debates in the law and religion interface, such as questions about 'law's religion' (cf. Berger 2018) or the construction of the concept of 'sincerely held belief' (cf. McCrary 2022). It is of course unrealistic to expect each scholar to become an expert in each of these different research fields. However, the more interdisciplinary curiosity exists, the more nuanced the resulting analyses will be. Our authors might variously identify with the sub-fields outlined above yet have entered into a conversation that hopefully will cross-fertilize future research, both their own and that of scholars who engage with this volume. I encourage researchers on the topic to sincerely engage with research from other angles and disciplines and to let it inform their questions and research designs in moving this field forward.

Secondly, asylum and conversion must be studied in a comparative framework for it to really render meaningful insights. The contributions in this book are based on a workshop held in June 2021, to which we invited anyone who worked on the topic from any disciplinary perspective and in any jurisdiction. While a small number of scholars on the topic were not able to participate, and a small number of those who participated were not able to contribute to this volume, we do believe that we collated submissions by the majority of those whose main research focus was the study of conversion and asylum at the time. While some of us had met beforehand, it was exciting for us to discuss the details of our research with other experts in the field. Given the relative novelty of the research field, however, we also noticed that many of our presentations covered similar ground in setting out the rationale for our respective research. Each of us was used to talking to non-specialist colleagues which involves lengthy descriptions of the parameters of why this research matters, how the asylum process works, as well as the uniqueness of religious-conversion claims. This leaves limited space to dig deeper into the specificities of our individual questions, approaches and analyses. Observing this dynamic was useful on the one hand because it confirmed the challenges raised by asylum and conversion identified above in our different settings. On the other hand, we noticed that the absence of authoritative frameworks setting out the terms of engagement with the topic also limited our focus on the specific questions this issue raises in our specific national or transnational settings. I hope that my contribution on asylum adjudications based on religious conversion to the *Handbook on Religion and Contemporary Migration* (Rose 2023), as well as this chapter, might offer such groundwork for future researchers to refer to and build on, allowing them to spend more time on the specificities of their own research contexts.

The discussions within the workshop and our subsequent working together on this volume have demonstrated that our comparative approach generates awareness of similarities and differences between disciplines and jurisdictions. These differences and similarities both matter profoundly. Working out the specificities of our contexts can help us to nuance the research outcomes and work towards conclusions that are attentive to the specific political–theological settlements and church–state relations of each asylum-receiving host state. Thus, those working in contexts with a strong national church (e.g. Finland, Austria) found that decision-makers have less understanding for converts shaped by the Christianity of free churches (cf. Hoellerer and Gill 2021). How the church–state relationship is organized in each context seems to further shape how decision-makers relate to the support and witness of church personnel, too. While we of course cannot claim full coverage of all research on asylum and conversion, to our knowledge there is no such research being conducted in the context of the UK, France, Italy, Greece or other prominent asylum-receiving countries,[3] which explains our focus on the chosen selection of mainly Western and Northern European countries in this book. The fact that the countries we were able to include in this book have attracted more research on the question of asylum and conversion (and some, such as Germany and Sweden, are represented by several authors) than other prominent asylum-receiving countries also merits attention. In part, this could be led back to the topic having hit more of a nerve with wider society, and thus seeming like a more prominent societal issue that needs to be investigated. It could also be due to asylum seekers' networks and choices – many Iranians, for example, choose Germany or Sweden as asylum destination, but when their asylum processes fail might move on to another country like the UK (which has been made easier since Brexit severed the UK from EU asylum frameworks). A further reason could be the relative acceptance rates of asylum seekers who base their claim on conversion. The UK, as mentioned above, for example, has a much higher acceptance rate for Iranian asylum seekers (who often base their claims on conversion) than other European countries, which means there are less legal challenges to accommodate such claims, hence perhaps less public dissatisfaction by church representatives (cf. Rose 2021). An as yet unexplored area of research in this context would be to trace how asylum seeker's religious identities change as they encounter different state churches and different church–state settlements. We hope that this volume might provide a significant foray into this cross-disciplinary and comparative approach to asylum and conversion to Christianity, and be of value to students, academics, and practitioners alike.

Notes

1 Fear of religious persecution also affects some religious minorities, converts to other religions or those who reject a dominant religious belonging altogether. Sometimes fear of religious persecution is intertwined with fear of political persecution and other reasons.
2 Stefan Vogler (2021), for example, traces how the categories of sexuality have emerged through case law.
3 This was accurate at the time of writing. We of course welcome any such research and look forward to engaging with scholars focusing on asylum and conversion in these and other jurisdictions in Europe and beyond.

Bibliography

Aarsheim, Helge (2019). 'Sincere and Reflected? Localizing the Model Convert in Religion Based Asylum Claims in Norway and Canada'. *Faith in the System? Religion in the (Danish) Asylum System*, Marie Juul Petersen and Steffen Jensen (eds.), 83–96. Aalborg: Aalborg University Press.

Akcapar, Sebnem Koser (2006). 'Conversion as a Migration Strategy in a Transit Country: Iranian Shiites Becoming Christians in Turkey'. *International Migration Review*, 40 (4): 817–53. https://doi.org/10.1111/j.1747-7379.2006.00045.x.

Berger, Benjamin L. (2018). *Law's Religion: Religious Difference and the Claims of Constitutionalism*. Toronto: University of Toronto Press.

Berlit, Uwe, Harald Doerig and Hugo Storey (2015). 'Credibility Assessment in Claims Based on Persecution for Reasons of Religious Conversion and Homosexuality: A Practitioners Approach'. *International Journal of Refugee Law*, 27 (4): 649–66. https://doi.org/10.1093/ijrl/eev053.

BPB (2023). 'Demografie von Asylsuchenden in Deutschland. Infografiken Zu Alter, Geschlecht Und Herkunft von Asylsuchenden'. 10 March 2023. https://www.bpb.de/themen/migration-integration/zahlen-zu-asyl/265710/demografie-von-asylsuchenden-in-deutschland/.

Bradley, Mark (2014). *Too Many to Jail: The Story of Iran's New Christians*. Oxford: Monarch Books.

BVerfG (2020). Beschluss der 1. Kammer des Zweiten Senats vom 03. April 2020, 2 BvR 1838.

Carlson, Darren (2021). *Christianity and Conversion among Migrants: Moving Faith and Faith Movement in a Transit Area*. Leiden: Brill.

Craig, Sarah and Karin Zwaan (2019). 'Legal Overview'. *Asylum Determination in Europe: Ethnographic Perspectives*, Nick Gill and Anthony Good (eds.), 27–49. Basingstoke: Springer.

Dahlvik, Julia (2019). 'Why Handling Power Responsibly Matters: The Active Interpreter through the Sociological Lens'. *Asylum Determination in Europe: Ethnographic Perspectives*, Nick Gill and Anthony Good (eds.), 132–54. Basingstoke: Springer.

Enstedt, Daniel, Göran Larsson and Teemu T. Mantsinen (eds.) (2020). *Handbook of Leaving Religion*. Leiden: Brill.

European Union Agency for Asylum (2022). 'Interviewing Applicants with Religion-Based Asylum Claims'.

Feneberg, Valentin, Nick Gill, Nicole Hoellerer and Laura Scheinert (2022). 'It's Not What You Know, It's How You Use It: The Application of Country of Origin Information in Judicial Refugee Status Determination Decisions – A Case Study of Germany'. *International Journal of Refugee Law*, 34 (2): 241–67.

Fine, Shoshana (2017). 'Holy Crossings'. *Borders and Mobility in Turkey*, Shoshana Fine (ed.), 105–24. Basel: Springer. https://doi.org/10.1007/978-3-319-70120-2_6.

Ganschow, Constantin Alexander (2021). *Die Konversion im Asylverfahren*. Potsdam: Universitätsverlag Potsdam.

Gibb, Robert and Anthony Good (2014). 'Interpretation, Translation and Intercultural Communication in Refugee Status Determination Procedures in the UK and France'. *Language and Intercultural Communication*, 14 (3): 385–99. https://doi.org/10.1080/14708477.2014.918314.

Good, Anthony (2009). 'Persecution for Reasons of Religion under the 1951 Refugee Convention'. *Permutations of Order: Religion and Law as Contested Sovereignties*, Thomas G. Kirsch and Bertram Turner (eds.), 27–48. Farnham; Burlington, VT: Ashgate.

Gräfin Praschma, Ursula (2019). 'Konvertierte Iraner und Iranerinnen im Asylverfahren'. *Entscheiderbrief – Informations-Schnelldienst 10/2019*, 2–4. BAMF. https://www.bamf.de/SharedDocs/Anlagen/DE/Behoerde/Informationszentrum/Entscheiderbrief/2019/entscheiderbrief-10-2019.pdf?__blob=publicationFile&v=4.

Gunn, Thomas Jeremy (2003). 'The Complexity of Religion and the Definition of "Religion" in International Law'. *Harvard Human Rights Journal*, 16: 189–215.

Hartikainen, Elina (2019). 'Evaluating Faith after Conversion'. *Approaching Religion*, 9 (1–2): 41–56. https://doi.org/10.30664/ar.80355.
Herlihy, Jane and Stuart W. Turner (2007). 'Asylum Claims and Memory of Trauma: Sharing Our Knowledge'. *British Journal of Psychiatry*, 191 (1): 3–4. https://doi.org/10.1192/bjp.bp.106.034439.
Herlihy, Jane and Stuart W. Turner (2015). 'Untested Assumptions: Psychological Research and Credibility Assessment in Legal Decision-Making'. *European Journal of Psychotraumatology*, 6: 1–5. https://doi.org/10.3402/ejpt.v6.27380.
Hoellerer, Nicole and Nick Gill (2021). 'Assembly-Line Baptism: Judicial Discussions of "Free Churches" in German and Austrian Asylum Hearings'. *Journal of Legal Anthropology*, 5 (2): 1–29.
Hurd, Elizabeth Shakman (2021). 'Freedom, Salvation, Redemption: Theologies of Political Asylum'. *Migration and Society: Advances in Research*, 4 (1): 110–23.
Jubany, Olga (2011). 'Constructing Truths in a Culture of Disbelief: Understanding Asylum Screening from Within'. *International Sociology*, 26 (1): 74–94. https://doi.org/10.1177/0268580910380978.
Kagan, Michael (2003). 'Is Truth in the Eye of the Beholder? Objective Credibility Assessment in Refugee Status Determination'. *Georgetown Immigration Law Journal*, 17 (3): 367–415.
Kagan, Michael (2010). 'Refugee Credibility Assessment and the "Religious Imposter" Problem: A Case Study of Eritrean Pentecostal Claims in Egypt'. *Vanderbilt Journal of Transnational Law*, 43 (5): 1180–230.
Karras, Benjamin (2018). *Missbrauch des Flüchtlingsrechts? Subjektive Nachfluchtgründe am Beispiel der religiösen Konversion?* Tübingen: Mohr Siebeck.
Kéri, Szabolcs and Christina Sleiman (2017). 'Religious Conversion to Christianity in Muslim Refugees in Europe'. *Archive for the Psychology of Religion*, 39 (3): 283–94. https://doi.org/10.1163/15736121-12341344.
Kim, Jaeeun (2022). 'Between Sacred Gift and Profane Exchange: Identity Craft and Relational Work in Asylum Claims-Making on Religious Grounds'. *Theory and Society*, 51 (2): 303–33. https://doi.org/10.1007/s11186-021-09468-8.
Kobelinsky, Carolina (2019). 'The "Inner Belief" of French Asylum Judges'. *Asylum Determination in Europe: Ethnographic Perspectives*, Nick Gill and Anthony Good (eds.), 53–68. Basingstoke: Springer.
Krannich, Conrad (2020). *Recht Macht Religion. Eine Untersuchung über Taufe und Asylverfahren*. Göttingen: V&R unipress.
Leman, Johan (2007). 'A "Lucan Effect" in the Commitment of Iranian Converts in Transit. The Case of the Pentecostal Iranian Enclave in Istanbul'. *Revue Des Mondes Musulmans et de La Méditerranée*, 120 (119–20): 101–14. https://doi.org/10.4000/remmm.4323.
Mayblin, Lucy (2017). *Asylum after Empire: Colonial Legacies in the Politics of Asylum Seeking*. Kilombo (Series). London: Rowman & Littlefield International.
McCrary, Charles (2022). *Sincerely Held: American Secularism and Its Believers*. Chicago: University of Chicago Press.

McDonald, Douglas (2016). 'Escaping the Lions: Religious Conversion and Refugee Law'. *Australian Journal of Human Rights*, 22 (1): 135–58. https://doi.org/10.1080/1323-238X.2016.11882161.

Miller, Duane Alexander (2015). 'Power, Personalities and Politics: The Growth of Iranian Christianity since 1979'. *Mission Studies*, 32 (1): 66–86. https://doi.org/10.1163/15733831-12341380.

Miller, Duane Alexander and Patrick Johnstone (2015). 'Believers in Christ from a Muslim Background: A Global Census'. *Interdisciplinary Journal of Research on Religion*, 11: n/a–n/a.

Musalo, Karen (2004). 'Claims for Protection Based on Religion or Belief'. *International Journal of Refugee Law*, 16 (2): 165–226. https://doi.org/10.1093/ijrl/16.2.165.

Öztürk, Ebru (2022). 'Finding a New Home through Conversion: The Ontological Security of Iranians Converting to Christianity in Sweden'. *Religion, State & Society: The Keston Journal*, 50 (2): 224–39.

Pernak, Benjamin (2018). *Richter als »Religionswächter«? Zur Gerichtlichen Überprüfbarkeit eines Glaubenswechsels*. Berlin: Duncker & Humblot.

Römer, Benedikt (2022). 'Elam in Exile. Religion and Nation among Iranian Christians in the Diaspora'. Doctoral Thesis. Bayreuth: University of Bayreuth.

Rose, Lena (2021). 'Churches Aren't Helping Asylum Seekers "Game" the Immigration System'. *The Conversation*, December. https://theconversation.com/churches-arent-helping-asylum-seekers-game-the-immigration-system-172361.

Rose, Lena (2023). 'Asylum Adjudications on the Basis of Religious Conversion'. *Handbook on Religion and Contemporary Migration*, Fiddian-Qasmiyeh and Anna Rowlands Rowper (eds.). Oxford: Oxford University Press.

Rose, Lena and Deborah Thebault (2018). 'Case Comment: What Kind of Christianity? A. vs. Switzerland'. *Oxford Journal for Law and Religion*, 7 (3): 543–50.

Rose, Lena and Zoe Given-Wilson (2021). '"What Is Truth?" Negotiating Christian Convert Asylum Seekers' Credibility'. *The Annals of the American Academy of Political and Social Science*, 697 (1): 221–35. https://doi.org/10.1177/00027162211059454.

Samahon, Tuan (2000). 'The Religion Clauses and Political Asylum: Religious Persecution Claims and the Religious Membership-Conversion Imposter Problem'. *The Georgetown Law Journal*, 88 (7): 2211–38.

Sonntag, Holger (2018). 'Testing Religion: Adjudicating Claims for Religious Freedom Brought by Iranians in the U.S. and Germany'. *Case Western Reserve Law Review*, 68 (3): 975–1057.

Spellman-Poots, Kathryn (2004). *Religion and Nation: Iranian Local and Transnational Networks in Britain*. New York: Berghahn Books.

Stadlbauer, Susanne (2019). 'Between Secrecy and Transparency: Conversions to Protestantism among Iranian Refugees in Germany'. *Entangled Religions*, 8. https://doi.org/10.13154/er.8.2019.8322.

Stene, Nora (2016). 'Christian Missionaries and Asylum Seekers: A Case Study from Norway'. *Nordic Journal of Human Rights*, 34 (3): 203–21. https://doi.org/10.1080/18918131.2016.1227589.

Theißen, Henning and Knud Boysen (2020). *Integration und Konversion. Taufen Muslimischer Flüchtlinge als Herausforderung für Kirchen Und Gesellschaft*, Amsterdam: Brill.

UNHCR (2004). 'Guidelines for International Protection: Religion-Based Refugee Claims under Article 1A(2) of the 1951 Convention and/or the 1967 Protocol Relating to the Status of Refugees'.

UNHCR (2019). 'Handbook on Procedures and Criteria for Determining Refugee Status and Guidelines on International Protection'. February: 1–278.

Vogler, Stefan (2021). *Sorting Sexualities Expertise and the Politics of Legal Classification*. Chicago: Chicago University Press.

Wheeler, William (2021). 'Conversion through Destitution: Religion, Law, and Doubt in the UK Asylum System'. *Refugees and Religion. Ethnographic Studies of Global Trajectories*, Peter van der Veer and Birgit Meyer (eds.), 239–56. London: Bloomsbury Academic.

2

Definitions of religion as gatekeeping: A discursive approach to asylum and Christian conversion in Finland

Helmi Halonen

Introduction

The Immigration Service concludes that your interest in and conversion to Christianity is more about things related to universal human values and good manners and does not accept as fact that Christianity in your case would be a permanent, personal, spiritual conviction.

(Decision 70[1])

The extract above is from the negative asylum decision of a young man from a Muslim background who converted to Christianity after arriving in Finland as an asylum seeker. His asylum decision highlights how by defining religion in a particular way – as a 'personal spiritual conviction' rather than 'universal human values' and 'good manners' – the immigration officer who wrote it delegitimates his claim for international protection.

Asylum determination is one of the very few contexts where Finnish civil servants have to attempt to define 'religion'. Finland, like much of Northern Europe, is a majority Protestant country where religion is generally considered to be a private matter. Though church membership has been in steady decline over recent decades, 68.7 per cent of the Finnish population still belonged to the Evangelical Lutheran Church of Finland in 2019. The Lutheran Church shares its official status as a national church with the Finnish Orthodox Church, the membership of which was 1.1 per cent in 2019 (Sohlberg and Ketola 2021: 50). Other significant religious minorities include Muslims, Jehovah's Witnesses and Jews as well as Catholics, Pentecostals and other Christian groups (Sohlberg and Ketola 2021: 52). Levels of religious observance are fairly low even among members of the Lutheran Church; according to survey data from 2019, only 8 per cent of church members attend services once a month or more. The same survey showed that only half the total population pray, and 21 per cent read the Bible more than once a year, a noticeably low percentage given that over two thirds of the population were members of the Lutheran Church at the time (Hytönen et al. 2021: 154; Salomäki 2021: 101; Sohlberg and Ketola 2021: 50).

Asylum seekers converting to Christianity after their arrival in Finland is not a new phenomenon. However, since 2016, it has happened on an unprecedented scale. The Finnish Immigration Service does not have statistics on asylum seekers' religious affiliations or grounds for asylum, though an Immigration Service expert estimated the total number of conversion-related asylum applications since 2016 to be around 1,500 (personal communication, 9 February 2020). While this is not a large proportion of the more than 50,000 asylum applications in the same period, the phenomenon was seen as significant enough to merit a response from the Immigration Service. They issued a press release on the subject in June 2017, advising that conversion to Christianity does not automatically guarantee refugee status in Finland (Finnish Immigration Service 2017).

This rise in the number of asylum seekers converting to Christianity followed a dramatic rise in the number of asylum seekers in general. In 2015, Finland registered over 32,000 asylum applications – a small number compared to many other EU countries at the time, but still a more than tenfold increase from the year before. A clear majority – over 20,000 – of these applications came from Iraqi citizens, with Afghanistan, Somalia and Syria as the next most common nationalities (Finnish Immigration Service 2015, 2023). The Finnish government at the time had a restrictive approach to immigration and asylum already before this significant increase in asylum applications. Unsurprisingly, the political response was focused on limiting access to asylum and removing so-called 'pull factors'. To this end, the government introduced several changes to immigration policy, including restricting asylum seekers' access to free legal aid, shortening appeal periods and tightening regulations around family reunification.

As an EU member state, Finland's asylum and immigration law follows EU directives and legislation. If an application for international protection is accepted for assessment in Finland under the Dublin regulation, the asylum determination process starts with an interview conducted by the Immigration Service. The decision to grant or refuse asylum is made based on this interview and any additional evidence presented by the claimant, usually by the same immigration officer who conducted the interview. The claimant has a right to appeal this initial decision first to the Administrative Court and, if necessary, to the Supreme Administrative Court.

The data for this chapter consists of asylum interview transcripts and corresponding decisions made by the Finnish Immigration Service between 2016 and 2021.[2] The chapter is based on a broader study that applies ideas from Discursive Study of Religion (DSR) to look at how immigration officers define religion in the process of assessing cases of religious asylum in Finland. A majority of this data concerns other religious groups, as Christian converts are not the only – or the largest – group seeking asylum on religious grounds in Finland.[3]

Out of the total data set of 250 case files, 50 are related to Christian conversion after departure from the country of origin, either in Finland or en route. The data set also contains cases where the claimant converted to Christianity already in the country of origin, but for the purposes of this chapter, I will focus on claimants who converted after departure. This is because the Finnish Immigration Service – as well as the UNHCR guidelines on assessing religious persecution claims – has different standards for assessing so-called *sur place* claims where the grounds for asylum emerged after the claimant's departure from the country of origin (UNHCR 2004). These claimants are often subjected to a more detailed questioning about the authenticity of their religious affiliation than claimants who were already under threat for having converted in their country of origin and left because of it. Out of these fifty cases, thirty-eight concern Iraqi citizens, nine Afghans, one Iranian and two from other nationalities. These cases concern conversion to either the Lutheran Church or minority Protestant Churches, notably Pentecostalism. No Orthodox or Catholic converts were featured.

Teemu Taira describes DSR as a field where '"religion" is understood as a floating signifier in the sense that it is historically, socially and culturally constructed and negotiated in various situations' (Taira 2022: 20). Thus, rather than studying 'religion' as an existing phenomenon or using it as an analytical concept, DSR scholars focus on what *counts as* religion in a particular context and, in more critical approaches, what is being *done* by framing religion in a particular way (see e.g. Hjelm 2014). From this perspective, in assessing the authenticity of a claimant's religious affiliation or the seriousness of religious persecution, immigration officers are effectively making decisions about what counts as religion – in other words, producing definitions of religion.

Critical discourse analysis is based on the premise that text production is a series of choices; Sara Mills, for example, argues that 'every text which has been produced could have been produced differently' (Mills 1995: 144; see also Fairclough 1992: 185). This means that in addition to looking at *what* is said, we should pay attention to what is implied or presupposed by phrasing it in a particular way, as well as what is omitted or sidelined. Discourse analysts have long held that language has the power to influence and actively (de-)construct social relations. Johanna Niemi-Kiesiläinen et al. (2006) point out that this is especially true of legal discourse since it is backed and legitimized by state power and has a direct impact on legal decision-making (Niemi-Kiesiläinen et al. 2006: 37). Similarly, T. Jeremy Gunn (2003: 195) argues that '[l]egal definitions do not simply describe the phenomenon of religion, they establish rules for regulating social and legal relations among people who themselves may have sharply different attitudes about what religion is and which manifestations of it are entitled to protection'.

Asylum determination is a residence permit process, and while individuals have a legal right to *seek* refugee status, it is within the receiving state's discretion to grant or refuse it (see Falk 2017). The asylum system can thus be conceptualized as an instrument of border control by which sovereign states get to choose who they admit within their borders and who they leave out. To the extent that this process involves assessing religion, defining religion in a particular way also becomes an instrument of this kind of gatekeeping.

For Lucy Mayblin (2017), the increasingly exclusionary asylum policies in Western Europe in recent decades, as well as the asylum system itself, have their roots in colonial ideologies of *differential humanity*. In this hierarchy, the humanity and thus the access to human rights that are accorded to an individual or group are determined by their 'modernity' – that is, their presumed closeness to an imagined benchmark of the rational, secular, Western European male (Mayblin 2017). This applies also in cases where modern Western European notions of 'religion' are used to assess the authenticity of the beliefs or affiliations of others.

Legal uses of 'religion' have tangible and serious consequences; in asylum determination, they can literally be a matter of life and death. Categorizing particular people, practices or groups as 'religious' legitimizes their claims for international protection, while defining religion in a way that leaves them out will serve to delegitimize those claims. My research thus asks what counts as religion in the Finnish asylum determination process, how these implicit definitions of religion are negotiated in asylum interviews and how they influence asylum decision-making.

Asylum determination through a discursive lens

Religion is rarely defined explicitly in asylum interview transcripts or decisions. Therefore, in order to study definitions of religion that are constructed in the process of determining religious asylum, we need to look at implicit ways in which immigration officers frame the concept. *Presuppositions* are implicit truth claims that are embedded in what is actually said (see e.g. Fairclough 1992: 120–1). For example, when a claimant is asked *why* they chose to convert to a different religion, the question already presupposes that religious conversion is a choice. Norman Fairclough also notes that contesting these presuppositions is particularly difficult in an interview setting where doing so will look like trying to dodge the question (Fairclough 1992).

The asylum interview is already a complicated interactive context. Marco Jacquemet (2009) has argued that the claimant and the interviewer have not only different institutional roles in the asylum interview, but often also different interests, priorities and expectations. These conflicting interests are not on an equal footing, however; on the contrary, the interviewer is in charge of the interaction, and also has the power to determine how the claimant's story is presented in the transcript (Jacquemet 2009: 533). In Fairclough's (1992: 152–8) terms, the interviewer employs *interactional control*; they typically govern turn-taking and the topics that are covered in the interview.

Importantly, the asylum narrative that makes it into the decision document is a product of this complex and asymmetrical social interaction rather than an accurate account of what the claimant actually thinks, feels or remembers (see e.g. Doornbos 2005; Maryns 2006; Skov Danstrøm and Whyte 2019). In Finnish asylum determination, the interview transcript is typed up by the immigration officer during the interview and should cover everything that is talked about, whether the interviewer considers it relevant or not. The decision document, meanwhile, only refers to those passages in the interview that have impacted the decision. Looking at the transcript and the decision document side by side reveals not only how the interviewer has interpreted and assessed those utterances from the claimant that have made it to the decision, but also which parts of the interview were not considered relevant for the decision and thus get left out of the asylum narrative completely.

John E. Richardson has called analysing discursive practice 'analysis of texts as they are embedded within, and relate to, social conditions of production and consumption' (Richardson 2007: 39). Looking at how the narrative changes between transcript and decision exposes underlying values and ideological structures in a way that studying one type of document in isolation cannot do. In the following sections, I will first outline the discourses of religion employed by Finnish immigration officers through presupposition, and then look at how alternative understandings are negotiated or omitted in creating the asylum narrative.

Private, active, apolitical: The official discourse

Immigration officers define 'religion', 'Christianity' or 'conversion' most directly through the questions they ask in order to determine the sincerity of the claimant's religious affiliation. I have identified two main discursive threads in these questions that I call *internal* and *active religion*. By internal religion, I mean discourses that treat religion as an individual cognitive or emotional matter, a question of knowing, believing or decision-making (see also Schlüter; Caglar and Ramsauer, this volume). Active religion, meanwhile, stands for a discourse of religion as something a claimant is expected to actively practice, often in particular conventional ways, such as praying, studying the Bible or attending church. Whether personal or communal, all of these forms of religious thought, belief and practice are contained within a separate religious sphere, and have little connection to political, societal or ethical issues.

This is unsurprising given that the concept of 'religion' already presupposes a distinction between 'religion' and the rest of life. DSR scholars have argued that the idea of 'religion' as a distinct category is a product of the particular context where it was coined – that is, Protestant Western Europe. Brent Nongbri, for example, calls religion 'anything that sufficiently resembles modern Protestant Christianity' (Nongbri 2015: 18). This Protestant model of understanding religion tends to focus heavily on religion as a personal belief system or, as Nongbri puts it, 'apolitical paths to individual salvation' (Nongbri 2015: 8). More troublingly, treating this kind of 'religion' as a universal human characteristic thus sets the Protestant European as a benchmark of humanity against which others can be judged (Arnal and McCutcheon 2013; Dubuisson 2003; see also Römer, this volume).

This becomes a concern particularly when 'religion' is used as a legal category. For Winnifred Sullivan:

> Religion – 'true' religion some would say – on this modern protestant reading, came to be understood as being private, voluntary, individual, textual, and believed. Public, coercive, communal, oral, and enacted religion, on the other

hand, was seen to be 'false'. The second kind of religion, iconically represented historically in the United States, for the most part by the Roman Catholic Church (and by Islam today), was, and perhaps still is, the religion of most of the world.

(Sullivan 2005: 17)

Sullivan thus argues that the 'religion' that is referred to in Western – and also international – law is not, in fact, what 'most of the world' mean by the term. Similarly, Peter W. Edge and Graham Harvey (2000) have argued that this understanding of religion as a matter of private, personal faith becomes problematic when it is naturalized in law and applied to people who conceptualize 'religion' in a different way (Edge and Harvey 2000: 7).

Previous studies have shown the problematic nature of using knowledge questions in determining the authenticity of a claimant's religious conversion in asylum hearings (see e.g. Kagan 2010; Meral and Gray 2016; Musalo 2004). The very use of knowledge questions, such as 'Why do Christians celebrate Christmas?' or 'Can you tell me something about the disciples of Jesus?', sets learning or studying as a prerequisite for a genuine conversion. A similar presupposition can be found also outside of these direct knowledge questions. The interview questions below likewise presuppose that religion is – at least to some degree – about knowledge:

> Q: You said you liked the Christian community and how people behaved and treated each other. Was there something in the teachings of Christianity and what it teaches that caught your interest?
>
> (Interview 45)
>
> Q: Describe to me how you converted even though you don't know much about Christianity.
>
> (Interview 209)

In the first extract, the interviewer implies that community is not a sufficient motive for conversion. In pressing the claimant to talk about the 'teachings of Christianity' instead, the interviewer is essentially placing 'teaching' ahead of 'community' – and assuming that how Christians 'treat each other' has nothing to do with 'the teachings of Christianity'. Similarly, the second interviewer directly questions the claimant's conversion because the claimant has admitted to not knowing much about Christianity – thus implying that conversion requires knowledge.

UNHCR guidelines on the assessment of religious persecution claims caution against relying on this approach and instead recommend 'allowing the claimant to explain the personal significance of the religion to him or her' (UNHCR 2004: 8). Prioritizing 'personal significance' over testing religious knowledge should work in the claimant's favour, but in practice this presents a different set of problems. In order to assess the 'personal significance' of religion in a claimant's life, Finnish immigration officers typically ask the claimant to reflect on their 'thoughts and feelings' related to conversion, or describe what Christianity or another related concept 'means to them personally':

> 94. I am still not clear on how your final internal conversion to Christianity happened on the level of thoughts, so to speak. Describe the process for me in more detail, the thoughts and feelings that you went through in your mind when you decided to convert to Christianity.
>
> (Interview 185)

> 45. What meaning does Jesus have for you?
> A: He is the lord, isn't he.
> 46. What does Jesus mean to you?
> A: He is my lord. But what how does he mean to me?
> 47. Does Jesus have some meaning for you?
> A: You mean Lord Jesus.
> 48. Yes.
> A: I don't know.
>
> (Interview 66)

Asking claimants to describe their 'thoughts and feelings' 'in detail' or explain what Jesus Christ 'means' to them is essentially a request for them to reflect on themselves in a complex and abstract way. When the second claimant finally replies 'I don't know', this is less about him not knowing what Jesus means to him than about him not understanding what he is being asked to do. More than the sincerity of a claimant's faith, these questions end up measuring their eloquence and capacity for abstract self-reflection.

Discourses of internal religion also include approaches where conversion is treated as a rational choice, as in the extracts below:

> 30. There are numerous religions in the world and within them numerous denominations, how did you come to the conclusion that Christianity and within it the Lutheran church would be the right way?
> A: Many things happened to me and I studied a lot about Christianity and the Lutheran church. [...] Of course I know that there are many different

religions in the world. This is a kind of matter of the soul and I felt in my soul that Christianity is the right faith and I don't differentiate between different churches. The Lutheran church felt right in my soul, and I don't differentiate between different branches of Christianity anyway. […]

(Interview 122)

50. When did your interest in Christianity begin? When did you start thinking that it might be a good option for you?
A: It is not an option, it is within me.

(Interview 114)

The interviewers in these extracts presuppose not only that conversion is a decision-making process, but also that this process involves comparison between 'numerous religions' or choosing from among different 'options' (see also Morgan and Schlüter, this volume). In contrast, neither of these claimants describes their conversion or their 'choice' of church as a rational decision. Rather, both refer to feeling and experience ('it felt right in my soul'; 'it is within me'). In a similar vein, claimants are also typically asked to explain why they 'chose' a particular congregation over others. Out of the entire data set of fifty conversion cases, only two claimants gave reasons related to the 'teaching' of different churches; for the majority, the rationale for choosing the church they attend had to do with location and accessibility, services in a particular language, or friends who attend the same church.

This focus on Christian conversion as a matter of individual faith, knowledge or choice is well documented in other recent and emerging research (see e.g. Blumgrund 2023; Hurd 2021; Rose and Given-Wilson 2021). In the Finnish data, however, it appears that this kind of 'internal' conversion alone is not enough. Genuine converts are also expected to actively practice their new religion in particular conventional ways, such as prayer, Bible study and attending church.

34. How do you practice religion alone, without the presence of the congregation?
A: This relationship in Christianity is slightly different from other religions. In other religions you have to do practices or rituals, but in Christianity it's open. You can be in contact with the Lord whenever and talk to him. And another thing is that I obey God's orders.
35. Tell me more concretely how you practice religion alone. Like do you pray, read the Bible and so on.

(Interview 68)

Here, the claimant answers a question about religious practice with a discussion of Christian principles regarding the relationship between believer and God – in other words, with exactly the kind of abstract reflection on personal faith and Christian doctrine that is demanded by interview questions that focus on subjective experience and knowledge (see also Römer, this volume). The interviewer, however, wants a list of 'concrete' actions he performs to practice his religion ('pray, read the Bible and so on').

> 57. Have you had any particular duties or responsibilities in the congregation?
> A: No.
> 58. Is it common in your congregation for members to participate in some way?
> A: Who do you mean?
> 59. Ordinary members who don't work for the church, ordinary people.
> A: They participate in prayer.
> 60. Is there a reason why you haven't participated?
> A: When you asked if I participate, I do, but I don't have any responsibilities.
> 61. I apologize, I did ask poorly. I meant is there a reason why you don't have responsibilities?
> A: I haven't noticed any such responsibilities in church.
>
> (Interview 16)

In addition to personal faith and practice, sincere converts are also expected to actively contribute to their congregations. In fact, the extract above shows how the focus is on the individual even when talking about community. Note how the claimant is not asked to describe his congregation or the community he belongs to, but to reflect on his individual role within it. The interviewer's questions about 'participating' imply that the claimant needs a specific reason for not having any special role or 'responsibilities' in his congregation.

These examples demonstrate the perceived importance of practising the new religion and contributing to a religious community. However, this by no means contradicts the understanding of religion as an essentially private, individual matter. On the contrary, all of these forms of religious practice and community life happen strictly within a separate 'religious' sphere, and have little to do with wider concerns. Even when claimants are asked about the influence of Christianity on their own lives, they are expected to discuss the impact of the conversion only on the private lives of themselves or their families, not on how they relate to the society around them.

Religion as morality: An alternative discourse

Though the official framing of 'religion', 'Christianity' or 'conversion' comes from the interviewer, claimants can – and do – negotiate and contest these understandings. One of the principal sites where this happens is around discussions of what I call *moral religion*, a discourse of religion as a way of living in the world and relating to other people. This type of religion-talk is largely absent from the questions interviewers ask, but noticeably common in the responses produced by claimants regardless of their origin or religious affiliation. A moral discourse of religion can involve anything from broader questions of good and evil to everyday choices related to things like sexual morals, substance use, or how to raise one's children. Fundamentally, when claimants employ a moral discourse of religion they talk about religion as a way of relating to society and, in Saba Mahmood's terms, 'organizing daily conduct' (Mahmood 2005:44). This is close to what Sullivan refers to as the 'religion of most of the world' – 'public, coercive, communal, oral, and enacted' (Sullivan 2005:17).

124. How is religion present in your life outside of this congregation?
    A: Yes it is present through love for other people. I'm not pessimistic. I just feel happy and I believe this is natural, too. Maybe it can't be put into words.
125. How do you practice your religion outside church events?
    A: I practice good manners, I'm honest, my life is filled with good deeds.
126. Have you concretely changed something in your behavior or everyday life after converting to Christianity?
    A: When I've been going to church, […] and when I heard about this, […] I quit drinking alcohol.
127. Has something else changed?
    A: There has been nothing important like that that I would have stopped doing, but generally my life has changed. I hope God forgives me for having been late on my way.
128. How has the everyday life of your family changed since […]?
    A: Of course the family have stayed together as a family and I feel like we have become closer since our conversion. In […] there was bickering, but since Christianity we don't have it any more and tolerate each other better.
129. Do you do something related to Christianity as a family outside church events?
    A: What do you mean exactly?

> 130. How do you practice Christianity aside from attending church events?
> A: Like I told you in the beginning, we practice good deeds and good manners. [...]
>
> (Interview 233)

> [...], you have been asked how going to church and taking up Christianity have impacted you and your life. You have replied that you have calmed down, feel love for other people and have become happier. [...] You have also mentioned love, honesty and forgiveness as features you associate with Christianity that are important to you. You have said you practice Christianity outside the congregation by following good manners, being honest and doing good deeds. You have also quit drinking alcohol. When asked specifically about it, you have also said you pray and read the bible. [...] Based on your coherent narratives, the Immigration Service accepts as fact that your family life has calmed down as a result of attending church and taking part in congregation activities. However, your narratives do not demonstrate how Christianity specifically has impacted said change.
>
> (Decision 233)

Here, the interviewer is trying to ask questions about religious practice in the sense described above – as specific, concrete 'religious' actions that the claimant is expected to take. For the claimant, in contrast, 'practising religion' and the changes brought about by conversion are primarily about how he behaves in his everyday life and relates to the people around himself ('love for other people'; 'good manners', 'good deeds', 'honest', 'quit drinking', 'tolerate each other').

Fairclough (1992: 140) has pointed out that doctor–patient interactions, as well as other social interactions that take place within a formal institutional framework, often follow a pattern where the doctor asks a question, the patient answers, and the doctor either does not accept the answer and asks the question again, or accepts it and moves on to the next topic. The same is true of asylum interviews. Note how the interviewer in the extract above asks essentially the same question over and over again in slightly different ways, signalling that the claimant's answers are not correct or sufficient.

The corresponding extract from the claimant's negative asylum decision gives an indication of how his narrative has been interpreted by the immigration officer. In the decision, the immigration officer considers praying and reading the Bible as important features of Christianity, and the fact that the claimant only brings these up 'when asked specifically' damages his credibility. Meanwhile the association of Christianity with moral concerns such as love, honesty and forgiveness is framed as only the claimant's subjective experience ('features you associate with Christianity'). Thus, because the things that motivated the claimant's conversion are not considered to be about 'Christianity specifically', the claimant's conversion is seen as insincere.

The same discrepancy between interviewer and claimant understandings of 'religion' becomes even more visible in the extract below:

> 46. What is your personal relationship with God like?
> A: God willing, this is a good relationship.
> 47. How do you maintain this relationship with your God?
> A: Like this society maintains it.
> 48. Please clarify this for me.
> A: What does God want from you, what does God want from people? That they don't do wrong, don't steal and don't have extra-marital sex. That they want good things for others.
>
> (Interview 213)

> You said that you maintain your relationship with God by doing God's will, meaning not doing wrong, not stealing and not having extra-marital sex. You do not maintain your relationship with God in other ways.
>
> (Decision 213)

In this example, by a 'personal relationship with God', this interviewer is presumably referring to a subjective and spiritual connection with the divine maintained through private, individual prayer. For the claimant, however, 'maintaining a relationship with God' means doing 'what God wants from people' – that is, living in a moral way. In his answers, religion cannot be separated from society and how we live in it; on the contrary, he essentially speaks about religion as a way of relating to society.

The asylum claim was later refused. In the grounds for the refusal, the above exchange is referenced with 'you do not maintain your relationship with God in other ways' – implying that maintaining a relationship with God should be about more than just leading a moral life. The interview extract does not, in fact, conclusively show whether or not this claimant feels and upholds the kind of personal connection with God that the interviewer expects from a sincere convert. All it does show is that for him, the concept of a 'relationship with God' means something different.

The connection between religion and society is likewise contested in the following extract from another interview and decision:

47. Explain in more detail what you said about not having boundaries, or that the boundaries you have are easy.

A: Christianity is easy and the boundaries are easy. For example, talking about Finland, everyone in Finland follows the commandments, I don't know how many of them are believers, it's enough that I look at how people live, how they respect nature and nature conservation in Finland and it's this Christianity, it's the right life. It's a clear life.

48. Could you still explain how you think these things are related to Christianity?

A: If we look at commandments, the same commandments are in the holy book. When especially we look at commandments. They repeat the life of Jesus. He explained to us everything about how a person should live.

[…]

75. What kind of feelings did you have when you became aware that you, that Christianity has started to appeal to you?

A: I have become open. I had many problems because of Islam. I was changed, a different person, I believe in myself. And I love people more. I stopped hating other religions, many nice things. Many things have changed, I don't remember all of them.

76. What do you mean, you became open?

A: Socially open, I accept other points of view, I'm not as radical. I accept everyone else. My way of thinking has become broad.

77. Can you still explain how you think these things are related to Christianity specifically and not for example this surrounding Finnish society?

A: It's the teaching of the holy book when you obey the commandments, how a person lives with others, how to love your enemies. I see all these things in the society in Finland. I don't believe everyone follows Christianity. I had taken up these habits. I've settled down in this country. And I'm a Christian.

(Interview 185)

Likewise, your narrative of how Christianity has changed you is very general and lacks specificity. […] When asked about your feelings after conversion to Christianity, you have said vaguely that you have become more open and that you believe in yourself more and love people more, in addition to which there are many things but you do not remember all of them. When asked what you mean by becoming more open, you have replied very shortly that you have become socially open and accept other people and criticism (transcript sections 75—76).

(Decision 185)

The interviewer in this extract is focused on separating Christianity and 'Finnish society' from each other. They don't see the claimant's talk of openness and tolerance, or following commandments and respecting nature, as related to religion. This is not just about the interviewer classifying these things as societal rather than religious, but also about 'society' and 'religion' being treated as separate and mutually exclusive categories to begin with. For the claimant, meanwhile, Christianity and Finnish society are interlinked and inseparable. He talks about religion as 'how a person should live', which in turn cannot be separated from societal issues or relations with others.

When this passage is referred to in the decision, these more societal concerns are missing completely – meaning that they were not considered relevant for the decision that was made. Simultaneously, they become erased from the claimant's official asylum narrative; based on the decision document alone, this conversation never even happened. Instead, the decision focuses on instances where the claimant talks about his increased openness and belief in himself. Without the more societal frame of the transcript, this, too, becomes contextualized as primarily a private individual matter rather than a societal or political one.

Charles McCrary (2022) argues that legal actors see religion as 'essentially not political, which is to say, not really arising from the real world' (McCrary 2022: 197). Therefore, religiosity that rejects a distinction between the 'religious' and the 'secular' – or religion and the rest of life – is not as readily recognized as real or authentic religion (McCrary 2022: 223–4). Immigration officers' reluctance to recognize a moral discourse of religion as 'really' religious can thus be traced back to secular ideas about the place of 'religion' in society.

Conclusion

Discrepancies between claimant and interviewer understandings of 'religion' matter because the claimant risks not appearing credible if their narrative falls outside of what the interviewer considers relevant, or contradicts the interviewer's presupposition of what 'religion' means. McCrary points out that religion is 'often most legible to agents of the secular state when expressed in familiar idioms and with particular affective comportments' (McCrary 2022: 174). In the case of Christian converts in the Finnish asylum determination system, this entails adhering to locally prevalent ideas of what 'religion' or 'Christianity' looks like: private, voluntary, apolitical and actively believed and practised in particular conventional ways.

Importantly, there is a gulf between this idea of authentic Christianity on the one hand and how Christianity is actually practised by the majority of Finnish locals on the other. Converts to the Lutheran Church, for example, are expected to pray, study the Bible and be active members in their congregations – all things that a majority of Finnish Lutherans do not regularly do (Hytönen et al. 2021; Salomäki 2021; Sohlberg and Ketola 2021). This ties to what Hurd calls 'religion as choice' (Hurd 2021: 113) – an assumption that if an individual has 'chosen' to belong to a particular religious group, they can be expected to actively believe in and practice it. Thus, standards of active and committed 'religiosity' can apply to foreign converts even if a majority of local church members do not meet those standards.

The definition of religion employed by Finnish immigration officers thus disadvantages two types of claimants. First, claimants who have difficulty with abstract self-reflection or learning and expressing factual information will find it difficult to 'prove' the sincerity or authenticity of their conversion. This disproportionately affects claimants without a higher education background, those with limited time and resources (such as parents with young children) and those who are struggling with their mental health. Secondly, this framing of religion also excludes claimants who understand religion as a moral or societal issue rather than just a set of beliefs and practices that remain within a clearly defined 'religious' sphere. This is a serious concern, as a majority of asylum claimants in the data – regardless of affiliation or background – discuss religion in this way at least to some degree.

It is important to note, however, that this type of analysis can only look at effect, not intent. The system privileges claimants who cut close to the imagined ideal of the 'modern', secular, Western European male (see Mayblin 2017), not necessarily because of a deliberate decision to do so, but because of the impossibility of objectively assessing the authenticity of religious conversion. It is unlikely that the Finnish Immigration Service or individual immigration officers purposefully define religion in a particular way in order to exclude particular individuals or groups. Rather, the results of this study show how a system where civil servants have to rely on their subjective understandings of an abstract concept such as 'religion' privileges claimants who share those understandings. Fundamentally, securing asylum on the grounds of religious conversion appears to require the ability to discuss conversion in terms that are familiar to the host society.

Notes

1. All extracts from the data are translated from Finnish by the author. Where possible, the translation reflects the structure, tone and occasional grammatical errors in the original documents. Any recognizable details have been removed and replaced by *[…]*.
2. The data set for the broader study this chapter is based on covers the period between 2014 and 2021 to include cases from before, during and after the so-called Refugee Crisis of 2015. The earliest decisions concerning Christian conversion in the data are from 2016, and the latest from 2021.
3. In the data set for this study, more than half of the cases concern Sunni Muslims from Iraq – the largest group seeking asylum on religious grounds in Finland according to the Immigration Service (personal communication, 9 February 2020). Other significant groups include Shi'a Muslims from Afghanistan, Jehovah's Witnesses from the Russian Federation, and atheist or non-religious claimants from Muslim-majority countries. The data also includes individual claimants from other religious minority groups (including established Christian minorities) as well as numerous cases where the claimant does not belong to a religious minority at all but is persecuted for perceived transgressions within their religious group.

Bibliography

Arnal, William E. and Russell T. McCutcheon, (2013). *The Sacred Is the Profane: The Political Nature of 'Religion'*. New York: Oxford University Press.

Blumgrund, Ilona (2023). 'Credibility Assessment of Religious Conversion in the Asylum Process: A Theological Analysis'. *Studia Theologica – Nordic Journal of Theology*, 77 (2): 125–52.

Doornbos, Nienke (2005). 'On Being Heard in Asylum Cases: Evidentiary Assessment through Asylum Interviews'. *Proof, Evidentiary Assessment and Credibility in Asylum Procedures*, Gregor Noll (ed.), 103–22. Leiden: Martinus Nijhoff.

Dubuisson, Daniel (2003). *The Western Construction of Religion: Myths, Knowledge, and Ideology*. Baltimore: Johns Hopkins University Press.

Edge, Peter W. and Graham Harvey (2000). 'Introduction'. *Law and Religion in Contemporary Society: Communities, Individualism and the State*, Peter W. Edge and Graham Harvey (eds.), 1–14. Aldershot: Ashgate.

Fairclough, Norman (1992). *Discourse and Social Change*. Cambridge: Polity Press.

Falk, Richard (2017). 'Refugees, Migrants and World Order'. *The Refugee Crisis and Religion: Secularism, Security and Hospitality in Question*, Luca Mavelli and Erin K. Wilson (eds.), 23–34. Lanham: Rowman and Littlefield.

Finnish Immigration Service (2015). *Turvapaikanhakijat 1.1.-31.12.2014.* https://migri.fi/documents/5202425/6161882/2014±Turvapaikanhakijat±%28fi%29.

Finnish Immigration Service (2017). *Miten kristityksi kääntyminen vaikuttaa turvapaikkapäätökseen?* Press release, published 12 June 2017. https://migri.fi/artikkeli/-/asset_publisher/miten-kristinuskoon-kaantyminen-vaikuttaa-turvapaikkapaatokseen-.

Finnish Immigration Service (2023). *Statistics.* https://tilastot.migri.fi/#decisions.

Gunn, T. Jeremy (2003). 'The Complexity of Religion and the Definition of "Religion" in International Law'. *Harvard Human Rights Journal*, 16: 189–215.

Hjelm, Titus (2014). 'Religion, Discourse and Power: A Contribution towards a Critical Sociology of Religion'. *Critical Sociology*, 40 (6): 855–72.

Hurd, Elizabeth Shakman (2021). 'Freedom, Salvation, Redemption: Theologies of Political Asylum'. *Migration and Society: Advances in Research*, 4: 110–23.

Hytönen, Maarit, Kimmo Ketola and Veli-Matti Salminen (2021). 'Everyday Religious Practice'. *Religion in Daily Life and Celebration: The Evangelical Lutheran Church of Finland, 2016-2019,* Hanna Salomäki, Maarit Hytönen, Kimmo Ketola, Veli-Matti Salminen and Jussi Sohlberg (eds.), 149–83. Vaasa: Church Research Institute Publications.

Jacquemet, Marco (2009). 'Transcribing Refugees: The Entextualization of Asylum Seekers' Hearings in a Transidiomatic Environment'. *Text & Talk*, 29 (5): 525–46.

Kagan, Michael (2010). 'Refugee Credibility Assessment and the "Religious Imposter" Problem: A Case Study of Eritrean Pentecostal Claims in Egypt'. *Vanderbilt Journal of Transnational Law*, 43 (5): 1179–233.

Mahmood, Saba (2005). *Politics of Piety: The Islamic Revival and the Feminist Subject.* Princeton: Princeton University Press.

Maryns, Katrijn (2006). *The Asylum Speaker: Language in the Belgian Asylum Procedure.* Manchester & Northampton: St. Jerome Publishing.

Mayblin, Lucy (2017). *Asylum after Empire: Colonial Legacies in the Politics of Asylum Seeking.* London: Roman & Littlefield.

McCrary, Charles (2022). *Sincerely Held: American Secularism and Its Believers.* Chicago: University of Chicago Press.

Meral, Ziya and Amanda Gray (2016). *Fleeing Persecution: Asylum Claims in the UK on Religious Freedom Grounds.* London: Asylum Advocacy Group and All-Parliamentary Group for International Freedom of Religion and Belief.

Mills, Sara (1995). *Feminist Stylistics.* London: Routledge.

Musalo, Karen (2004). 'Claims for Protection Based on Religion or Belief: Analysis and Proposed Conclusions'. *International Journal of Refugee Law*, 16 (2): 165–226.

Niemi-Kiesiläinen, Johanna, Päivi Honkatukia and Minna Ruuskanen (2006). 'Diskurssianalyysi ja oikeuden tekstit'. *Oikeuden tekstit diskursseina*, Johanna Niemi-Kiesiläinen, Päivi Honkatukia, Helena Karma and Minna Ruuskanen (eds.), 21–41. Helsinki: Suomalainen lakimiesyhdistys.

Nongbri, Brent (2015). *Before Religion: A History of a Modern Concept.* New Haven: Yale University Press.

Richardson, John E. (2007). *Analysing Newspapers: An Approach from Critical Discourse Analysis*. Basingstoke: Palgrave.

Rose, Lena and Zoe Given-Wilson (2021). '"What Is Truth?" Negotiating Christian Convert Asylum Seekers' Credibility'. *The ANNALS of the American Academy of Political and Social Science*, 697 (1): 221–35.

Salomäki, Hanna (2021). 'Worship, Church Ceremonies and Christian Holidays'. *Religion in Daily Life and Celebration: The Evangelical Lutheran Church of Finland, 2016–2019*, Hanna Salomäki, Maarit Hytönen, Kimmo Ketola, Veli-Matti Salminen and Jussi Sohlberg (eds.), 91–135. Vaasa: Church Research Institute Publications.

Skov Danstrøm, Matilde and Zachary Whyte (2019). 'Narrating Asylum in Camp and at Court'. *Asylum Determination in Europe: Ethnographic perspectives*, Nick Gill and Anthony Good (eds.), 175–94. Cham: Palgrave Macmillan.

Sohlberg, Jussi and Kimmo Ketola (2021). 'Religious Communities in Finland'. *Religion in Daily Life and Celebration: The Evangelical Lutheran Church of Finland, 2016–2019*, Hanna Salomäki, Maarit Hytönen, Kimmo Ketola, Veli-Matti Salminen and Jussi Sohlberg (eds.), 45–66. Vaasa: Church Research Institute Publications.

Sullivan, Winnifred Fallers (2005). *The Impossibility of Religious Freedom*. Princeton: Princeton University Press.

Taira, Teemu (2022). *Taking 'Religion' Seriously: Essays on the Discursive Study of Religion*. Leiden: Brill.

UNHCR (2004). *Guidelines on International Protection: Religion-Based Refugee Claims under Article 1A(2) of the 1951 Convention and/or the 1967 Protocol Relating to the Status of Refugees*. Geneva: UNHCR.

3

Credibility assessment in asylum claims based on religious conversion in Germany: A qualitative sociological analysis

Anne K. Schlüter

When does the secular state consider an individual's confession of faith credible? Since 2015, this question has become increasingly important in Germany, and many other European countries, because of the rise in Christian baptisms among refugees from Muslim backgrounds.[1] Given most of these converts come from Iran or Afghanistan, where conversion to Christianity is persecuted as a form of apostasy, many of them include their conversion as grounds for persecution in their asylum claim. As state authorities suspect that, under such circumstances, baptisms may be primarily opportunistic, i.e. a means to improve the chances of being granted refugee status, the question of the 'sincerity' of the religious conversion often becomes a topic of focus during the assessment of asylum claims.[2] In Germany, the difficult task of addressing this question is performed by officials of the Federal Office for Migration and Refugees (BAMF), who undertake the initial examination of asylum claims, and by administrative judges, who re-examine the cases in the event of an appeal against the BAMF's decisions. As federal German courts have largely refrained from defining what constitutes a 'sincere' religious conversion and how credibility is to be assessed in these cases, BAMF officials and judges have a lot of leeway in the definition they apply.

As in other European countries, these 'state tests' of religious conversions have been highly debated in Germany in recent years and several media outlets have run headlines such as 'Christian check in court' (Deutschlandfunk 2018), 'The lie detector' (ZEIT 2019) and 'Judges deny Christians their faith' (FAZ 2019).[3] Church representatives, in particular, have criticized the BAMF and administrative courts for conducting extensive religious knowledge exams and often ignoring the statements of the pastors acting as witnesses in these cases. From the churches' perspective, it is often not those who are truly 'sincere' about their religious conversion that are legally recognized as 'refugees', but those who are most eloquent or luckiest in terms of who is assigned to decide on their case. However, a decision by the Federal Constitutional Court in April 2020 has put an end to the churches' hopes surrounding a substantively new legal interpretation regarding these cases for the time being. In its decision, the court confirmed the view of the Federal Administrative Court, according to which state authorities are not bound by the opinion of the pastors and must reach an independent conclusion about the 'religious identity' of any applicants (BVerwG 2015; BVerfG 2020).

Given the heated debate on this topic in Germany and other countries, the question of how refugee status determination (RSD) processes are conducted when a conversion to Christianity is involved has been receiving increased academic attention. The existing scholarship[4] falls broadly into three categories. One vein of research examines the legal framework surrounding these claims by analysing national and supranational regulations, directives and case law (Aarsheim 2019; Ganschow 2021; Karras 2017; Madera 2022; McDonald 2016; Pernak 2018; Sonntag 2018; Thebault and Rose 2018). The other two veins of research, while also taking the legal framework into account, focus on the day-to-day handling of religious conversion claims by asylum authorities and courts. They include, firstly, studies that undertake a systematic analysis of official documents issued in these cases, i.e. written decisions and, to a lesser extent, hearing transcripts (Kagan 2010[5]; Karras 2017: 245ff.; Blumgrund née Silvola 2023; Halonen in this volume) and, secondly, studies that place a greater emphasis on asylum practices by also drawing on ethnographic observations of hearings and/or interviews with decision-makers and other actors in the field (Hoellerer and Gill 2021; Krannich 2020: 197ff.; Rose and Given-Wilson 2021). Researchers from across these different approaches have repeatedly emphasized that credibility assessments in conversion-based asylum claims often rely heavily on religious knowledge testing and are based on presuppositions about religion and conversion that privilege a Western religious understanding (for a detailed overview, see Rose 2023; Selim et al. 2023). Regarding the practical side of the process, previous research has also shown how courtroom power dynamics, including the role of interpreters (Rose and Given-Wilson 2021), as well as rumours about supposed 'assembly-line baptisms' performed by certain church communities influence decision-making processes (Hoellerer and Gill 2021).

The present study, which outlines some of the preliminary findings of an ongoing sociological research project on asylum and conversion, adds to the existing scholarship by approaching the topic from a perspective that is not only empirical but also theoretical, that is, it is built upon the perspective of the sociological theory of multiple differentiation. By emphasizing the difference between the law as an abstract system and the law as practice, it is argued that, for a more profound understanding of how conversion-based asylum claims are processed, it is insufficient to rely on the analysis of legal regulations and written documents alone. Therefore, through the combination of court ethnography, analysis of judgements and qualitative interviews with decision-makers, the present study examines how credibility assessment in the asylum claims of Christian converts is conducted, *in practice*, by administrative judges in Germany. This study differs from previous ethnographic approaches by investigating specific formal and informal strategies used in judicial decision-making, i.e. 'test strategies' for assessing the 'sincerity'[6] of the religious conversions. It will be demonstrated that, although written judgements often read quite similarly, in practice individual judges differ significantly in the way they reach decisions. This is not only because they rely on their individual religious understandings when processing these claims, but also because of other factors such as their courtroom management style, their degree of experience with such cases and the different weight they place on various aspects when making their final decisions on refugee status. In this context, it is also shown that judges' decision-making involves tacit knowledge – a fact that has repeatedly been highlighted in the general academic debate on the asylum process (e.g., Affolter 2021; Dahlvik 2018; Jubany 2011) but has, thus far, received little attention in research on conversion-based claims. This article argues that the wide divergence in recognition rates among individual decision-makers identified in previous research (Karras 2017) and confirmed here can only be explained if all of these practical aspects are taken into account.

Law as a system and law as practice

As previously mentioned, the theoretical framework of this study is built on the sociological *theory of multiple differentiation* (TMD) by the German sociologist Joachim Renn (2006a, 2006b), which is also known as *social translation theory*. While this section outlines some of the basic assumptions of TMD and their implications for this study, it is not possible to give a comprehensive account of the social theoretical foundations here. However, it should be noted that the theory claims to combine systems theory and pragmatism (Renn 2006a) and is, therefore, particularly suitable for the analysis of sociological questions concerning the relationship between micro and macro contexts.

Building on the work of the systems theorist Niklas Luhmann (2012, 2013 [1997]), a key assumption of TMD is that modern society is characterized by the existence of different *social systems*, such as politics, economics, law, religion and science, each of which operates through its own inner logic and performs a unique function for society as a whole. For example, the function of the political system is to make collectively binding decisions, while the legal system provides stability of expectations, and the religious system offers a means for coping with contingency. However, according to TDM, functional differentiation is only one of several structural principles of modern society. Furthermore, TMD describes modern society as differentiated in a *vertical* way. In this context, there are four types of social subunits that are classified according to how they assign meaning to notions and actions (on a scale from more abstract to more specific). In addition to the functional *systems*, these are formal *organizations*, cultural *milieus* and individual *persons*. What is important here is that, according to TMD, each individual social subunit in modern society – i.e. each system, each organization, each milieu and each individual – constitutes a closed context of meaning, in other words, it speaks its own 'social language'. Regarding the empirical case presented here, this can be illustrated by the fact that the religious conversion of an asylum seeker has a different meaning for the converted individual (e.g. identity formation) than it does, for example, for the respective religious organization (e.g. acquisition of a new member), the legal system (the RSD, in accordance with the applicable law) or the individual judge who is assigned to decide on the asylum claim (reaching a decision). Given that linear transmission of meaning is not possible between individual social subunits, TMD concludes that '*social translation processes*' are constantly taking place in modern society.

In light of these general theoretical considerations and regarding the sociology of law, TMD implies that law in modern society manifests itself not only as a functional system (Luhmann 2004 [1995]), but also in less abstract, non-systemic forms, such as legal cultures and legal practices that are carried out by individuals and milieus. It is then assumed that there are complex 'social translation relations' between these levels (Nell 2020). Regarding the *judicial adjudication process* under discussion here, this means, in simplified terms, that the law (as a system), in its trans-situational and abstract format, has to be 'translated' into *legal practice* when being applied to a specific case. In this sense, the responsible judge must make a *pragmatic interpretation*[7] of the relevant law that is, necessarily, based on both explicit knowledge of legal norms and organizational (role) requirements, and forms of *tacit, i.e. non-verbalisable knowledge*[8] they possess as a member of a particular professional milieu (i.e. the judicial milieu). Insofar as it is relevant to the case, this process also involves more person-dependent (tacit and explicit) knowledge from non-legal contexts (e.g. from the field of religion). From the perspective of the TMD, however, the 'translation' of law into practice is understood as only one side of the judicial adjudication process. This follows from the assumption that there is a systematic difference between *judicial decision-making*, which is carried out in practice and for which, among other things, tacit knowledge is also relevant, and the written and, thus, propositionally structured *legal justification* of the decision, i.e. the judgement. As the latter must be communicatively connectable to the abstract 'language' of the legal system, judicial decisions must, in turn, be 'translated back' into appropriate and explicit legal criteria and terms.

Against the backdrop of the TMD and the 'social translation relations' between the law as an abstract system and the law as practice described here, it is evident that, for a deeper understanding of judicial adjudication processes on any given issue, it is generally not sufficient to rely only on the analysis of legal regulations and written judgements. For this reason, the present study focuses on the question of how credibility assessment in asylum claims based on conversion to Christianity is conducted *in practice* at German courts, asking about *specific strategies for judicial decision-making*, i.e. 'test strategies' for assessing the 'sincerity' of religious conversion. Based on the theoretical assumption about the systematic difference between *judicial decision-making* and *legal justification*, it is thereby assumed that not all strategies that are applied during the practical process of decision-making are reflected in the written judgements. Therefore, the following sections distinguish between *formal* and *informal* test strategies. While both are used in the practice of decision-making, they differ in that the former also claim validity in the written judgements, whereas the latter become invisible when the decision is 'translated back' into the 'language' of the legal system.

Methods

The data for this study consists, firstly, of eleven self-generated transcripts of appeal hearings of converted asylum seekers that were observed at two German administrative courts between August and November 2019 (H1 to H11). At all hearings, the applicant themselves, either a single judge or a panel of judges, a lawyer and an interpreter were present. Sometimes representatives of the BAMF acted as defendants. Furthermore, in about half of the hearings, pastors or other parishioners attended as witnesses. After carrying out the court ethnography, the corresponding legal judgements for the observed cases were obtained through public request. These serve as a second source of data (J1 to J11). Thirdly, this study relies on five semi-structured interviews with administrative judges that were conducted during the same period (I1 to I5). The additional insight gained from the interviews was particularly significant because all interviews were carried out with judges with whom the researcher had come into contact through the observed hearings. For this reason, it was possible to refer directly to the hearings and, for example, ask why the judges had asked specific questions.

Data analysis was carried out based on *grounded theory*, as this method allows an open approach to a topic and is also able to structure a large amount of data (Glaser and Strauss 1967; Strauss 1987). Following the recommended coding steps, the different test strategies presented in the next section were identified.

Practical test strategies for assessing the 'sincerity' of religious conversion

The first and most important finding of the present study is that – although the written judgements often read quite similarly, partly using the same standard passages – the hearings were carried out very differently by the individual judges. While the following test strategies for assessing the 'sincerity' of religious conversion were found to be typical, i.e. frequently applied at the courts examined, this does not mean that every judge used them in the same way. Indeed, it became apparent that the judges varied in terms of which strategies they applied and, even more so, in how they applied them. In this context, the judges' individual understanding of religion played an important role, as will be demonstrated in more detail below, as did their individual courtroom management style. It was observed that the judges systematically differed in whether they relied more on open-ended or closed-ended questions (see also Kagan 2010), whether they let applicants talk for any length of time or interrupted them prematurely to record their statements, and how much time they allocated for questions about religious conversion in the hearings. Furthermore, the judges were found to differ greatly in how they evaluated the results of different tests and weighted them for their final decisions on refugee status. All of this resulted in extremely divergent recognition rates in conversion-based asylum claims at the courts under study, ranging from about 5–10 to about 80–90 per cent among the judges interviewed.[9]

On the question of how the 'sincerity' of religious conversion is assessed in practice, this data analysis identified seven different test strategies. Five of them can be considered *formal* test strategies and two of them *informal*:

1. Assessment of events in the country of origin (*formal*)
2. Assessment of religious knowledge (*formal*)
3. Assessment of motives (*formal*)
4. Assessment of religious practice (*formal*)
5. Assessment of testimonies (*formal*)
6. Case comparison (*informal*)
7. 'Overall impression' (*informal*)

Referring to the findings of Thomas Scheffer (2001: 171f.), who conducted a comprehensive study of the German asylum process, it can be noted that some of these test strategies are carried out actively. This means that judges confront the applicants with certain questions and expect them to provide appropriate answers. In other cases, however, the assessment is conducted passively, in the sense that judges constantly and silently check all the statements made by the applicants (as well as those left unmade) according to certain criteria.

While the two informal test strategies are characterized by the fact that they find no counterpart in the 'language' of the legal system (see section above), the five formal test strategies are not surprising, at least at first glance. Even though this study proposes a different classification, they are generally consistent with national and supranational legal recommendations for credibility assessment in religion-/conversion-based asylum claims (e.g. Berlit et al. 2015; UNHCR 2004). However, as should have become clear by now, the fact *that* certain aspects play a role in judicial decision-making does not say much about *how* they do so. Therefore, the following discussion of the individual test strategies sheds some light on the different types of *questions* judges ask in hearings and on the *criteria* they use to evaluate various statements.

Assessment of events in the country of origin

The first formal test strategy addressed here is the *assessment of events in the country of origin*. This strategy focuses on assessing whether certain persecution-related incidents in the applicants' home countries, usually before the migration process, occurred as claimed. It is important to note that this test strategy is not applied exclusively in asylum cases in which religious conversion is asserted; rather, it is a common strategy used in the assessment of many asylum claims. As applicants cannot usually provide papers or documents to prove the threat of persecution they face, recognition of their refugee status often depends on the credibility of the events that allegedly led to the flight (EASO 2018; UNHCR 2013).

In the asylum cases of Christian converts, the assessment of events in the country of origin may refer directly to the religious conversion of the person in question, but it does not have to. Such an examination may occur if the given applicant claims that they had already turned to Christianity before the migration process, but not if they report having started the conversion process later. In addition, it is sometimes the case that the migration was allegedly triggered by other events, such as persecution for political activities, and this may also be assessed for credibility. In the hearings observed, typical questions under discussion in this test strategy included, for example, whether it was credible that the applicants had attended a house church in their home country, whether they had actually been in contact with members of Christian minorities before their flight (e.g. with Armenians in Iran; see Römer in this volume) and whether they had indeed been persecuted by state authorities.

Throughout the research, it was found that the assessment of events in the country of origin is both a passive and an active strategy. As the analysis of the judgements indicates, it was continuously applied during the hearings in the form of a silent examination of all statements made by any given applicant about incidents related to persecution in their home country. However, verifiable statements were also elicited by the judges through specific questions, for example, by asking about the initial reasons for seeking asylum or how and when the applicant first had contact with Christianity. Moreover, it became apparent that the credibility of the relevant events was primarily evaluated based on three criteria: firstly, whether the statements were *plausible*, i.e. whether it was feasible that certain events took place as the applicant claimed; secondly, all statements were checked for *consistency* with other statements made during the appeal hearing and in the BAMF interview and with those made by witnesses or in related cases (e.g. cases of family members); and thirdly, all statements were checked for their *degree of detail*. While these criteria are consistent with the general recommendations for credibility assessment in the asylum process (e.g. EASO 2018; Hungarian Helsinki Committee 2013), previous research has already pointed out that while judges do rely on official expert knowledge, i.e. country-of-origin-information, they also draw on other forms of knowledge, such as their 'common sense' and knowledge acquired through previous cases, when applying them (e.g. Affolter 2021; Dahlvik 2018; Herlihy et al. 2010; Johannesson 2012; Jubany 2011; Scheffer 2001). Without being able to go into further detail here, it can be stated that this observation was confirmed by the findings of the present study.

Generally speaking, it is important to note that, in the cases of converted asylum seekers, the assessment of events in the country of origin is a strategy that is only indirectly related to the core question of the 'sincerity' of the religious conversion. This is so because it is possible that applicants may be lying about the initial reasons that triggered their migration process (or may have lied about it in their interview with the BAMF) but nevertheless be 'genuine' Christians at the time of their appeal hearing. In such cases, they would also be legally entitled to receive recognition of their refugee status (Karras 2017). The logic of this strategy, thus, involves a 'detour'. Firstly, the assessment of the credibility of the stated pre-flight events serves to evaluate the general credibility (*Glaubwürdigkeit*) of the applicant in question. Secondly, conclusions are drawn from this about the credibility of the applicant's current religious identity (*Glaubhaftigkeit*). As a result, the judges were found to give this strategy very different weight in their final decisions on refugee status. While for some of the judges interviewed, the asylum applications stood or fell with the credibility of the stated pre-flight events, other judges gave more weight to the current religious identity of each asylum seeker and were thus willing to 'overlook smaller contradictions' in the statements regarding events in the country of origin. One of the judges even refrained from asking about pre-flight conversion-related events altogether. In the interview, the judge explained that, in most cases, they would not believe those narratives anyway and that they were, therefore, only interested in the 'here and now' of the religious conversions. A notable observation in this context was that the more importance the judges attached to the assessment of pre-flight events in their final decisions on refugee status, the lower their recognition rate.

Assessment of religious knowledge

A second formal test strategy is the *assessment of religious knowledge*. In contrast to the former, this strategy aims to directly assess whether the given applicant is a 'genuine' Christian at the time of the appeal hearing. In this regard, in line with previous research (see above) and Halonen's study in this volume, the first key finding is that religious knowledge tests were actively applied in some form in all of the hearings observed. In the interviews, the judges expressed a common understanding that knowledge is an indispensable 'foundation' of a 'true' religious identity ('If someone knows nothing at all, how can he then say: I believe in this or that?', I2).

However, despite this consensus, the questions that were asked in the hearings varied widely, ranging from *basic knowledge questions*, i.e. questions about the religious content to which there are predefined correct answers (e.g. 'What happened at Easter?', H10),[10] to more *theological questions* (e.g. 'What is the difference between God in Christianity and God in Islam?', H8) to more *open, personalised questions* (e.g. 'What is your favourite story in the Bible?', H4, H6). Although different question styles were often combined, the judges were found to set different priorities (see also Kagan 2010). For example, one judge who revealed in the interview that they are a practising Christian and active church member, relied more frequently on basic knowledge questions, while theological questions and an associated search for 'contradictions' in Christian doctrines itself (e.g. 'Why did Jesus have to die if God is an almighty figure?', H4) were popular with a judge who emphasized several times in the interview that they were a committed atheist. In this sense, it was confirmed that when assessing religious knowledge, judges draw on knowledge from their personal religious socialization as well as on their individual religious understandings to a large extent (see also Karras 2017; Rose and Given-Wilson 2021).

Assessment of motives

Another formal, actively applied test strategy observed in many hearings can be referred to as the *assessment of motives*. The judges were observed, in general, as expecting applicants to be able to provide a reason *why* they converted to Christianity and, often, why they turned away from Islam. In several of the cases observed, applicants were also asked to justify why they had chosen a particular *Christian denomination* or *certain church community*. In terms of the statements being evaluated, in certain cases, motive testing may overlap with event testing. Nevertheless, the two are analytically distinct as motive testing does not focus on the credibility of the events but on the question of whether the given reasons for the conversion are considered convincing from the judges' perspective. In line with the strong emphasis on knowledge assessments (see section above), it became apparent throughout the research that the judges generally expected a 'sincere' conversion to be based on a preceding conscious engagement with Christian teachings. Furthermore, claims were considered particularly convincing when applicants could justify their turn to Christianity with an identity crisis they had previously suffered due to certain biographical experiences. Given this focus on intellectual and biographical motives, it was found that other types of motives were generally not viewed as 'legitimate' grounds for a 'sincere' conversion. Although it was not necessarily considered negative if applicants stated that they had initially attended church or developed an interest in Christianity because of 'affective conversion motives', i.e. attachments to community members as grounds for conversion (Lofland and Skonovd 1981), the judges nevertheless assumed that a 'genuine' change of faith must ultimately be based on other (in such cases, subsequently arising) motives.[11] Finally, it was observed that during the assessment of motives, the date of the applicants' baptism was also taken into consideration. If, for example, the baptism took place shortly after the BAMF announced a negative asylum decision, the judges often saw this as an indication of opportunist conversion motives. These different observations correspond to the findings of previous studies (Hoellerer and Gill 2021; Krannich 2020; Rose and Given-Wilson 2021) as well as to those presented by Halonen and Ramsauer/Çağlar in this volume.

Assessment of religious practice

The *assessment of religious practice*, as a fourth formal test strategy, was actively performed to at least some extent in all the hearings observed (see also Halonen in this volume). In terms of *church practice,* applicants were generally expected to have participated in a baptism course before being christened. They were also expected to regularly attend church services, take part in further church activities and maintain personal contact with other parishioners. Nevertheless, the fact that a claim to church practice was found credible did not automatically convince the judges of the 'sincerity' of the religious conversion. Church practice was, instead, considered a necessary, rather than a sufficient, condition for the recognition of refugee status. In this context, the judges argued that it may 'only' serve integrative or even opportunistic functions and may not necessarily be based on an intellectual engagement with Christian doctrines and/or a spiritual search for meaning – factors that were considered prerequisites for a 'sincere' conversion (see section above).

As the judges generally considered other forms of religious practice more 'effective' for assessing the 'sincerity' of religious conversion, in many of the observed hearings, questions were asked about the applicants' *individual* religious *lifestyles* or potential *missionary activities*. Here, again, the types of questions varied greatly depending on the individual judge, for example, from the applicants' practice of prayer (e.g. 'How do you feel when you pray?', H1) to outward signs of their Christianity (e.g. 'Were you married in a Christian ceremony?', H5) to their practical orientation towards Christian rules of conduct (e.g. 'Which commandments do you see as practically binding for you?', H7).

Assessment of testimonies

The *assessment of testimonies* by pastors or other members of the applicants' church communities was identified as the final formal test strategy. As previously noted, pastors or other parishioners acted as witnesses in about half of the hearings observed. However, consistent with Rose's (2023) observation, it was noted that the judges attached little importance to the specific content of such testimonies when it came to the core question of the 'sincerity' of the religious conversions. In this sense, none of the judgements analysed substantially based the decision on refugee status on witness testimony. One reason for this is that state authorities, as explained above, are required, by law, to assess the credibility of the conversion-based asylum claims independently. In addition, the judges interviewed also articulated a suspicion that pastors and other parishioners would testify in favour of the applicants on principle.

Case comparison

The first of the two informal test strategies, i.e. forms of assessment that are not mentioned in the written judgements but are nonetheless relevant to the practical process of decision-making, can be referred to as *case comparison*. Case comparison is a passive strategy through which the statements made by any given applicant are continuously considered in relation to the statements of any previous applicants and evaluated based on both an individual and a collective judicial milieu-based body of experience. Similar to the assessment of events in the country of origin, case comparison is a test strategy that is not specific to cases involving Christian converts, rather, it is applied in all asylum cases involving credibility issues (see Jubany 2011; Liodden 2019; Scheffer 2001).

One important finding of the present study is that case comparison is effective in at least two ways. First, over time, a *minimum standard* is established that applicants have to fulfil in order to be successful. This became particularly evident throughout the research regarding parish certificates and witness testimonies. While the specific content of the testimonies was seen as less decisive (see above), it turned out to have a direct negative impact on the applicants' chances of recognition if they belonged to a church that was well known to the court but at the same time could not provide any up-to-date certificates or testimonies from parishioners to support their claim. Based on other hearings, the judges were aware that certain pastors usually issued certificates and accompanied their church members to court. This experience was transferred to the individual cases at hand so that applicants who were unable to present testimonies from certain pastors found themselves needing to explain this during the hearings ('J: And why is Mother X not here today? I know from other hearings, she usually comes along.' H3).

In addition to a general minimum standard, as a result of case comparison, the *originality* of the applicants' statements was found to be another important criterion used to determine the 'sincerity' of religious conversions. As the statements of individual converts were often viewed as quite similar, for example, in regard to the persecution-related events experienced, conversion motives or certain religious teachings, this led to a general distrust among the judges, who were less likely to attribute the convergence of narratives to similar life experiences than to tactical collusion among the converted asylum seekers:

> J: [...] based on experience, the more experience you have, the higher the rate of rejection simply because one has heard so many stories so many times. Things you thought of at the beginning as 'yes wow, that's totally convincing and unique' may, after three, four, five, six, seven, eight years, turn out to be: 'I've heard that a hundred times. That is what they all tell each other about.' Although this also has its dangers because you might become a bit prejudiced and lose sight of the individual case.
>
> (I1)

All the statements made by applicants and witnesses during the hearings were, therefore, constantly subject to comparison with 'standard versions' (Scheffer 2001: 165), i.e. statements typically made in previous cases. Based on the logic of case comparison, it followed that those applicants, in particular, were believed to be 'sincere' converts who, in the eyes of the judges, succeeded in standing out from the crowd (e.g. by making especially personal references to Christian doctrines). However, as the quotation above indicates, the likelihood of a 'unique' portrayal might generally decrease with the number of cases that a respective judge has heard.

One observation worthy of further investigation is that the degree of originality required seemed to vary for members of different church communities. This research indicates that applicants who belonged to churches with a large number of converted asylum seekers among their membership faced a particularly high need to stand out. In such cases, it even occurred that the test strategy of case comparison became explicit in the hearings. For example, in the following hearing sequence, the judge asked the pastor how the applicant would stand out compared to the other asylum seeking members of his community:

> J: Well, this is a little bit targeted. You have a lot of community members.
> P: Hm.
> J: I have had many of them sitting here in front of me. Some were successful, if I remember correctly, some were not. That's clear. That's why I ask the question because there are so many of them. The first question would be: What stands out to you about him in particular? So, what is the particular element that makes you say, in this respect, I am going testify in his favour today […]?
>
> (H5)

However, as case comparison contradicts the legal logic of case-by-case orientation and because it is partly based on tacit knowledge, it is usually not referred to in the written judgements.

Overall impression

The second informal test strategy is the 'overall impression'. This term, which was repeatedly invoked by the judges themselves, refers to a spontaneous and intuitive assessment of the 'sincerity' of religious conversion based on the physical co-presence of the judges and applicants in the hearings. As a kind of 'gut feeling', the overall impression can take all of the above forms of assessment as well as the given applicant's body language into account. In this sense, it was found that the judges considered the most credible applicants to be those who succeeded not only in emphasizing their Christian identity through the content of their statements, but also in transmitting a certain feeling when presenting themselves ('There must be a spark, so to speak', I2). In this respect, it may be that an applicant passes most or even all of the above tests, but judges are still not convinced of the 'sincerity' of their religious conversion. Based on the overall impression, as can be seen in the following interview excerpt, judges distinguish between presumed 'genuine' Christians and presumed 'actors', i.e. those who are accused of having engaged with Christianity 'on a purely intellectual' level:

J: [...] and in her case I had ... She had an immense amount of knowledge but I just couldn't shake the feeling ... It was my deep, inner impression that this person had dealt with this matter on a purely intellectual level. She was damn good at it. But there was a lack of any personal reference. There was nothing. It was ... I totally believe her that she didn't want to be a Muslim. We believe that in most cases. But she wasn't a Christian either.

(I1)

As the overall impression is based on tacit knowledge, i.e. its formation cannot be fully articulated, and because it is considered less neutral than other forms of assessment (Hungarian Helsinki Committee 2013; EASO 2018), it is usually not represented in the written judgements. However, based on studies on general credibility assessment in the asylum process (Affolter 2021; Jubany 2011; Kobelinsky 2019), as well as the judges' statements in the interviews, it can be assumed that this test strategy plays at least some role in the assessment of all asylum claims made by Christian converts. Thus, four out of five judges interviewed reported that they would also pay attention to the facial expressions and gestures of the applicants. In particular, because conventional credibility assessment strategies, such as the assessment of events in the country of origin, are only partially effective in the processing of conversion claims (see above), there is even reason to suspect that the overall impression is more important in these claims than in others. However, the weight that is ultimately given to the overall impression in the final decision on refugee status is expected to vary not only from judge to judge but also from case to case. Given this, it is also thought to depend on whether a decision is pronounced immediately after the hearing or later after a (re)review of the official hearing transcript and other documents in the case file.[12]

Conclusion

Against the backdrop of the sociological theory of multiple differentiation, which points to the importance of distinguishing between the law as an abstract system and the law as practice, the present study focused on how administrative judges in Germany conduct, in practice, credibility assessments in conversion-based asylum claims. More specifically, it raised the question of which specific 'test strategies' judges use when determining the 'sincerity' of religious conversions. The study distinguished between formal strategies, which, when used, are referred to in the written judgements, and informal strategies, which, being based on tacit knowledge and/or contradicting the rules of legal justification, become invisible when decisions are 'translated back' into the 'language' of the legal system. Through court ethnography, the analysis of judgements and qualitative interviews with decision-makers, this study identified five formal test strategies (assessment of events in the country of origin, religious knowledge, motives, religious practice and testimonies) and two informal test strategies (case comparison and overall impression) that were frequently applied at the courts examined. However, it was found that individual judges vary greatly in terms of how they make use of and weight the results of the various tests in their final decisions on refugee status, which leads to highly divergent recognition rates. Overall, this study demonstrated that, in order to gain a more profound understanding of the asylum process in cases involving Christian converts, it is essential to take various aspects of practical decision-making, including different individual understandings of religion, courtroom management styles, the degree of experience with such cases and tacit knowledge into consideration.

Regarding the scope of the study, it needs to be emphasized that the findings do not claim to be comprehensive. From a theoretical perspective, this study has focused on the vertical 'social translation relations' between the law as a system and the law as practice. However, in the context of TMD, another question more focused on horizontal 'social translation relations' would be how religion is 'translated' into the 'language' of law in the asylum process. That is, it would ask: how does the individual meaning that applicants themselves ascribe to their religious conversion differ from that of the legal system and the legal practice, and thus, what shifts in meaning occur as a result of the 'translation processes'? Furthermore, as the analysis presented here is based on a sample of two administrative courts, it is conceivable that other important factors which were not identified here could feature at other German administrative courts. Moreover, it should be noted that the data for the analysis was collected in 2019 and was, like the data for the previous ethnographic studies focusing on RSD in conversion-based asylum claims in Germany, collected before the change in the German government in December 2021, the Taliban's reinvasion of Afghanistan in August 2021, Russia's invasion of Ukraine in February 2022 (and the associated rise in refugee numbers), and the protests against the Iranian regime that began in September 2022. It is conceivable that all these events will impact how credibility assessments are conducted in conversion-based asylum claims, not only legally but also practically. In terms of further research, a larger sample with more recent data would, for these reasons, be of particular value.[13] In addition, given that (almost) all ethnographic studies on conversion-based asylum claims in Germany to date have focused on the judicial part of the asylum process, it would be insightful to examine how credibility assessments are conducted in these cases on the administrative level of the BAMF, and how their practices differ from those of the courts.

Based on the judicial decision-making practices identified here, this study has several potential implications for practitioners involved in the asylum process. As it was found that individual judges differ greatly in how they conduct the process and, therefore, also in their recognition rates, this study suggests that there is a need for a stronger standardization of credibility assessments in conversion-based asylum claims. However, given the 'social translation relations' between the law as a system and the law as practice, it is also clear that such standardization cannot be achieved through stronger legal regulations alone and any reform must directly address decision-makers, for example, by providing training on both procedural and content-related aspects. Regarding the direction of standardization, previous studies have already recommended that open-ended, narrative questions, reflections on cultural and religious presuppositions, a greater focus on religious practices rather than religious knowledge, and a stronger consideration of testimonies of parishioners could be a good way forward (Kagan 2010; Karras 2017; Rose 2023; Rose and Given-Wilson 2021; Selim et al. 2023). Based on the present findings, we can add two additional factors to this list. The first relates to the observation that the more weight judges give to the credibility of pre-flight events in their final decisions on refugee status, the lower their recognition rate. However, given that the time of the hearing is ultimately decisive for the persecution prognosis, one could argue that decision-makers should generally focus on the current religious identity of the applicants. Secondly, the findings indicate that because of constant case comparison, the recognition rates of decision-makers might decrease with the number of cases they have heard. While other studies suggest that it is essential that decision-makers have experience in handling the relevant cases (e.g. Selim et al. 2023), this study argues that this could also lead to unintended side effects. Hence, as a corrective measure, it is advisable that conversion-based asylum claims should, as a standard, be decided on by a panel of both experienced and inexperienced decision-makers rather than by a single judge.

Notes

1   In the absence of relevant statistics, it is not possible to give a precise figure for the total number of refugees who have converted to Christianity in Germany.

However, the broad media coverage on the topic since around 2016 indicates that the phenomenon is of considerable empirical relevance (e.g. Deutschlandfunk 2017; ZEIT 2016). According to one of the judges interviewed for this study, the number of converts in the asylum cases of Iranians heard at their court was about 90 per cent at the time of the interview in 2019, whereas it had been only about 10 per cent a few years earlier.

2   For a general legal background on the topic, see Rose in this volume. For the specific German legal framework, see BVerfG (2020), as well as Karras (2017), Sonntag (2018), Pernak (2018) and Ganschow (2021).

3   These titles and all verbatim quotations in this chapter were translated from German into English by the author.

4   The state of research presented herein is based on German and English publications.

5   Kagan's study does not focus on asylum claims by Christian converts in Europe but on religion-based asylum claims by Eritrean Pentecostals in Egypt. However, the study provides many insights relevant to the cases discussed here.

6   It is important to note that this study itself does not make any assumptions about the 'true' religiosity of the applicants. For a discussion of conversion motives and narratives of refuges from Muslim backgrounds, see, for example, Morgan, Fossdal and Römer in this volume, as well as Akcapar (2006), Kéri and Sleiman (2017), Stadlbauer (2019), Petersen and Jensen (2019), Krannich (2020) and Öztürk (2022).

7   In this sense, legal interpretation is understood as a situation of 'pragmatic rule application', in which the rule does not dictate how it is applied within the specific situation but rather requires a situationally appropriate interpretation (see Nell 2020: 179ff.). The fact that the law must always be interpreted is not, of course, a groundbreaking insight. However, an important contribution of a sociology of law informed by the TMD is the emphasis on tacit knowledge in the process (see note 8).

8   The term 'tacit knowledge' (Polanyi 1966) characterizes a form of practical knowledge about how to act in specific situations. It differs from explicit, propositionally structured knowledge in that it cannot be articulated linguistically (see Renn 2006a: 274f.). The distinction between tacit and explicit knowledge used here corresponds, broadly speaking, to Gilbert Ryle's (1949) distinction between 'knowing how' and 'knowing that'.

9   These figures are based on the self-assessments of the interviewed judges regarding their individual recognition rates in conversion-based asylum claims. As all judges stated that they had already decided on a considerable number of such cases, it can be ruled out that the large differences found are due to chance. In general, there are no official statistics on recognition rates in conversion-based asylum claims in Germany.

10 Basic knowledge questions were observed in some of the hearings, but to a much lesser extent than was expected given the claims made in the media reports and previous studies. The judges themselves attributed this to their concern that the applicants could easily prepare for such questions and that the knowledge presented might, therefore, have 'merely' been memorized rather than reflecting actual religious commitment.
11 As a mystical conversion experience, for example a religious dream (see Vähä-Savo and Koivuluhta in this volume) was not given as the decisive motive in any of the cases observed, it is not possible to say how the judges would evaluate such a claim. In line with the focus on intellectual motives, however, it became apparent that the judges generally had a rather processual understanding of religious conversion.
12 Judges can choose between two options: pronouncing a decision immediately following the oral hearing or delivering the written decision within two weeks.
13 While the present study focused primarily on general trends as well as the differences in the assessment practices of individual judges, the data collected also indicates systematic differences between the individual courts. The author is currently investigating these phenomena, among others, in her aforementioned research project, for which a second survey phase was started in December 2022.

Bibliography

Aarsheim, Helge (2019). 'Sincere and Reflected? Localizing the Model Convert in Religion Based Asylum Claims in Norway and Canada'. *Faith in the System? Religion in the (Danish) Asylum System*, Marie Juul Petersen and Steffen Bo Jensen (eds.), 83–95. Aalborg: Aalborg University Press.

Affolter, Laura (2021). *Asylum Matters: On the Front Line of Administrative Decision-Making*. London: Palgrave Macmillan.

Akcapar, Sebnem Koser (2006). 'Conversion as a Migration Strategy in a Transit Country: Iranian Shiites Becoming Christians in Turkey'. *International Migration Review*, 40 (4): 817–53.

Berlit, Uwe, Harald Doerig and Hugo Storey (2015). 'Credibility Assessment in Claims Based on Persecution for Reasons of Religious Conversion and Homosexuality: A Practitioners Approach'. *International Journal of Refugee Law*, 27 (4): 649–66.

Blumgrund née Silvola, Iona (2023). 'Credibility Assessment of Religious Conversion in the Asylum Process: A Theological Analysis'. *Studia Theologica – Nordic Journal of Theology*. https://bit.ly/42MBJCh (last accessed 29 March 2023).

BVerfG (2020). Beschluss vom 03.04.2020, Az. 2 BvR 1838/15.

BVerwG (2015). Beschluss vom 25.08.2015, Az. B 40/15.

Dahlvik, Julia (2018). *Inside Asylum Bureaucracy: Organizing Refugee Status Determination in Austria*. Cham: Springer.

Deutschlandfunk (2017). 'Flüchtlinge lassen sich taufen'. https://bit.ly/3I1STmT (last accessed 3 February 2023).

Deutschlandfunk (2018). 'Christencheck vor Gericht'. https://bit.ly/3hyt0gB (last accessed 3 February 2023).

EASO (2018). 'Judicial Analysis: Evidence and Credibility Assessment in the Context of the Common European Asylum System'. https://bit.ly/3jEiZTF (last accessed 14 March 2023).

FAZ (2019). 'Richter sprechen Christen den Glauben ab'. https://bit.ly/3K7wAKH (last accessed 3 February 2023).

Ganschow, Constantin Alexander (2021). *Die Konversion im Asylverfahren*. Potsdam: Universitätsverlag Potsdam.

Glaser, Barney G. and Anselm L. Strauss (1967). *The Discovery of Grounded Theory: Strategies for Qualitative Research*. Chicago: Aldine.

Herlihy, Jane, Kate Gleeson and Stuart Turner (2010). 'What Assumptions about Human Behaviour Underlie Asylum Judgments?' *International Journal of Refugee Law*, 22 (3): 351–66.

Hoellerer, Nicole and Nick Gill (2021). '"Assembly-Line Baptism": Judicial Discussions of "Free Churches" in German and Austrian Asylum Hearings'. *Journal of Legal Anthropology*, 5 (2): 1–29.

Hungarian Helsinki Committee (2013). 'Credibility Assessment in Asylum Procedures: A Multidisciplinary Training Manual', Vol. 1. https://bit.ly/3kKuNRo (last accessed 14 March 2023).

Johannesson, Livia (2012). 'Performing Credibility: Assessments of Asylum Claims in Swedish Migration Courts'. *RETFÆRD ÅRGANG*, 35 (3): 69–84.

Jubany, Olga (2011). 'Constructing Truths in a Culture of Disbelief: Understanding Asylum Screening from Within'. *International Sociology*, 26 (1): 74–94.

Kagan, Michael (2010). 'Refugee Credibility Assessment and the "Religious Imposter" Problem: A Case Study of Eritrean Pentecostal Claims in Egypt'. *Vanderbilt Journal of Transnational Law*, 43 (5): 1179–233.

Karras, Benjamin (2017). *Missbrauch des Flüchtlingsrechts? Jus Internationale et Europaeum 134*. Tübingen: Mohr Siebeck.

Kéri, Szabolcs and Christina Sleiman (2017). 'Religious Conversion to Christianity in Muslim Refugees in Europe'. *Archive for the Psychology of Religion*, 39: 283–94.

Kobelinsky, Carolina (2019). 'The "Inner Belief" of French Asylum Judges'. *Asylum Determination in Europe: Ethnographic Perspectives*, Nick Gill and Anthony Good (eds.), 53–68. London: Palgrave Macmillan.

Krannich, Conrad (2020). *Recht macht Religion: Eine Untersuchung über Taufe und Asylverfahren*. Göttingen: Vandenhoeck & Ruprecht.

Liodden, Tone Maia (2019). 'Making the Right Decision: Justice in the Asylum Bureaucracy in Norway'. *Asylum Determination in Europe: Ethnographic Perspectives*, Nick Gill and Anthony Good (eds.), 241–62. London: Palgrave Macmillan.

Lofland, John and Norman Skonovd (1981). 'Conversion Motifs'. *Journal for the Scientific Study of Religion*, 20 (4): 373–85.

Luhmann, Niklas (2004 [1995]). *Law as a Social System*. Oxford: Oxford University Press.

Luhmann, Niklas (2012/2013 [1997]). *Theory of Society*. Vol. I and II. Stanford: Stanford University Press.

Madera, Adelaide (2022). 'The Intersection between Refugees and Religion: The Challenge of Assessing Religiously Based Asylum Claims in the European Legal Framework'. *International Journal for Religious Freedom*, 15 (1/2): 121–39.

McDonald, Douglas (2016). 'Escaping the Lions: Religious Conversion and Refugee Law'. *Australian Journal of Human Rights*, 22 (1): 135–58.

Nell, Linda (2020). *Die multiple Differenzierung des Rechts: Eine pragmatistisch-gesellschaftstheoretische Perspektive auf den globalen Rechtspluralismus*. Weilerswist: Velbrück Wissenschaft.

Öztürk, Ebru (2022). 'Finding a New Home through Conversion: The Ontological Security of Iranians Converting to Christianity in Sweden'. *Religion, State & Society*, 50 (2): 224–39.

Pernak, Benjamin (2018). *Richter als 'Religionswächter'? Zur gerichtlichen Überprüfbarkeit eines Glaubenswechsels: Asylverfahren von Konvertiten in Deutschland und Großbritannien im Vergleich*. Berlin: Duncker & Humblot.

Petersen, Marie Juul and Steffen Bo Jensen (eds.) (2019). *Faith in the System? Religion in the (Danish) Asylum System*. Aalborg: Aalborg Universitetsforlag. https://bit.ly/3LPwmZV (last accessed 6 February 2023).

Polanyi, Michael (1966). *The Tacit Dimension*. Chicago: University of Chicago Press.

Renn, Joachim (2006a). *Übersetzungsverhältnisse: Perspektiven einer pragmatistischen Gesellschaftstheorie*. Weilerswist: Velbrück.

Renn, Joachim (2006b). 'Indirect Access: Complex Settings of Communication and the Translation of Governance'. *Sociology of Translation*, Arturo Parada and Oscar Diaz Fouces (eds.), 191–211. Vigo: University of Vigo Press.

Rose, Lena (2023). 'Asylum Adjudications on the Basis of Religious Conversion'. *Oxford Handbook on Religion and Contemporary Migration* (online edn, Oxford Academic, 22 March 2023), Elena Fiddian-Qasmiyeh and Anna Rowlands (eds.). https://bit.ly/3NFClmt (last accessed 9 July 2023).

Rose, Lena and Zoe Given-Wilson (2021). '"What Is Truth?" Negotiating Christian Convert Asylum Seekers' Credibility'. *ANNALS, AAPSS*, 697: 221–35.

Ryle, Gilbert (1949). *The Concept of Mind*. New York: Barnes & Noble.

Scheffer, Thomas (2001). *Asylgewährung: Eine ethnographische Analyse des deutschen Asylverfahrens*. Stuttgart: Lucius & Lucius.

Selim, Hedayat, Julia Korkman, Peter Nynäs, Elina Pirjatanniemi and Jan Antfolk (2023). 'A Review of Psycho-Legal Issues in Credibility Assessments of Asylum Claims Based on Religion'. *Psychiatry, Psychology and Law*, 30 (6): 760–88.

Sonntag, Holger (2018). 'Testing Religion: Adjudicating Claims of Religious Persecution Brought by Iranians in the US and Germany'. *Case Western Reserve Law Review*, 68 (3): 975–1057.

Stadlbauer, Susanne (2019). 'Between Secrecy and Transparency: Conversions to Protestantism among Iranian Refugees in Germany'. *Entangled Religions*, 8. https://bit.ly/3MasVhj (last accessed 14 March 2023).

Strauss, Anselm L. (1987). *Qualitative Analysis for Social Scientists*. Cambridge: Cambridge University Press.

Thebault, Deborah and Lena Rose (2018). 'Case Comment: What Kind of Christianity? A. vs. Switzerland'. *Oxford Journal for Law and Religion*, 7 (3): 543–50.

UNHCR (2004). 'Guidelines on International Protection: Religion-Based Refugee Claims under Article 1A(2) of the 1951 Convention and/or the 1967 Protocol relating to the Status of Refugees', HCR/GIP/04/06.

UNHCR (2013). 'Beyond Proof: Credibility Assessment in EU Asylum Systems'. https://bit.ly/345vRdH (last accessed 14 March 2023).

ZEIT (2016). 'Neuanfang als Christ'. https://bit.ly/3K70IWD (last accessed 14 March 2023).

ZEIT (2019). 'Der Lügendetektor'. https://bit.ly/3htUfJ1 (last accessed 14 March 2023).

4

Making the convert speak: The production of truth and the 'apparatus of conversion' in Austria

Markus Elias Ramsauer and Ayşe Çağlar

There is a judicature by the Higher Administrative Court which I consider to be illegitimate. It basically says that we, the judges or the agency must check if he changed religion out of deep inner conviction. Out of deep! Inner! Conviction! This is a pretension!

(A judge at the Federal administrative Court in Vienna, Austria, December 2020)

I can say that the standpoint which you are proclaiming is more or less the cosmology, which is to be found in Spinoza and Nietzsche, in simpler words. So, I also try to classify that and look if this conviction is in accordance with classical religion-critical arguments.

(A scholar serving as an expert witness at a court in Vienna, October 2021)

We also examined our asylum seekers. We asked about their knowledge. But also repeatedly told them that they can and should express themselves emotionally.

(A Protestant church member in Vienna, September 2021)

Introduction

These three quotes hint at the challenges the actors in the field of asylum seekers' conversion process in Austria repeatedly face and have to engage with. Furthermore, they draw our attention to *the peculiar kind of knowledge* required to determine the truth about the asylum seeker and his/her conversion. However, the truth finding about the asylum seeker's conversion is never complete without the voice of the asylum seeker, i.e. without making the convert speak. On the basis of empirical research conducted between 2019 and 2021 in Vienna, which included interviews with judges, legal representatives, asylum seekers, journalists and members of religious institutions, together with the review of policy and court documents and decisions, this chapter explores how the space for the voice of the convert in Austrian courts is constituted and negotiated by various actors at a particular conjuncture. As the bigger part of asylum applications was filed by persons from predominantly Muslim countries like Syria, Afghanistan, Iraq and Iran, our focus is on the asylum procedures of primarily Afghanis and, to a lesser extent, citizens from the Republic of Iran who arrived in Austria during the so-called European refugee crisis of 2015.

As our opening quote from a judge at the Federal administrative Court (*BVwG*) clearly states, the evaluation of faith poses problems to the secular logic of the state, since the *unprovable needs to be made provable* outside of the religious logic. This is true for asylum cases based on conversion to Christianity, as well as for the adaption of an atheist or agnostic worldview, since for all three cases it is the alleged apostasy which potentially constitutes a reason for persecution. Here it is important to note that the evaluation of whether or not the asylum claims could be considered to be credible and whether or not the acclaimed 'identity' could be confirmed to be 'true' shows striking similarities in the ways evidences of 'truth' are produced and evaluated in the asylum cases of the LGTBQ+ people from countries where they are subject to persecution.[1]

In exploring the dynamics, mechanisms and the workings of these 'regimes of proof', we argue that the concept of *apparatus* (as it was developed primarily by Agamben 2009; Foucault 1975, 1976; and later by Feldman 2011, 2012)[2] is useful to explore the interrelations within an assemblage of actors and the negotiations of asylum claims based on religious conversion. It enables us to address how indicators of what is considered to be a 'true' conversion are produced, negotiated and practised. In exploring the workings of the conversion apparatus, we highlight the location and the role of the members of religious and non-religious institutions, as well as their strategies in making the respective conversion narratives legible/audible, thus 'acceptable'. This process is marked by the tensions between different understandings of *how one knows what one knows*. We then conclude with the role of rumours, hearsay and scepticism in this process and underline the tropes through which the relationship between the state and the convert, but also for inter and intra dynamics of the congregations, are framed and imagined.

The Austrian context of asylum seeking and conversion

The year 2015 saw a significant rise in asylum applications in Austria from 28,064 in 2014 to 88,340.[3] The greatest portion of these applications came from Syrian and Afghani citizens who arrived in Austria and had to go through the official asylum procedure: this consists of an initial interview by the Austrian police, whereafter the newcomers are summoned to a hearing at the first asylum court, the *Bundesamt für Fremdenwesen und Asyl* (*BFA*), which decides their legal status. Whereas for Syrians the rate of positive asylum decisions was at 81 per cent in 2015, only 30 per cent of Afghani asylum applicants were granted asylum in Austria. In 2019, the initial year of our research, the *BFA* acceptance rate for Afghan citizens in 2019 was still below 40 per cent though the Afghan cases were the most numerous. This led to a great number of decisions being appealed and brought to the second court, the *Bundesverwaltungsgericht* (*BVwG*). There, a considerable amount of cases came to be based on the claim of religious persecution (both conversion to Christianity and apostasy, i.e. the adaption of an atheist or agnostic world view).

This also has to do with the often year-long asylum procedures during which asylum seekers can undergo identity changes which in turn could lead to asylum-relevant danger of persecution in the case of a return to the country of origin, thereby constituting additional grounds for an asylum claim (*Nachfluchtgrund*). If the appellant could make a credible claim that he/she would be persecuted because of his/her religious identity, they would be granted asylum.[4] Persons who failed to do so were often accused of fake conversion (*Scheinkonversion*), meaning that they were trying to make use of a conversion claim just for the sake of getting an asylum status.

A diverse set of actors contribute to negotiations about the 'genuineness' of an asylum seeker's conversion. For our research we focused on the ones listed below while paying less attention to others like the superior courts *Verwaltungsgerichtshof* (*VwGH*) and *Verfassungsgerichtshof* (*VfGH*), court interpreters, court staff and documents, police officials, country of origin information[5] and international law.

In the process of determining an asylum seeker's status, if their initial asylum application is rejected by the *BFA*, the asylum seeker may choose to appeal the decision, which then confers upon them the legal status of an appellant (*Beschwerdeführer*). The appellant then presents their case at the second court, the BVwG, where the court evaluates their actions both inside and outside the space and time of the asylum hearing. The judges as representatives of the Bundesverwaltungsgericht review the BFA decision. In doing so, their assessment is not confined to legal aspects but also includes the factual issues of an asylum case. The judges at the BVwG are in charge of the hearing's procedure, as well as of formulating and justifying their decision about the asylum seeker's status. The latter is often accompanied by a legal representative who assists the asylum seeker in their defence, offering support in the form of preparation, guidance and advocacy both prior to and following the hearings.[6]

Similarly, persons from (a-)religious institutions often act as the asylum seeker's allies. We will discuss their respective role and their diverse performances in the production of truth about an asylum seeker's identity in detail in the later in the chapter. What is essential to know is that these persons can act as witnesses and/or as persons of trust.

Lastly, here we need to mention the impact of the *Bundesamt für Fremdenwesen und Asyl*. Following an interview with the asylum seeker, the BFA declares its decision. If this decision gets appealed by the asylum seeker, the BFA seeks to defend its initial decision at the BVwG, either in written form or with a representative present at the hearing.

The apparatus

An analytical lens of apparatus[7] is useful to address the dynamics and processes of the asylum seekers' conversion beyond a simple focus on '[t]he Institutional Logic in Assessment of Asylum Applications'[8] as well as beyond questions of whether or not someone is really, i.e. sincerely and sustainably, converted or only in pretence; whether or not asylum seekers are frauds who manipulate refugee protection to find a better way of life (Kagan 2003: 368). Instead it enables us to focus on an active field of an assemblage of diverse actors and their interrelations through which subjects are produced as 'officially' converted or non-converted. This is the *apparatus of conversion*. This framework allows us to address and capture the truth-finding dynamics of the claims of conversion as well as the heterogeneity and the diversity of actors (institutional, non-institutional individual and state) involved beyond any kind of ascribed coherence to their acts. Though the relations between the actors and the negotiations of conversions are far from being equal and are embedded within power asymmetries, they are neither dominated by a sole sovereign agent regulating their operations, nor is there a built-in coherence into this field.

Furthermore, by establishing realms of truth, knowledge and morality by defining what counts as right and wrong, be it in a moral or in an epistemological sense, the apparatus opens and shapes a space for subject positions, i.e. assigning different actors certain positions and ranges of agency. Thus, the *apparatus of conversion* has a decisively productive/constitutive element to it, meaning that the asylum seeker, as officially converted or not-converted, is produced/constituted within the workings of the apparatus and its operations. She or he is produced as a governable subject. This way, a living being is reduced to a manageable figure.[9]

The productive/constitutive aspect of the apparatus is important, as it enables us to move away from the question of intentionality, that is whether or not the asylum seeker is 'really' converted. What is important is that the person is constituted as *a subject* with a convert identity in interaction with the apparatus. Thus, within this framework, it is necessary to concentrate on the workings of the juridical discourse though without ascribing a determining role. The actors in the field are subjected to the logics of the apparatus, but at the same time it allows them to exert power via their performance.[10] In order to do so successfully, these performances must comply to the rules of what Thomas Scheffer, in reference to Wittgenstein, calls 'the language game of asylum assessment'.[11] Failing in one's performance can, for example, take the form of referring to obsolete legal aspects, getting lost in irrelevant details, talking when not allowed, etc. This potential failure deprives the respective statements and actions from their assertive power. Apparatus is a conjunctural formation. Thus, the production of truth within the workings of the apparatus is dependent on the particular configuration of the discursive and institutional space, time and position of the actor. The rules for what counts as a meaningful statement, in what form (tone) and most importantly what counts as a true statement are produced through the apparatus. This is how the unprovable is made provable within the *apparatus of conversion*.

Furthermore, apparatuses have a strategic nature in that they emerge as a strategic answer to a specific historical setting, especially to a crisis. As Paul Rabinow in his reading of Foucault's apparatus theory in *Discipline and Punish* points out, an apparatus must be seen as '[a] response [...] to crises or problems [whereas] the term "problem" [is to be understood as] a historical conjuncture that raises power/knowledge questions to those governing.'[12] It is therefore important to understand the emergence of an apparatus in relation to a particular conjuncture rather than a free-flowing structure which could be applied at any time or place. In our case, the conjuncture was the 'refugee crisis' of 2015, when the number of asylum applications in Austria rose from 1,503 (2013) to 28,064 (2014) and subsequently to 88,340 cases in 2015.[13] For the years 2014–16, the highest number of applications was submitted by migrants with a Syrian or Afghan passport. For Syrians, the rate of positive asylum decisions was at 81 per cent in 2015; however, in the same year only 30 per cent of the Afghan citizens were granted asylum in Austria. This discrepancy can be explained by the civil war in Syria presenting a much clearer picture in terms of the impossibility for a return to the country of origin, compared to the more ambiguous claims of persecution due to religion, sexuality or membership of a social group brought forward by Afghan citizens.

In the cases of the asylum claims based on the fear of religion-based persecution, it was not only the sheer number of asylum applications which constituted a challenge to the state institutions, but also the asylum applications' non-compliance with the secular notions of facts and proof (demanded by the courts). Asylum applications based on conversion often operate outside the secular state's 'comfort zone' of objective facts. They are nevertheless to be negotiated inside its institutions. Very different spheres of life, institutions, discourses and actors are brought together into the truth-finding field of asylum seekers' conversion. Again, this is what the concept of apparatus enables us to address.

Of course, the issue of conversion-based asylum applications did not only appear in the years 2014/15, but already was implicit in the Geneva Convention of 1951. For example, in 1998, a Congolese priest had to sing a prayer in Latin to the asylum officials to prove his sincerity.[14] Furthermore, the guidelines from the Austrian Catholic and Protestant Churches concerning conversion and asylum in 2014/15,[15] demanding thorough examinations of the converts' motives, are both indicators of the emerging conversion apparatus in the second half of the 2000s in Austria and of the political climate dominated by suspicion against allegedly fraudulent refugees occupying judicial and religious institutions and the public discourses.[16]

The 'fact-finding process' of the conversion apparatus

The first statements one hears when talking to persons in the field about the *'fact-finding process'* in asylum conversions is usually marked by aporia like: *'How should one assess that? No one can look inside another person'*. This statement by a judge indicates clearly the hard time judges have in assessing the cases. As we experienced during the fieldwork, asylum cases based on religious claims are often causes for confusion about the state actors' tasks and methods. This confusion is mainly due to the respective jurisdiction which holds that a conversion or an atheist lifestyle has to be internalized to a degree that it would not be reasonable to expect the person to suppress his/her beliefs.[17] One judge at the *BVwG* formulated his stance towards the internalization of religious beliefs as follows: '[T]he judges or the agency [*Behörde*] must check if he changed religion out of deep inner conviction. Out of deep! Inner! Conviction! This is a pretension [*Das ist vermessen*].'[18] All these confusions and challenges led to the in-practice establishment of a number of indicators through which a true conversion could be detected. The important thing here is that these indicators, no matter how contestable they are,[19] are expected to work as the pieces of a puzzle of a coherent, credible and verbalized conversion narrative in the asylum procedure upon which the authenticity of the conversion claim would be assessed.

In our research, we found that the fact-finding process of the credibility of conversion claims were evaluated on five areas, namely on the nature of knowledge, positioning against the former religion, the timing and pace of conversion as well as the audience of conversions, and the convert's performance (see also the chapters by Halonen and Schlüter in this volume).

Knowledge

A particular kind of knowledge and its mode of acquisition are important in the evaluation of the conversion claims of the asylum seekers. When analysing decision texts from the court, one frequently finds statements like the following: 'The appellant would know the three prayers Our Father, the Creed and the "prayer of Mary". Furthermore, the appellant recited Our Father and named the sacraments.'[20] The frequency of similar passages in asylum decision texts suggests that factual knowledge about the denomination most often does play a role in asylum decisions based on conversion. One must note, however, that these questions are but one part of knowledge which is required from an asylum seeker.

Another set of questions concerns the way this new knowledge has influenced the person individually and how they have incorporated it in his/her everyday life.[21] Thus, the knowledge should become part of his/her life. For this reason, *personal* questions become part of assessing the knowledge of the 'convert' and they should not be responded to in alleged truisms like 'Jesus is love' as these can appear as something learnt by heart.

For the case of proclaimed atheists/agnostics, knowledge-based questions can take on a more complex nature and be posed, for example, in the form of knowing the difference between atheism and agnosticism.[22] The asylum seekers are expected to answer philosophical questions about their atheist worldviews. It is clear that the capacity to answer these questions is, of course, highly dependent on the appellant's education, his/her verbalization skills as well as on the 'transformative filter'[23] of the court interpreter. This dependence, especially on education which conforms to secular understandings of knowledge, also adds a class dimension to the negotiation since, for example, people working in agriculture tend to be less familiar with official state procedures than journalists.

Rejection of the former religion

The asylum seeker is expected to justify his/her choice of converting by referring to the potential flaws in his/her former belief system. In fact, the 'traces' of this old system in his/her testimony can be interpreted as evidence against the internalization of conversion.[24] Again, the appellant should formulate his/her justification in his/her own words and abstain from using phrases like 'In Islam, women have no rights' without further elaborating on that statement. At one point a comprehensive knowledge on the differences between religions and congregations, i.e. histories of Christianity in Europe and the unfolding of its diverse implementations,[25] is expected; on the other hand, the simple formulation style of the narratives in one's own words becomes an indicator of the claim's authenticity.

Temporality of the conversion

Like the delicate balance between the coherence and incoherence as well as the elaborated and simple style of the narratives of the conversion narratives, the temporality of conversion is intricate. A conversion desire/process initiated right after arrival in Austria can be interpreted as a sign of a strategic conversion. Judges doubt the statements of asylum seekers who have been in contact with a church very soon after their arrival, since this could suggest a potential 'asylum strategy' behind this move.[26] However, if the conversion process is only initiated after a first or second negative asylum decision, this is often met with suspicion by the *BFA* and the *BVwG*.[27] Therefore, to join a congregation only after a negative asylum decision can also be seen as an indicator of a so-called 'fake conversion' (*Scheinkonversion*).

Temporality of conversion enters into the truth-finding processes in yet another form. An internalized and sincere conversion is expected to take a certain amount of time; that is to say not only the timing of the conversion, but also its *pace* plays a crucial role in assessing the 'truth' of conversion claims. Here it is ironic that stories based on Christian notions of epiphany are usually not regarded as credible.

The audience of conversion/public knowledge

It is not only the content, the timing and pace of its acquisition and the internationalization of particular knowledge about the religion which are crucial for establishing the credibility of the converts' claims. The asylum seekers are expected to have spoken publicly with other people about their conversion, or make it public via social media, etc. Thus, the audience becomes an integral part of the conversion's 'truth'. This constitutes a very delicate and possibly a very dangerous situation for the converts. If they do not make their conversion public, they lower their chances for asylum in Austria. If they display and make their conversion public, they run into the danger of being exposed in their 'home' and 'diasporic' communities, thus making them more vulnerable to condemnation, violence and persecution in case of a return.

Altogether these indicators of a sincere 'credible' conversion share a common characteristic in that they constitute a picture of the converted subject, whose actions are not strategic or fully coherent; that is, the converted subject is expected not to act 'rationally'. At one point there should be a coherence in the convert's narrative; on the other hand, he or she should not be following a rational coherent narrative. Instead, the asylum seeker is expected to present his/her conversion narrative within a delicate temporal dimension, publicly but also out of its context, that is to say stripped from its potential consequences in the case of a return.

Convert's performance

The aptitude of answering questions about religion, for example, in an unfamiliar environment is highly dependent on the appellant's education (see Halonen in this volume), and his/her performance and verbalization competencies. In order to provide a meaningful statement, the 'converts' must present and narrate their experiences in compliance with the parameters established by the apparatus of conversion.

This process essentially involves not only the asylum seekers' performances but also a number of further players which contribute to the production of the plausibility of the convert's voice. Here, we found out that the members of religious or non-religious associations employed three common strategies to make the asylum seeker's voice become audible to the judicial institution. These are the strategies through which the convert is made to speak. The space for his/her voice is construed through the specific characteristics of the fact-finding processes of the conversion apparatus.

Experts embedded into the conversion apparatus

One peculiarity of asylum cases based on conversion is the increased role expert witnesses play in the decision-making process. The crucial role the witnesses play in the decision-making processes marks a distinction from other asylum cases for which witnesses are rarely available.[28]

Already at the interview at the *Bundesamt für Fremdenwesen und Asyl*, persons from the asylum seeker's (a-)religious institutions are allowed to be present as persons of trust; however, this does not give them the right to intervene in the procedure. This is also true for the hearings at the *Bundesverwaltungsgericht*, where persons of trust are usually obliged to remain silent during the interrogation.

The quasi-expert status of the church official as witness can be conceptualized in two ways. First, they operate as experts on matters concerning knowledge about the respective congregation, like the importance of specific holidays, its ritual procedures, its authorities, its hierarchical structures, its belief system, the meaning of baptism, etc. However, the role of the expert witness becomes complicated due to the aforementioned criteria of the knowledge being made part of the self, or internalized. In addition to their role in checking the nature, scope and depth of the religious knowledge of the convert, they are expected to provide knowledge and make statements about the asylum seekers personally, beyond the knowledge and the content of their faith. Thus, in addition to the expert knowledge about Christianity, a witness contributes to the truth-finding process in conversion claims by drawing on knowledge about his/her acquaintanceship with the asylum seeker and their beliefs.

However, we need to note that church officials would frequently question the state officials' insistence on the personality of the 'convert' in assessing someone's faith by referring to the state officials' lack of feeling (*Gespür*), sensibility

(*Empfinden*) or ability to grasp the essence of Christianity. This epistemic stance of 'I believe in order to understand' is illustrated by the quote by a protestant priest: '[The official] cannot sense that if she is not inside of it.'[29] The emphasis on feeling poses a problem for state actors, since it evades their classificatory, distanced and 'objectified' understanding of 'fact finding' that is supposed to mark the secular logic of the state.

Another aspect of church members' multifarious involvement in the asylum procedure of the converts is their role prior to the court hearings. Church members often prepare the asylum seekers. As a supplement to the regular building of a knowledge corpus in baptism preparation or in discussions at atheist meetings, preparations are often directed at the official asylum procedure. In interviews, the members of (a-)religious institutions usually emphasized that the activities like baptism preparation were entirely separated from this court preparation.

Besides making the asylum seeker familiar with the official procedures, the preparations often revolve around knowledge about Christianity. Based on prior experiences, (a-)religious institutions draw up lists of questions which are found to be commonly asked at court hearings. These lists circulate inside the institutions, building a basis of knowledge which can then be studied by asylum seekers to prepare them about expressing how the new way of life manifests itself for the asylum seeker. A former court witness remarked in an interview, 'We also examined our asylum seekers [laughs]. Asked about their knowledge. But also repeatedly told them that they can and should express themselves emotionally.'[30] 'Expressing themselves emotionally' is important to present one's own religion in a way that goes beyond answers which can easily be learnt by heart. Besides 'emotionally embody[ing], in the courtroom, what they reveal in the text of their testimony',[31] asylum seekers should also be able to explain how they interpret certain bible passages or philosophical questions.

A third aspect of the religious officials' roles concerns the production of documents. Besides the statements provided by witnesses at court as well as the preparation/training process of the asylum seeker, *documents* play an important role in the production of truth about one's conversion. Documents are found to be a way of complying with the courts' standards in establishing a credible conversion narrative. Written documents play a powerful role in 'the structuring of identities and circumstances'.[32] The most widespread forms of documents in this context are probably the baptism certificate as well as written statements by church members, indicating that the appellant has indeed taken part in religious activities. Along the baptism certificate as the most widely known document, other evidence concerning the baptism includes photos of the ceremony or – as in the case of an atheist organization – attendance lists which are handed out at the regular meetings, where the asylum seekers can sign in to prove their continuous involvement in the community.

There are, however, also other forms of documents used in the process, one of which especially drew our attention, since it very clearly shows how the 'noise' of an inner change of identity is put into an acceptable and audible, thereby usable, form.

These are documents produced about the religious attitude of atheist or agnostic asylum seekers on the basis of a semi-structured interview. The interviewee expresses his/her philosophic world views, which are later reformulated by the atheism expert in the manner of one of our opening quotes about Spinoza and Nietzsche, when he says that the expressed view would comply an established philosophical cosmology.

These documents are titled as 'survey concerning the religious attitude of xy [*Gutachten zur religiösen Einstellung von xy*]'. They represent the outcome of a semi-structured interview conducted by the expert which she or he describes as 'pos[ing] questions which one must pose in order to find out if someone advocates an atheist worldview relatively consequently and ordered'.[33] Besides the classification of the asylum seekers' utterances in an acceptable epistemic frame, these surveys are thought of as occupying a powerful position due to the expert status of their author. The latter (potentially) concludes the survey with the assessment that the asylum seeker would 'sincerely and honestly advocate an atheist position'.

People from (a-)religious institutions, even if they are not summoned as witnesses at the *Bundesverwaltungsgericht*, can furthermore obtain the role of a quasi-witness via the use of documents, occasionally described as a 'letter of recommendation [*Empfehlungsschreiben*]'. Here, the community members declare that they know the convert and that they can confirm his/her regular and active contributions. One must, however, be aware that these letters of recommendation can also be used by state officials as indicators of the fraudulent character of a conversion if the asylum seeker is not able to answer questions in the manner of 'you were described as this and that or that you do this and that in a Christian way. Why? Explain what was meant by that!'[34]

In short, the usage of documents, alongside the hearing preparation and the witness statements, all illustrate how a conversion is performed, not only by the asylum seeker, but also by other players such as the church members mentioned here. While the persons in the field occasionally draw on differing epistemic systems, they – as part of the apparatus – produce a 'unified' narrative of truth, relying on these very different types of knowledge. The conversion apparatus produces but also builds upon 'regimes of proof',[35] within which different forms of 'data' are produced as evidence of claims and the determination of credibility.

Rumours and inter- and intra-congregational tensions

The truth-finding process is entrenched in scepticism, rumours and hearsay. We found instances of these rumours going in various directions. In addition to the scepticism from the state actors concerning the realness of the conversion, this disbelief can also be anchored in the inter-congregational dynamics and tensions as a whole; this is especially the case for lesser-known churches like Pentecostals (especially in Austria). Furthermore, there are intra-congregational rumours as illustrated by the following quote from a Catholic Church official: 'These [congregations] appeared in 2015 from abroad [and] were very active in 2016 and practically only did weekend courses. 30 people in the lecture room in Linz. Saturday preparation, Sunday baptism.'[36] In this case, the scepticism is addressed to 'smaller' and non-state congregations. It illustrates a dynamic in which the institution itself can be accused of accepting members 'only' as to raise their chances for asylum or to increase the number of members in the congregation.[37]

Suspicion towards other congregations is, however, also present in communities with no standardized ways of member acceptance. This is based on claims that in the Catholic Church, baptism, for example, would be only bound to a member certificate. A member of a Free Church who stressed the personal aspect of baptism stated that for him, 'it looked like that those two who consciously said, "no, we are not only getting baptized in pretense [*des Scheins wegen*] but we really take it seriously and only get baptized when we are ready and convinced", they had a handicap in the end which is somehow sad'.[38] What becomes apparent in both statements is that the discourse about fake conversions has certainly entered the congregations.

While it was confirmed by informants that members of national churches have a higher rate of positive asylum decisions,[39] one should move the question of power of (a-)religious institutions beyond the binary of 'national' or 'free' churches to a global scale.[40] The inter- and intra-congregational power struggles all find their way into the 'registers of doubt', which become integral part of the truth-finding processes of the conversion apparatus.

Whereas the sincerity of a conversion is usually not to be doubted in non-asylum cases, since it could hardly serve non-spiritual interests,[41] in the case of asylum, doubt and scepticism have a central role in the working of the apparatus. Operating as hidden registers, they mark the truth-finding processes. Traces of this sceptical attitude can be found in personal statements as well as in official church documents stating that it would be especially important to the Catholic Church to thoroughly check on asylum seekers' motives behind the wish to get baptized. The rationale behind this examination is that only by taking these measures can the institution obtain its powerful position by distinguishing between 'real' and 'fake' converts. This is very much about guarding their authority.

In lieu of a conclusion

We have shown that the space within which the convert is made to speak in the asylum processes is produced by several state and non-state actors within an active and conjunctural field. The convert's voice becomes audible not because of its content, but by the performance of how, when, at what pace and in relation to what kind of publics and authority a particular kind of knowledge is acquired, lived through, and communicated, and by whom it is evaluated. Converts' utterances become audible and act as performatives only in relation to this space strongly marked by emotions, but also by canonized 'knowledge' about the former religion, in our case Islam. A method of knowing, which Ann Stoler aptly identifies to be prevalent in the colonial archives, marks the conversion apparatus: 'Evidential truths derived from rumor, visual proof, hearsay, emotives, and the written word, each called upon as "fact" (or disparaged as unreliable) depending on who conveyed them, where and when.'[42] These truth registers, as is the case with all performatives, should be recognized as such by the main institutional players involved in this process so that they become credible. It is ironic that rumours acquire a central place within the diagnostics of the 'truth-fact-finding' of the asylum-conversion processes and in its hierarchies of credibility. Rumours are also central in establishing a fertile battle ground for the negotiation of inter- and intra-congregational power and dominance. While trying to identify the transformative nature of conversion for the asylum-convert within this apparatus, this process unleashes a transformative process on the churches and particularly on the canonization of Christian belief.

Notes

1. Kocak 2022.
2. Foucault 1975; Foucault 1976; Agamben 2009; Feldman 2011: 375–95; Feldman 2012.
3. This increase followed a period of relatively stable number of asylum applications between 13,000 and 17,500 in the years 2006–13. In 2022, after the start of the Russian attack on Ukraine, the number reached a peak of 108,781 applications.
4. With the re-establishment of the Taliban regime in 2021 the situation for Afghani citizens in Austria has changed, since the Austrian state has suspended deportations to Afghanistan.
5. On the topic of Country of Origin Information, see van der Kist, Dijstelbloem and de Goede 2018: 68–85; van der Kist and Rosset 2020: 663–79; Gibb and Good 2013: 291–322.
6. Whereas until 2021 this was mainly done by NGOs or private lawyers, now the state-owned *Bundesagentur für Betreuungs – und Unterstützungsleistungen* (*BBU*) has taken over most of the cases.
7. The concept of apparatus refers to a heterogeneous ensemble of mechanisms and knowledge structures, which maintains and reproduces the exercise of power within the social body. Building upon Foucault, Agamben and Feldman use it to analyse the mechanism through which a set of relations between disconnected actors and diverse phenomena such as discourses, institutions, architectural forms, regulatory decisions, laws, administrative measures, scientific statements, philosophical, moral and philanthropic propositions are established. Foucault 1975, 1976; Agamben 2009; Feldman 2011, 2012.
8. Wikström 2014: 210–18.
9. Agamben 2009.
10. Butler, in her theory of performativity (1990), refers to the ways discursive practices produce or enact by naming or by utterance. Performance here refers to the way the asylum seeker is constituted by his/her *acts* of utterances/discursive practices rather than representing an already-constituted subject.
11. Scheffer 2003: 427 [translation by the authors].
12. Rabinow 2003: 54.
13. This followed a period of relatively stable number of asylum applications between 13,000 and 17,500 per year from 2006. Before that, the conflicts in Afghanistan and Chechnya had led to a peak in 2002 with close to 40,000 applications. https://www.bmi.gv.at/301/Statistiken/files/Jahresstatistiken/Jahresstatistik_Asyl_2016.pdf (accessed 5 December 2021).
14. Scheffer 2003: 430.

15 Bischofskonferenz 2015: 9–14; Theologischer Ausschuss der Generalsynode der Evangelischen Kirche 2014.
16 The question of the (non-)authenticity of asylum seekers' conversions increasingly became a topic in the media coverage in Germany and Europe. See Stadlbauer 2019.
17 VwGH 20.07.2020, Ra 2019/14/0608.
18 Interview 17 December 2020.
19 Snow and Machalek 1984: 167–90.
20 BVwG 28.01.2021; W1742158420-1/19E, 7.
21 This approach is often based on 'Western notions of Christianity'. See Madziva and Lowndes 2018: 83; Thebault and Rose 2018: 543–50.
22 BVwG 16.07.2020; W1232196188-1, 51–2.
23 Wikström and Johansson 2013: 94.
24 Tuan Samahon highlights the questionability of such an understanding of conversion, since converts would often take on heterodoxic beliefs. See Samahon 2000: 2221–24.
25 This dynamic is also discussed in Ramsauer 2021; Hoellerer and Gill 2021: 1–29.
26 Hoellerer and Gill 2021.
27 This stance seems to neglect the notice made by Samahon that 'Conversion often occurs during adversity'. See Samahon 2000, 2223.
28 For the hearings dealing with claims not based on conversion, expert knowledge can be introduced via surveyors or country of origin information.
29 Interview 19 October 2021.
30 Interview 13 September 2021.
31 McKinnon 2009: 215.
32 Dahlvik 2013: 304.
33 Interview 22 October 2021.
34 Interview 19 October 2021.
35 Sriraman 2018.
36 Interview 11 December 2020.
37 Ramsauer 2021; Hoellerer and Gill 2021.
38 Interview 13 March 2021.
39 See, for example: https://www.katholisch.at/aktuelles/136008/konversion-als-asylgrund-experte-sieht-verbesserungen-bei-behoerde (accessed 4 November 2021).
40 Çağlar and Schiller 2018; Schiller and Çağlar 2015: 40–61.
41 An exception being (alleged) 'fake conversions' in order to become eligible to be a godfather or godmother.
42 Stoler 2022.

Bibliography

Agamben, Giorgio (2009). *'What Is an Apparatus?' and Other Essays*. Stanford, CA: Stanford University Press.

Bischofskonferenz, Österreichische (2015). 'Richtlinien der Österreichischen Bischöfe zum Katechumenat von Asylwerbern'. *Amtsblatt der Österreichischen Bischofskonferenz*, 64 (1): 9–14.

Butler, Judith (1990). 'Performative Acts and Gender Constitution: An Essay in Phenomenology and Feminist Theory'. *Performing Feminisms: Feminist Critical Theory and Theatre*, Sue-Ellen Case (ed.), 270–82. Baltimore: Johns Hopkins University Press.

Caglar, Ayse and Nina Glick Schiller (2018). *Migrants and City-Making Dispossession, Displacement, and Urban Regeneration*. Durham; London: Duke University Press.

Dahlvik, Julia (2013). 'Institutionelle Einsichten: Die Bedeutsamkeit von Schriftlichkeit und Dokumenten Im Prozess der Bearbeitung von Asylanträgen'. *Migration und Integration – Wissenschaftliche Perspektiven Aus Österreich. Jahrbuch 2/2013*, Julia Dahlvik, Christoph Reinprecht and Wiebke Sievers (eds.), 301–17. Göttingen: V&R unipress.

Feldman, Gregory (2011). 'If Ethnography Is More than Participant-Observation, Then Relations Are More than Connections: The Case for Nonlocal Ethnography in a World of Apparatuses'. *Anthropological Theory*, 11 (4): 375–95.

Feldman, Gregory (2012). *The Migration Apparatus: Security, Labor, and Policymaking in the European Union*. Stanford, CA: Stanford University Press.

Foucault, Michel (1975). *Surveiller et Punir: Naissance de La Prison*. Paris: Gallimard.

Foucault, Michel (1976). *Histoire de La Sexualité. 1, La Volonté de Savoir*. Paris: Gallimard.

Gibb, Robert, and Anthony Good (2013). 'Do the Facts Speak for Themselves? Country of Origin Information in French and British Refugee Status Determination Procedures'. *International Journal of Refugee Law*, 25 (2): 291–322.

Glick Schiller, Nina, and Ayse Caglar (2015). 'Beyond Methodological Ethnicity and towards the City Scale: An Alternative Approach to Local and Transnational Pathways of Migrant Incorporation'. *Rethinking Transnationalism: The Meso-Link of Organisations*, Ludger Pries (ed.), 40–61. London: Routledge.

Hoellerer, Nicole and Nick Gill (December 2021). 'Assembly-Line Baptism: Judicial Discussions of "Free Churches" in German and Austrian Asylum Hearings.' *Journal of Legal Anthropology*, 5 (2): 1–29.

Kagan, Michael (2003). 'Is Truth in the Eye of the Beholder? Objective Credibility Assessment in Refugee Status Determination'. *Georgetown Immigration Law Journal*, 17 (3): 367–415.

Kist, Jasper van der, and Damian Rosset (2020). 'Knowledge and Legitimacy in Asylum Decision-Making: The Politics of Country of Origin Information'. *Citizenship Studies*, 24 (5): 663–79.

Kist, Jasper van der, Huub Dijstelbloem and Marieke de Goede (2018). 'In the Shadow of Asylum Decision-Making: The Knowledge Politics of Country-of-Origin Information'. *International Political Sociology*, 13 (1): 68–85.

Kocak, Mert (2022). 'Migration Industries and Transnational Governance of Queer Migration: Bureaucratization of Sexuality and Gender in Turkey'. PhD Thesis.

Madziva, Roda and Vivien Lowndes (2018). 'What Counts as Evidence in Adjudicating Asylum Claims? Locating the Monsters in the Machine: An Investigation of Faith'. *Science and the Politics of Openness: Here Be Monsters*, Sarah Hartley, Brigitte Nerlich, Sujatha Raman and Alexander Smith (eds.), 75–94. Manchester: Manchester University Press.

McKinnon, Sara L. (2009). 'Citizenship and the Performance of Credibility: Audiencing Gender-Based Asylum Seekers in U.S. Immigration Courts'. *Text and Performance Quarterly*, 29 (3): 205–21.

Rabinow, Paul (2003). *Anthropos Today: Reflections on Modern Equipment*. Princeton, NJ; Oxford: Princeton University Press.

Ramsauer, Markus E. (2021). 'Who Creates What? The Apparatus of Conversion'. Master's Thesis.

Samahon, Tuan N. (2000). 'The Religion Clauses and Political Asylum: Religious Persecution Claims and the Religious Membership-Conversion Imposter Problem'. *The Georgetown Law Journal*, 88 (7): 2221–38.

Scheffer, Thomas (2003). 'Kritik der Urteilskraft – Wie die Asylprüfung Untentscheidbares in Entscheidbares überführt'. *Migration Steuern und Verwalten: Deutschland vom späten 19. Jahrhundert bis zur Gegenwart*, Jochen Oltmer (ed.), 423–58. Göttingen: V&R unipress.

Snow, David A. and Richard Machalek (1984). 'The Sociology of Conversion'. *Annual Review of Sociology*, 10 (1): 167–90.

Sriraman, Tarangini (2018). *In Pursuit of Proof: A History of Identification Documents in India*. New Delhi: Oxford University Press.

Stadlbauer, Susanne (2019). 'Between Secrecy and Transparency: Conversions to Protestantism among Iranian Refugees in Germany'. *Entangled Religions*, 8: 69–93. https://doi.org/10.13154/er.8.2019.8322.

Stoler, Ann L. (2022). *Interior Frontiers: Essays on the Entrails of Inequality*. Oxford: Oxford University Press.

Thebault, Deborah, and Lena Rose (2018). 'What Kind of Christianity? A v Switzerland'. *Oxford Journal of Law and Religion*, 7 (3): 543–50.

Theologischer Ausschuss der Generalsynode der Evangelischen Kirche (2014). 'Handreichung des Theologischen Ausschusses der Generalsynode der

Evangelischen Kirche A. und H.B. in Österreich für Taufanfragen, Taufunterricht und Taufe von Asylsuchenden'.

Wikström, Hanna (2014). 'Gender, Culture and Epistemic Injustice: The Institutional Logic in Assessment of Asylum Applications in Sweden'. *Nordic Journal of Migration Research*, 4 (4): 210–18.

Wikström, Hanna and Thomas Johansson (2013). 'Credibility Assessments as "Normative Leakage": Asylum Applications, Gender and Class'. *Social Inclusion*, 1 (2): 92–101.

5

Material conversions: Exploring the materiality of asylum seekers' conversion narratives in Norway

Olav Børreson Fossdal

Introduction

This chapter employs the perspective of materiality to investigate Iranian asylum seekers' conversion narratives in Norway. I use Lewis Rambo's seven-stage model for religious conversion,[1] as a starting-point, and elaborate on four of its stages to explore how the perspective of materiality can be included. The four stages are *context, encounter, interaction* and *commitment*. My findings show that different physical objects are given agency by asylum seeker converts at various stages during the conversion process. This means that there is a connection between the converts' intentions for religious change and the material objects being used during the process of conversion. Using the perspective of materiality, I specifically look for the meaning behind objects. These meanings are stretched and placed outside of objects' physical capabilities, generating an agency that becomes visible between physical things and humans. The data for this chapter was collected using a two-part interview methodology.[2] In addition to the interviews, I analysed twenty conversion cases from Norwegian courts with special attention to material objects. I suggest that examining religious conversion through objects can offer an alternative avenue of understanding that broadens assessments of individuals' religious convictions. Additionally, I argue that immigration authorities should actively include questions about asylum applicants' relationship to religious objects, when considering the credibility of religious conversions. However, simply questioning applicants about material objects is inadequate if the implication of the answers is not sufficiently understood. Therefore, authorities should move beyond a superficial examination of materiality and prioritize a deeper understanding of its significance. This chapter offers a comprehensive framework that can guide decision-makers in this task.

Asylum seeker conversion cases in a Norwegian context

To contextualize my findings, we begin with some background on the Norwegian treatment of asylum cases. Seeking asylum is a human right which is stated in the United Nations' Universal Declaration of Human Rights and agreed to by almost all member states in 1948, including Norway.[3] Additionally, freedom of religion is a constitutional right in Norway. However, a dilemma occurs for Norwegian authorities receiving applications for protection based on claims of religious conversion. Norway cannot deny asylum to people who, because of their religious conviction, might face persecution in their country of origin. Simultaneously, due to a strict immigration policy, asylum cannot be granted to all who seek it. Therefore, being granted asylum in Norway is not always an easy feat. All Western countries have put in place deterrence policies so that they can avoid non-refoulement obligations like processing claims, providing food, housing and attracting more asylum seekers (Parekh 2020: 128). These initiatives intend to make it harder to receive asylum and to prevent large numbers of asylum seekers from entering. The juridical framework of conversion cases in Norway is constituted in the Immigration Act, specifically chapter 4, *Residence permit for foreign nationals in need for protection (asylum)*.[4]

In Norway, every asylum seeker must go through an application process where their claim for asylum is processed, investigated and questioned by the authorities. This includes the assessment of credibility of religious conversion claims. Additionally, the risk of persecution, on grounds of religious conversion, in the applicant's country of origin is also considered before the authorities decide on the outcome of the application.

All applications for asylum in Norway are first handled by the Directorate of Immigration (UDI). The UDI conducts interviews that determine the applicant's claim for asylum in Norway, including the credibility of religious conversions. If the UDI rejects an applicant's claim, he or she can appeal to the Immigration Appeal Board (UNE). The UNE was established as an independent executive office in 2001, operating on behalf of the Justice Department. In short, this means that no politically elected official, MP or otherwise, can interfere with the appeal board's processing of asylum cases. The reason for establishing the UNE was due to an increase in cases, leading to heightened pressure and executive work for the Department and Minister of Justice. Additionally, critique was directed towards the Justice Department, fearing the workload would hinder a due process of law (Grythe 2009: 367). An asylum seeker convert arguing for the credibility of their conversion can appear in person and make their case in a board hearing. In a board hearing, three people decide the outcome of the case together: a board leader who is employed by the UNE and two members from outside the institution. Most of these applications were previously processed internally without the asylum seeker being present. From 1 August 2021, asylum seeker converts were given an enhanced right to have their case processed by the UNE. Additionally, the right to provide witnesses for the applicant was strengthened. The reason for these changes was due to the special challenges of fact-finding and evidence, when mapping out a person's religious conviction[5]. Most applicants in religious conversion cases that the UNE processes are from Afghanistan[6] and Iran.[7] Today, Afghan converts, who are believed to have a valid claim for their religious conversion, receive protection in Norway because of the high risk of persecution they face at the time of writing. However, the situation is different for Iranians. According to the UNE, it is possible for some, but not all, Iranian converts to live their life as Christians in Iran without fearing persecution. The key challenge for the UNE is determining how each convert chooses to live out their Christian faith. This implies that an outward religious lifestyle, both vocal and visual, is seen to lead to a greater risk of persecution in Iran. The UNE can either reject the applicant's claim or change the UDI's initial decision. If the UNE rejects the applicants claim, he or she can take their case to court. Cases regarding asylum seekers and religious conversion have been prosecuted at all three levels of the Norwegian court system.[8] In this chapter, I include twenty cases like this. Before I provide my analysis of these, I will examine what potential the perspective of materiality can offer when researching religious conversions.

Religious conversion from the perspective of materiality

The perspective of materiality on religious conversion is increasingly becoming a topic of scholarly interest. There are several reasons for this, but one might credit some of this heightened attention to the *material turn* within religious studies. Among other things, this field of study has revealed that material things, practices and symbols can be interpreted for the religious meanings they carry (Hazard

2013). This perspective also challenges a Western historical bias towards religion as primarily being a system of *belief*. Scholars of material religion challenge this bias, and stress that religion is very much a material phenomenon. This becomes even more evident when we look at religious conversions. In this context, Helena Kupari notes that even though research on conversion and materiality is growing, it is still a perspective that seldom is included in scientific theories and definitions of conversion as a religious phenomenon (Kupari 2023: 2). According to Kupari, this is not so surprising given the conventional understanding of conversion in social scientific scholarship, namely that conversion involves radical changes in the individual's consciousness (i.e. that conversion is a mental event and therefore essentially 'immaterial'). This conventional understanding tends to overshadow the potential that the perspective of materiality offers. For instance, the possibility of exploring what role local epistemology and material creativity plays in conversion processes (Bennett 2022: 30). A reason for applying Lewis Rambo's seven-stage model in this chapter is to show that objects have continuous relevance for asylum seeker converts throughout the process of conversion. It is also an attempt to demonstrate why the perspective of materiality can and should be included in theoretical assessments of conversions as a religious phenomenon. Including this perspective is especially relevant regarding asylum seeker converts applying for protection. This group of converts must prove their religious conviction to immigration authorities and courts and, as we will see, use objects to do this. It is therefore important that authorities correctly consider the material dimension of religious life. For appeal boards, like the UNE, that struggle with challenges of fact-finding and evidence in these types of cases, it can be fruitful to actively include questions about converts' relationship to material objects. Examining religious conversion through objects can offer an alternative avenue of understanding that complements and expands on the conventional focus on personal faith and belief, thus creating a broader assessment of an individual's religious conviction.

In the preface of his book, Rambo writes that the limitations of sociological literature in the field became apparent to him when developing his model. He stresses the need for interdisciplinary perspectives on religious conversion. Consequently, the model he developed can be categorized as a holistic approach to the phenomenon of religious conversions (Groonen 2010: 40). This means that even though Rambo does not consider a material perspective on conversion specifically, his model allows for this perspective to be included. It must be mentioned that Rambo does mention aspects of religion that can be studied from the perspective of materiality. For instance, he mentions cultural symbols

(Rambo 1993: 25), salient features of religion (Rambo 1993: 88) and religious actions (Rambo 1993: 114), all of which can become important aspects of any conversion process. Still, Rambo does not go into detail regarding the physicality and material properties of these conversion aspects. As a supplement to Rambo's model, this chapter therefore shows how these aspects can be manifested physically through materials and objects. Specifically, based on findings in my own research interviews with asylum seeker converts, I show how objects are important in the conversion stages *context, encounter, interaction and commitment*.

Objects as proof: Determining the credibility of conversion claims in Norwegian court rooms

Before conducting my interviews, I analysed several 'conversion cases' from Norwegian courts, looking for references to material objects. In this chapter, I have included an analysis of twenty cases from Norwegian courts.[9] These cases cover a ten-year period from 2012 to 2022. I use these cases to illustrate a wider argument: that focusing on material objects can provide further depth to decision-makers' understanding of religious conversions. In the following analysis I highlight two discoveries: that material objects are referenced to and blend in with asylum seekers' overarching testimonies for religious protection in Norway, and that the Bible is the most common object mentioned in these testimonies. This matters because biblical knowledge is important in these hearings generally (see other chapters). However, the Bible as a religious object itself should also be more regarded because of its physical capabilities and the various religious meanings it carries for asylum seeker converts.

There are certain commonalities in these testimonies and references to objects play supporting roles in these. For instance, asylum seeker converts are expected to provide the court with a verifiable timeline of conversion. One way converts do this is by showing pictures to the court from their baptism,[10] or religious wedding.[11] The photographs become part of the wider presentation of evidence along with testimonies from witnesses – like congregation members or religious leaders, and baptismal certificates with dates and signatures. Religious imagery[12] in the domestic sphere can also be used as an example of genuine religious commitment by the convert. Having an active role within a congregation is also often stressed by the converts as an example of credible religious conviction. They prove this by referencing to various usages of the Bible. For instance, by participating in Bible study groups,[13] or translating passages or sermons for other members.[14] I will return to the frequent mentioning and various usages of the Bible in these cases shortly. Another common element in these testimonies is how converts express a strong desire to missionize and/or expose their Christian identity in the public sphere. One example of this can be wanting to establish an underground home-church upon return to their country of origin. Objects can be mentioned in this setting too, for instance, by distributing pamphlets[15] or wearing visible religious jewellery.[16]

The most common object that asylum seeker converts mention is the Bible. This book came up in all twenty cases. When referred to in this setting, the Bible is largely used in two ways. First, it is referred to as part of different religious practices the convert is involved in. These practices include participation in Bible study groups, reading scripture in church and quoting from it when evangelizing to others. A second way is referring to it as a specific religious object. The Bible is mentioned when the converts stress the illegality of possessing or distributing the book in their country of origin. Additionally, participating in smuggling the Bible to Iran in large quantities has in one case been used as an argument for a type of Christian activity that puts the convert in risk of persecution.[17] Interestingly, the Norwegian courts seem to pay little attention to the content of the Bible itself. What is important to the courts seems to be how this book becomes part of an explicit religious expression. Less consideration is directed to the theological arguments that the asylum seeker, or their witnesses, puts forward. In other words, that the object itself and what it can symbolize is more important in this context. Building on from this, it stands to reason that the Bible keeps being mentioned because its usage can be regarded, by the courts, as outward and visual Christian activity. To a degree, the usage of the Bible in various settings demonstrates the converts' attempts to be perceived as an 'authentic' Christian in the eyes of the court. This can in turn strengthen their claim of a valid conversion, in addition to stressing their risk of persecution should they return to their country of origin. As we will see, the Bible is also mentioned by my interlocutors, but in other ways. I will look closer at other aspects of the Bible and how its agency can shift and thus affect a conversion process.

Cultural *contexts*: The shifting agency of religious symbols

To fit the perspective of materiality into Rambo`s model, we first need to locate an aspect of the many contextual dimensions that can include references to objects. Context, in general, refers to the circumstances that form a given setting, in terms of which it can be interpreted and understood. When it comes to the contexts surrounding religious conversions, we must understand these as a vast panorama of conflicting, confluent and dialectical factors that both facilitate and repress conversions (Rambo 1993: 20). The vastness of contextual circumstances that affect religious conversions is so grand that it is not so much a stage in the stage model, but rather, as Rambo puts it, a total environment in which a conversion transpires. Because of this, I want to look more closely at a specific one of these contextual dimensions. Rambo refers to this one as 'culture and context'.

According to Clifford Geertz, 'culture is not a power, something to which social events, behaviours, institutions, or processes can be casually attributed; it is a context, something within which they can be intelligibly – that is, thickly – described' (Geertz 1973: 26). If this is true, it should also imply, as Webb Keane notes, that social categories such as culture must 'have some material manifestation that makes them available to, interpretable by, and, in most cases, replicable by other people: bodily actions, speech, the treatment of objects, and so forth' (Keane 2008: 114). Using these insights, we can conclude that cultural processes, such as conversions, cannot happen outside of cultural contexts. Moreover, for conversions to occur, and reoccur over time, they must happen in ways that make them recognizable and take semiotic form. Lastly, I want to add that the material manifestations of religious conversions do not only happen at the beginning of a conversion but, as my following examples in this chapter show, both endure and change during the process. This must be paid attention to in credibility assessments of religious converts.

The most prominent symbols of the Christian and Islamic faith are their sacred texts, the Bible and the Quran. One could perhaps argue that the authority of these religious symbols is rooted in their textual content. This, of course, is true, but not the full picture. The Bible and the Quran must also be regarded as objects with agencies stemming from their physicality. This becomes observable to us when we look at how Iranian asylum seeker converts from Islam to Christianity specifically relate to and utilize the Bible. To approach these matters reflexively, it would help to give an impression of the cultural and religious contexts that surround the Iranian converts in their country of origin.[18]

From the point of view of Islamic teaching, Muslims and Christians are among *din-e hanif*, puritanical/monotheistic religions, and both are offspring of Ibrahim with their roots to the divine (Afshari 2021: 284). This means that Christianity is acknowledged, and Islamic teaching allows for Christians to live within Muslim communities. However, Sharia law prohibits Christian leaders to rule over

Muslims. Secondly, only some Christian groups, mainly Orthodox and Catholic, are regarded as a 'religious minority' in Iran. Laws are implemented in the Iranian constitution that seek to secure some of their civil rights as a minority. But not all Christian denominations are regarded as a religious minority by the state. This privilege is granted to specific ethnic-religious groups, such as Armenians, Assyrians and Chaldeans. This means that belonging to a (Christian) religious minority is more connected to ethnicity, than to the individual's freedom to choose a religious identity. Thirdly, the Iranian government despises Protestant Christianity, calling it *Messihiat-e enherfy* (deviant Christianity) (Afshari 2021: 285). The reason for this is mainly because Protestantism is associated with Western Europe and the United States, and because protestant missionary movements from these countries increased their activity in Iran during the twentieth century.

The converts I interviewed were Iranians, Protestants and critical of the Iranian regime. They do not, in other words, fit in to any of the above-mentioned 'criteria' for living out their religious lives in accordance with the regime's (limited) perception of religious diversity. Given that there seems to be little room for them in the Iranian religious landscape, the question of how they utilize and relate to religious symbols as part of their conversion process is exceptionally relevant. Iranian converts receiving, buying or having the Bible in their possession is part of what starts their conversion process. For converts the Bible is regarded as the truth, an authority and a teacher. It is also an object that is kept secret. However, the initial reaction to the book can be quite reluctant. All these capabilities show how the relationship to physical symbols is affected by converts' cultural contexts.

In my interviews I heard converts talk about how sceptical they were at first towards the Bible. One convert, Maryam, who converted in Norway together with her whole family, talked about the first time they were invited to a birthday party in a church. The family decided to go, mainly because they knew that there would be other Iranians there. But before they went, they all agreed to throw away any Bible they might receive. Another convert, Farad, first visited a church because they gave out free food and showed movies. Afterwards, he threw the Bible he had received in a trash can outside the building. When I asked Farad why he did that, he said: 'I didn't know anything about what it said (the Bible). I only knew that it was the book for the Christians and that they were wrong.' This attitude towards the Bible is closely connected to Iranian cultural contexts generally, and more specifically the religious authority that the Quran symbolizes.

Though all converts I talked to claimed not to have been particularly religious prior to their Christian conversion, the dominant status of Islam was still woven into their country's cultural fabric. This can mean that the position of Islam shapes the new converts' contextual dimensions in such a way that adhering to them, by possessing other religious literature, represents a rupture with what is acceptable within an Iranian context. The hesitation of accepting the Bible as a gift is not rooted in its content, which most Iranian converts are unaware of in the beginning. The reason is because it is an object associated with Christianity. Therefore, within an Iranian cultural context, it is frowned upon. The Quran is also a symbol given agency outside of its textual content. For instance, when storing a Quran written in Arabic, it should be separated from other non-Islamic books and placed on the highest shelf within the cupboard. In addition to these specificities, many interlocutors describe how unattainable its content is. In its standardized form the Quran is written in Arabic, a language most Iranians do not understand. For these converts then, the Quran is more a token of the Islamic faith than a direct source of religious knowledge. Iranian asylum seeker converts' initial relationship to these two objects reveals a contextual presupposition embedded in culture, vital for the initiation of the conversion process.

The aforementioned reluctance continues after the Bible is in the converts' possession. However, these feelings are no longer directed towards the book itself, but to the converts' social surroundings. The converts' relationship to the book changes from reluctance to secrecy. In my interview with Mehdi, I showed him a picture of the Quran and the Bible lined up next to each other. While reflecting on his relationship to the two books, he told me the story of his meeting a Christian in Tehran who gave him his first Bible.

> I took the Bible that the Christian gave me. I went home and started to read. I had no teacher. I sat alone at home, reading. After my family had left the house and no one was home, I read. It was not allowed to have a Bible at home. If anyone found out, I would be put in jail. So, I read in secret. I read fast. I was like a hungry man who finally found food!

Keeping an object secret from family and using it in solitude also tells us a lot about the desire to materialize a possible newfound religious identity, even if it challenges the cultural contexts that surround the converts. In her article *Between Secrecy and Transparency*, Susanne Stadlbauer explores the concept of secrecy among asylum seeker converts in Germany. She writes: 'In terms of secrecy, the converts learn to acquire Christian practices and rituals in secret in Iran and are concerned about hiding them from the Iranian public or even from family members' (Stadlbauer 2019: 3). In addition to being an object that represents Christianity, for some converts, the Bible represents a new source of religious information. Many read the text thoroughly and, like Mehdi, develop an interest in theology through their own studies of the Bible and other Christian literature.

The first *encounter*: Seeking out a religious space

Different physical objects are given agency at different stages during the conversion process. Arguably one of the most important stages of any conversion process is the first encounter with the new religion. Meeting members for the first time, reading scripture or entering a new religious space can all be contributing factors when an individual makes the decision to convert. Encounters with a new religion happen through people, such as missionaries, or through salient features of a religion, such as objects of worship (Rambo 1993: 87–8). Let us take a closer look at how salient features and objects can play an active part in conversion narratives. I asked Cyrus if he could tell me when he first came to learn about Christianity. He shared:

> It all started when we drove past a church in Iran. I was maybe 13 or 14 years old. I asked my father what it was, and he said that it was a church. He then told me a bit about it, and I became very curious. I really wanted to go inside and see what it was like because the building was so different from everything else. I talked to a classmate of mine, and we decided to go have a look and see what it was like. The first time we went, we came in and figured that we probably had to light a candle. So, we did. We also realized that we had to sit down, and when we after a while decided to leave, we stood up and started walking out. But then we were told not to turn our backs to the altar. We had to, kind of, walk backwards. I liked it. I went back with the same classmate a second time. We did all the same things. Both times we went, there were no priest. It was just hymns sung in Armenian, playing over the speaker system. I liked it. It was something completely different from the mosque. I liked it very much. Everything with the cross, the altar, everything.

Notice how Cyrus' first encounter with Christianity does not contain reflections on substantial elements of Christian theology. His conversion narrative illustrates how it is not always intellectual properties such as dogmas, values and morality that spark an interest in religion. How Christianity differs from Islam, in terms of perceptions of the divine, is not discussed either. He does make a comparison to the mosque, but does so merely in a practical sense, indicating that expected behaviour and bodily practices differ. Of course, one can argue that these forms of practices have a root in some form of authority, for instance, in religious texts. By the agency of interpretation and theological debates, these have been developed through history. Over time, authoritative figures projected these to their intended audiences, making various practices, rites and creeds appear natural through claims of authenticity. From there on, the answers to the question of 'why do we do the things we do?' are always directed back at authoritative figures. This circular relation between authority and projection is common in all cultural traditions (Martin 2017).

However, my point is that some new converts can be completely unaware of these types of authoritative discourses. Cyrus had no previous knowledge of the types of practices typical or common for the church he visited, and naturally so. Instead, upon reflecting on his first encounter, he pointed to the uniqueness of the Armenian Christian practices and material culture. His appreciation of these things came from the fact that they were present in that religious space. The experience gained from Cyrus' first encounter with Christianity is not a deeper theological understanding of the faith, rather merely 'liking it', i.e. the various agencies of his physical surroundings are still what resonated with him. He even explicitly noted that there were no priest present. Rather, the very specific material culture of the church was what sparked Cyrus' interest. Thus, the church building, candles, pew benches, the altar, music and the cross played a major part in the beginning of this conversion narrative. Rambo states that encounters reveal the levels of access to knowledge about a new religion (Rambo 1993: 94). As we have seen, people, clergy and missionaries are not the only providers of this type of religious knowledge. Material objects and surroundings can also be formative in the early encounter stage of conversion.

Interacting with the cross: Using objects in daily religious practices

Alireza showed me a picture of an object very dear to him. It was a small handmade wooden cross, approximately 5–7 cm tall with sanded edges. A Christian activist (CA)[19] sent it to him via mail, while Alireza was detained at Norway's National Police Immigration Detention Centre. In the detention centre, and every night since then, Alireza places this cross in the palm of his hand and holds onto it while sleeping. He says, 'Now, I can't sleep without it.' In the morning, when he wakes up, he places the cross on his nightstand and starts the day with a morning prayer. After telling me this, Alireza smiled and we both chuckled. Talking about sleeping and specific preferences linked to this practice has a certain intimate and vulnerable element to it. The joint laughter that followed was a non-verbal way of admitting this, but also render it as harmless to the interview setting that we were in.

In the interaction stage, the convert learns to experience religion beyond the intellectual level. One way to do this is through religious actions that are regularized, sustained and intentional and which are fundamental to the conversion experience (Rambo 1993: 114). Converts utilize physical objects in their conversion process as parts of religious practices. Bourdieu views practices, in general, as operating directly upon the body, structuring the corporeal level and the very dispositions (i.e. thoughts, feelings, attitudes and perceptions) that generate meaningful human activity (Winchester 2008: 1757). What is important to notice about any practice is how it recognizes the body's relationship to the everyday social order. In addition to conducting practices privately or with other people, humans also utilize objects in their various practices. Objects and other 'non-human' entities are important to include in an observation of practices. This is because, as Julius Bautista notes in the book *The Spirit of Things*, objects at least have the potential of possessing agency, personhood, sovereignty and volition (Bautista 2012: 2). In other words, it should be recognized that there is a connection between the subjects' intention behind a practice and the things (body, spaces and objects) being used. For example, a Christian can ascribe specific meanings to the practice of lighting a candle in a church. Regardless of the meaning, the practice itself requires physical elements such as a body, a church, votive candle stands, a candle, fire, etc.

To use religious practices as an analytical concept means that one concentrates on the connections between the various daily, routine and unconsciously reproduced habits that shape and reproduce this field and its inhabitants (Bender 2012: 281). In ethnographic fieldwork, for instance, a researcher can observe various religious practices such as prayer or meditation. Doing this can teach us more about what religious subjects do and why they do it. An interesting aspect to the analytical category of religious practices is that researchers' scope is not limited to observing practices that are 'strictly' religious. It might be just as fruitful to include other (typically profane) practices as well.

With this in mind, there are several interesting points to the story about Alireza's wooden cross and how he uses it. Firstly, the 'religious nature' of this practice must be addressed. The practice of sleeping is not religious in and of itself. However, the perspective on practice turns our focus towards the processes that make certain things (activities, ideas, institutions) recognizably religious (Bender 2012: 275). The practice of sleeping becomes, in this case, recognizably religious for two reasons: (1) Alireza holds a cross (religious object) in his hand over night, and (2) he attributes specific meanings of comfort and security to the object, which are rooted in his religious conviction. Alireza is sharing the story about the cross to illustrate that he literally keeps a token of his faith with him at night. The story also shows how an object's agency can change when used in different contexts by a subject. Consequently, there are reasons to suggest that the practice of sleeping can be a religious one in Alireza's case. It is also evident that one reason this is a religious practice is because a specific object is being used. It is an object that has a biography and is given an agency by the user.

One other remark to this story is whether the usage of objects in religious practices is dictated by authoritative discourses, or if this usage is a product of the convert's own will. According to Rambo's model, in the interaction stage the potential convert either chooses to continue the contact and become more involved, or the advocate[20] works to sustain the interaction in order to extend the possibility of persuading the potential convert to convert (Rambo 1993: 102). The duality between convert and religious actor is closely related to the scholarly discussion of whether a convert is an active or passive element in the conversion process. The analytical shift towards 'the active convert' represents something of a paradigm shift within the field of conversion studies (Richardson 1985). But when it comes to the relationship between religious actors, asylum seeker converts and material objects, there is, as far as I can tell, no consensus about this 'active/passive' dichotomy. Therefore, this remains an important discussion within the field of asylum seekers and religious conversion.

To explore this further, one could say that Alireza is constructing a specific form of agency to the cross which he aims to 'fit in' to his own imagined or interpreted idea of 'typical' everyday Christian life. In other words, doing something because it is inspired by a specific religious authority – such as a myth, a leader or a group – making him a (more) passive element in his own conversion. This could imply that religious practices are primarily rooted in some form of authoritative discourse. In other words, that converts do not make conscious and individual decisions when conducting religious practices. However, in the case of Alireza, this is not the full picture. The reason for this is based on the very specific context that Alireza was in when he developed this religious practice. He described his time at the detention centre as a time of great solitude, with deep psychological implications. Even though he did correspond with Norwegian

CAs, it still seems implausible that they would provide such a specific guideline as 'how to sleep in a Christian manner' (if such a thing even exists). There were no specific instructions from the CA, who gave the cross to Alireza, on how to use it. Instead, he found a way to use it as part of a practice when constructing a new Christian identity.

From this example, we can see how the convert actively adapts parts of a Christian material culture in a highly individualized fashion. It also suggests that asylum seeker converts, who often spend a great deal of time in solitude, can be extra prone to develop these individualized relationships to religious objects. Without adhering to specific guidance from a given religious authority, the asylum seeker convert are freer to utilize religious objects as they please. This opens a room for religious expression, experimentation and creativity that, to a large extent, are tailored to the converts' own needs and preferences. This means that in addition to interacting with a religious community, i.e. 'the practice of fitting in' (with its own rules, practices, objects, habitus, etc.), an asylum seeker convert will also practice their new religion in ways that are strictly their own – and, importantly, use objects in ways that only have meaning and can be explained by them. In this case, an interaction occurred because an object was provided by a religious actor (CA) and given to the asylum seeker convert. The convert independently developed a religious practice using an object, that in turn became a part of the interaction stage.

Negotiating *commitment* – objects at home: Collecting, crafting and materializing the faith

Commitment involves observable events or rituals that demonstrate the converts' surrender to a new religion, such as baptisms or oral conversion testimonies (Rambo 1993: 135). However, commitment is not only executed in terms of rituals or testimonies. Religious commitment also refers to the degree to which a person adheres to his or her religious values, beliefs and practices, and uses them in daily living (Worthington et al. 2003: 85). The emphasis on usage in daily life is important to keep in mind when it comes to the perspective of materiality. When conducting my interviews, I discovered that several interlocutors decorated their homes with religious symbols and objects. Objects, especially domestic ones, like home altars, shrines or imagery, are part of the converts daily surroundings. Assembling, collecting and crafting objects for the home is, in my view, also a way of measuring religious commitment. There are two reasons for this. One is that religious domestic objects are given agency meant to direct the convert's memory and attention towards their religious values and beliefs in the everyday. The second reason is that religious commitment is thereby sustained over time. Surrendering oneself to a new religion does not happen overnight, and a newfound religious identity needs to be continuously negotiated by the convert. Using objects as a visual reminder can assist the convert in their religious commitment. A closer examination of examples from three of my interviews provides depth to these arguments.

Alireza showed me a picture of an altar in his home. On a table were several familiar objects that symbolize the last days of Jesus' life from the New Testament: a thorn crown, nails, a pouch with silver coins, communion cup and a framed note that says: 'He did it for you' referring to the biblical myth of Jesus sacrificing himself for humankind. When looking at this home shrine, Alireza is reminded of this essential Christian myth. Additionally, he talked about how this story resonated with his own. Like the biblical narrative about Jesus, Alireza had, because of his conversion to Christianity in Iran, also been a victim of betrayal, violence and torture. Constructing these types of biographical narratives that, to a degree, align with religious stories is not uncommon. This phenomenon is also well documented within narrative theory (e.g. Flood 1999). What is striking however, is how these narratives can take a physical form. A need to materialize religious myths, in a either large or small scale, seems to be a common theme amongst many Christians across the world. In his book *Materializing the Bible*, author James Bielo notes that 'materializing the Bible works as an authorizing practice to intensify intimacies with scripture and circulate potent ideologies' (Bielo 2021). Another way of visually portraying a new religious commitment is through collecting objects.

Cyrus also showed me an altar in his home. On the table there were several objects that he and his girlfriend had collected. The objects were souvenirs from trips, gifts and things found in nature. At the back of the altar, leaning up against the wall were small, framed images of Jesus, Mary and Mary Magdalene. In the foreground, an antler, several stones and seashells in different shapes and colours were displayed. To the right is a small wooden cross with sanded edges. Cyrus picked it up and demonstrated how easily it fitted in his hand. He told me that he kept a smaller cross like this one in his pocket and occasionally holds on-to it during the day. To the left there was a bell and a larger ornamented cross made of metal. The cross was a gift from a congregation he joined a few years prior.

While Catholics are the Christians most noted for their shrine building, Protestants also build shrines. Cyrus' shrine reveals a synergy between religious imagery, objects and symbols, put together with things found in nature. This tells us that religious lives are connected to physical places. The objects extracted and collected become memorabilia that ultimately are linked to the process of conversion. Both these examples show how objects can be used when committing to a new religious tradition. Either by materializing its myths or by collecting various objects to a meaningful whole. The third example shows how a time-consuming activity, like crafting an object, can also be an example of a physical representation of religious commitment.

Omid had a woven image of Jesus in his living room, which he and his weaving tutor made together. It depicts Jesus in close proximity to that of Warner Sallman's portrayal *Head of Christ* from 1940. Omid made it in Turkey and talked about the specific techniques needed to create the knots and layers of thread. Specifically, he explained how the knots are tied to warps, which are vertical strands running up and down, keeping the piece together. The colours, shades of brown, red, white and blue, are made from natural resources, he said. He pointed out the difficulty and high level of craftsmanship involved and made several connections to the famous tradition of Persian carpetmaking.

Commitment to a new religion by collecting and crafting objects related to it can be seen as a way of 'surrendering' into a new religious identity. The examples above are very much a demonstration, in a physical sense, of the converts' religious identity and therefore in accordance with Rambo's category of commitment. However, the word 'surrender' that Rambo uses when defining this stage of the conversion process is perhaps a bit dramatic. Gathering, crafting and collecting objects is not so much a surrender to something, as it is submerging and devoting oneself into an interest in a given religious tradition. A key element here is that the process of commitment in a material sense takes time. For any convert to display this type of submersion and devotion visually means that the person is consciously negotiating their degree of commitment.

Conclusion

One prominent component of the theory of material conversions to Christianity is that different physical objects are given agency at various stages during the conversion process. For instance, objects are important at the very beginning. To some converts raised in societies religiously dominated by Islam, Christianity can represent a type of otherness different from the cultural and religious contexts of their childhood. The contexts surrounding the convert may lead to a feeling of reluctancy towards an object like the Bible, not because of its content, but for what this book is associated with. For converts, these feelings eventually change and are replaced with secrecy, but also curiosity. A pull towards the physical otherness of Christian material culture and merely 'liking it' sparks this curiosity when converts encounter a religious space for the first time. Later, converts start interacting with the objects, and develop religious practices in their daily lives. As an act of attempting to 'fit in' a convert might also appropriate objects and symbols to express themselves and their newfound religious identity. In this study, a notable point is that asylum seeker converts interact with objects in a highly individualized fashion and utilize these in religious practices they develop themselves. Objects also reveal a submersion and devotion to religious commitment. Religious commitment is continuously negotiated over time and can take physical form. Physical objects become visual reminders of commitment and are given agency that directs the converts attention towards religious values and beliefs in the everyday. This includes, materializing religious myths, collecting memorabilia or crafting religious objects for the home. Material objects can also represent the convert's life and biographical circumstances – for instance, their struggle to leave their country, imprisonment, torture or solitude. They can also represent a sense of calm, fulfilment and gratitude. Objects can be used and made visible by the converts in public spheres as well, for instance, when converts hand out pamphlets, Bibles or wear a cross necklace.

In the case of asylum seeker converts referencing objects to appeal boards and in court hearings, the capabilities of objects change and become public to the authorities. Objects are referenced to and blend in with the converts overarching testimony for asylum in Norway. There are thematic commonalities in these testimonies and asylum seeker converts make references to objects when talking about their baptisms, active roles in a congregation, mission activities and visual religious lifestyles in the domestic and/or public spheres. However, the Bible is the most common object mentioned in various contexts in these testimonies. This shows that the Bible is an important object in the asylum seekers conversion process to Christianity, not just in relation to knowledge about it, and therefore worthy of attention to its material form from both scholars and authorities. Focusing on materiality is important because there are material dimensions to all religions and converts will relate to some form of material culture during their conversion process. In Norway asylum seeker converts have been given an enhanced right to have their cases processed by the appeal board, the UNE. The reason for this is because of challenges of fact-finding and evidence these authorities face when handling these cases. As research on the topic of asylum seeker converts continues to increase, it is paramount that immigration authorities stay open to adapt new perspectives when processing these types of asylum claims. It is not enough for authorities to simply consider materiality when assessing a claimant's credibility. They must also pay attention to the right aspects of materiality and use this information to inform their evaluations. By providing a comprehensive framework for decision-makers to navigate this task, this chapter offers a guide to authorities that aims towards a more nuanced and accurate assessment of asylum seeker claimants' credibility. Exploring the connections between asylum seeker converts' intentions for religious change and the things being used during the process of conversion will add greater of understanding when considering applicants' cases.

Notes

1   The seven-stage model was presented in Lewis Rambo's book *Understanding Religious Conversion* from 1993. It is a holistic approach to the phenomenon of conversion, and the book includes examples of religious conversions to many religious traditions. The seven stages include context, crisis, quest, encounter, interaction, commitment and consequence.
2   From August to December 2022, I interviewed nine Iranian asylum seeker converts. Seven of the interlocutors had been granted asylum in Norway. Two of them were accepted through the UN. Two were still awaiting a decision. I conducted two-part interviews. The first part was conducted as Photo-Elicitation Interviews (PEI), which are interviews in which the conversation starts with and is based on pictures (Harper 2002). Using pictures is meant to create an alternative avenue for conversation. It also encourages the informant to take a more active role in the interview setting, thus levelling the power imbalance between researcher and subject. I showed pictures depicting various known objects of Christian material culture and encouraged the interlocutors to talk freely about what they associated with the images. I also asked them to bring/show me pictures that were important to their religious life. Since I could not know in advance how the interlocutors would respond to the PEIs, I also prepared additional questions. The second part was therefore a qualitative narrative interview. Here I wanted to learn more about the interlocutors' background and journey through the conversion process. The participants' names used in this chapter are pseudonyms.

3   Eight nations abstained from the vote in 1948, but none dissented.
4   In short: 'a foreign national who is in the realm or at the Norwegian border shall, upon application, be recognized as a refugee if the foreign national has a well-founded fear of being persecuted for reasons of ethnicity, origin, skin colour, religion, nationality, membership of a particular social group or for reasons of political opinion. Or faces a real risk of being subjected to the death penalty, torture or other inhuman or degrading treatment or punishment upon return to the country of origin' (Immigration Act, §28, 2008). Section 30 of the Immigration Act mentions religion specifically. 'Religion shall in particular be deemed to include religious beliefs and other life stances, participation in, or intended abstention from formal worship in private or in public, whether alone or in community with others, other acts or expressions of opinion related to the religion or life stance of the person concerned, forms of individual or collective conduct dictated by religious or life stance-based convictions, freedom to convert to another religion or a different life stance' (Immigration Act, §30, 2008).
5   For a more in-depth investigation of credibility assessments in cases of this nature, I suggest reading the chapter authored by Schlüter in this volume.
6   Asylum seekers to Norway from Afghanistan (2015–21): Total (8,003), Cases processed by the UDI (7,881), Granted Asylum under §28a of the Immigration Act (1,031), Rejection (4,633).
7   Asylum seekers to Norway from Iran (2015–21): Total (1,843), Cases processed by the UDI (1,727), Granted Asylum under §28a of the Immigration Act (823), Rejection (802).
8   These are the District Court, Courts of Appeal and Supreme Court.
9   This data is part of an ongoing larger project, drawing on a greater number of legal decisions. I limit my analysis here to the twenty cases mentioned because cases from the years 2012–22 provide valuable insights and trends in the legal system over the past decade.
10 TOSLO-2012-197243.
11 LB-2014-169798.
12 LB-2015-168682.
13 LB-2019-12979.
14 LB-2020-151148.
15 LB-2014-81162.
16 LB-2010-134086.
17 LB-2014-169798.
18 For a more comprehensive exploration of Protestantism in Iran, please see the chapter written by Römer in this volume.
19 Christian activist is a term I use when talking about people who, for reasons of religious conviction and in different ways, involve themselves in cases regarding,

but not limited to, Christian asylum seeker converts' struggle for Norwegian citizenship. The concept is developed from Stene's theorization of Christian activism: 'In which asylum seekers are viewed as people in desperate need, but also as a new, local "mission field"' (Stene 2020: 212). These activists differ in denominational belonging. Still, they are characterized for interacting with asylum seeker converts, mission work, creating online support groups, fundraising, providing legal aid and alerting newspapers and other media.

20 Rambo refers to advocates as missionaries and/or missionary enterprises, and notes that their activities embrace numerous considerations regarding their views, motivations and strategies towards possible converts (1993: 66–86). In the context of asylum seeker converts, an advocate can also be a Christian activist.

Bibliography

Afshari, Sara (2021). 'Marginalization and Negotiation of Boundaries: The Case of the Armenian Church in Iran'. *Mission Studies*, 38 (2): 278–96.

Bautista, Julius (2012). *The Spirit of Things: Materiality and Religious Diversity in Southeast Asia*. Ithaca, NY: Southeast Asia Program, Cornell University.

Bender, Courtney (2012). 'Practicing Religions'. *The Cambridge Companion to Religious Studies*, Robert A. Orsi (ed.), 273–95. Cambridge: Cambridge University Press.

Bennett, Alison (2022). 'Objects of Catholic Conversion in Colonial Buganda: A Study of the Miraculous Medal'. *Journal of Religion in Africa*, 51 (1): 27–64.

Bielo, James S. (2021). *Materializing the Bible: Scripture, Sensation, Place*. London: Bloomsbury Academic.

Flood, Gavin (1999). *Beyond Phenomenology: Rethinking the Study of Religion*. London: Cassell.

Geertz, Clifford (1973). *The Interpretation of Cultures: Selected Essays*. New York: Basic Books.

Groonen, Henri (2010). *Religious Conversion and Disaffiliation*. New York: Palgrave & Macmillan.

Grythe, Trine (2009). 'Klageorganet Utlendingsnemda (UNE)'. *Utlendingsrett*, Runa Bunæs, Kristin Ottesen Kvigne and Bjørn Vandvik (eds.), 367–81. Oslo: Universitetsforlaget.

Harper, Douglas (2002). 'Talking about Pictures: A Case for Photo Elicitation'. *Visual studies*, 17 (1): 13–26.

Hazard, Sonia (2013). 'The Material Turn in the Study of Religion'. *Religion and Society*, 4 (1): 58–78.

Keane, Webb (2008). 'The Evidence of the Senses and the Materiality of Religion'. *The Journal of the Royal Anthropological Institute*, 14 (1): 110–27.

Kupari, Helena (2023). 'The Ambiguous Role of Materiality in Transitions to Orthodox Christianity in Contemporary Finland'. *Religion* (ahead of print): 1–21.

LOV-2008-05-15-35. 'Act Relating to the Admission of Foreign Nationals into the Realm and Their Stay Here (Immigration Act)'. Ministry of Justice and Public Security, Entry into force 1 January 2010. https://lovdata.no/dokument/NLE/lov/2008-05-15-35.

Martin, Craig (2017). *A Critical Introduction to the Study of Religion*. London: Routledge.

McDannell, Colleen (1995). *Material Christianity: Religion and Popular Culture in America*. New Haven, CT: Yale University Press.

Parekh, Serena (2020). *No Refuge: Ethics and the Global Refugee Crisis*. New York: Oxford University Press.

Rambo, Lewis (1993). *Understanding Religious Conversion*. New Haven, CT: Yale University Press.

Richardson, James (1985). 'The Active vs. Passive Convert: Paradigm Conflict in Conversion/Recruitment Research'. *Journal for the Scientific Study of Religion*, 24 (2): 119–236.

Stadlbauer, Susanne (2019). 'Between Secrecy and Transparency: Conversions to Protestantism among Iranian Refugees in Germany'. *Entangled Religions*, 8 (1): 68–93.

Stene, Nora (2020). 'Leaving Islam for Christianity: Asylum Seeker Converts'. *Handbook of Leaving Religion*, Daniel Enstedt, Göran Larsson and Teemu T. Mantsinen (eds.), 210–19. Leiden: Brill.

Winchester, Daniel (2008). 'Embodying the Faith: Religious Practice and the Making of a Muslim Moral Habitus'. *Social Forces*, 86 (4): 1753–80.

Worthington, Everett L., Nathaniel G. Wade, Terry L. Hight, Jennifer S. Ripley, Michael E. McCullough, Jack W. Berry, Michelle M. Schmitt, James T. Berry, Kevin H. Bursley and Lynn O'Connor (2003). 'The Religious Commitment Inventory-10: Development, Refinement, and Validation of a Brief Scale for Research and Counseling'. *Journal of Counseling Psychology*, 50 (1): 84–96.

6

Building belief: Navigating moral tensions through category work while assisting converted asylum seekers in Finland

Valtteri Vähä-Savo and Venla Koivuluhta

Introduction

In 2015 Finland received a record-breaking 32,476 asylum seekers, which was a huge increase compared to previous years (Laine and Salmi-Niklander 2017). This was accompanied with a backlash from right-wing groups and politicians demanding stricter immigration policies. However, the asylum seekers were also met by volunteers trying to help them settle in. The volunteer work was partly organized by well-established non-governmental organizations (NGOs) but there were also grassroots movements involved. Religious organizations and individuals with ties to religious communities also ended up playing a prominent role either as members of a congregation or through NGOs and grassroots movements (e.g. see Välimaa, Vähä-Savo and Hiitola 2022). Representatives of religious groups also spoke in public on behalf of asylum seekers and organized demonstrations against what they considered as inadequate practices by the immigration officials.

Our study focuses on volunteer support persons who have helped asylum seekers whose asylum claim is based on fear of persecution due to religious conversion from Islam to Christianity. A support person is someone that an asylum seeker asks to come along to the interview. They can be laymen or possess legal or other relevant expertise. However, they do not have the same status as legal counsels. Their participation is dependent on permission from the Finnish Immigration Service (Migri) and it is common that they are not given permission to talk during the interview. Based on our interviews with the volunteers, they have significant and complex roles (cf. Caglar and Ramsauer in this book). They are often also involved in the religious induction and teaching of the asylum seekers, which may lead to enduring relationships.

At the same time, people with religious ties have been accused of taking advantage of the vulnerable situation of asylum seekers in order to convert them and gain more congregants (see Huhtanen's (2018) article in the largest subscription newspaper in Finland, *Helsingin Sanomat*). There have also been suspicions that volunteers may coach asylum seekers to give the 'right answers' to the Migri, which may lead to fraudulent claims being accepted. The Migri, in response, tries to minimize the influence of support persons by controlling their right to speak during the asylum hearings. It is emphasized that the asylum seekers need to 'speak in their own words'. This puts the support persons in an awkward position. They want to help the asylum seekers both with questions of faith and the asylum proceedings. Yet, they are well aware of the allegations laid against them. Our interviewees unanimously condemned the idea of 'teaching to the test'. However, they also acknowledge that it can sometimes be extremely difficult to evaluate whether people have truly converted. This raises a moral dilemma as the volunteers wonder to what extent they should act as gatekeepers and avoid supporting suspicious asylum applications. It can also be hard to determine where to draw the line between giving too much advice and properly preparing a person for an asylum interview. Hence, the supporters find themselves constantly navigating morally treacherous waters (cf. Kim 2022).

While the Evangelical Lutheran Church of Finland is very influential in Finland, our interviews show that religious volunteers did not form a unified group with a centralized leadership. Many religious people volunteered independently and the members of the Evangelical Free Church of Finland were very active. As the number of asylum claims based on a fear of persecution due to a religious conversion has begun to rise, the work of religious volunteers has also risen in significance. As the Migri evaluates the threat posed by religious conversion to an individual and whether the conversion appears genuine, many religious volunteers would offer written testimonies on the behalf of asylum seekers or accompany them to the interviews.

It is easy to conceive of asylum interviews as encounters between immigration officials and asylum seekers, while overlooking the other actors involved (lawyers, translators and support persons). For example, studies have shown the great significance of translators in the interaction during the interviews

(Gibb and Good 2014). The role of support persons who take part in – or give advice concerning – the asylum hearings has been less studied. However, our data shows that they take care of important tasks that affect both the asylum seekers and the interview situations. Some of their work is carried out during asylum interviews, but most of it takes place in other venues. That is why we have included in our dataset interviews also with advisors and support people who have not attended actual asylum interviews.

Our sociological study examines how the volunteers who support and guide people seeking asylum based on religious conversion negotiate conflicting demands and responsibilities. We explore how the volunteers make sense of the moral dilemmas involved in their voluntary work and define their own moral responsibilities. We are interested in their understanding of the proper guidelines and norms that a support person should follow. The data set for the article consists of seventeen interviews, which were conducted as part of a bigger sociological research project that interrogates how experts and officials measure 'inner truth' of individuals in different contexts. Drawing mainly on membership categorization analysis (Garfinkel 1967; Sacks 1992), our analysis finds that the advisors use – knowingly or not – four different strategies of category work to handle the moral tensions pertaining to their tasks: (1) going formalist, (2) going psychological, (3) invoking a moral proxy and (4) evoking national interests. All of these strategies involve a different way of articulating moral responsibilities to the various categories of actors that are involved in the asylum procedures: who is responsible for what and how should the various groups of actors behave.

Volunteer assistance work with asylum seekers and moral problematics

Refugee support may be carried out by individual volunteers, professionals (e.g. case workers, translators and lawyers) and NGOs. Volunteering entails heterogeneous forms and activities. The volunteer work and its effects may be unpredictable, ambiguous and contradictory, as the well-documented tension between volunteering and politics demonstrates (e.g. Karakayali 2017; Vandevoordt and Verschraegen 2019). Fleischmann and Steinhilper (2017), for example, have documented how volunteering may at the same time have both anti-political and potentially politically transformative effects.

Scholars have also considered the pivotal role of emotions involved in refugee volunteer work. Emotions are central to volunteering experience (Karakayali

2017) – they help mobilize, motivate and sustain volunteering activities (Doidge and Sandri 2018). Studies have examined the role of specific emotions, such as compassion (Maestri and Monforte 2020; Wagner 2022) and empathy (Doidge and Sandri 2018). The studies show that emotions are not separate, but connected to action, morality and politics. Maestri and Monforte (2020), for example, show how volunteers continuously negotiate moral and emotional dilemmas as well as normative logics of refugees' 'deservingness'. This way they also render the meaning of compassion fluid and constantly shifting. Indeed, compassion may also reproduce unequal power hierarchies by victimizing refugees and by distracting from the more structural conditions of global inequality (Fassin 2012; Karakayali 2017).

Researchers have only recently started to explore the phenomenon of volunteering from the perspective of volunteers themselves. Refugee support work does not merely represent a case of individual good-will but is embedded in wider political and moral landscape. Hoppe-Seyler (2020) has explored the emotional, reflective and practical realities of volunteering. According to her, volunteering experience is often characterized by conflict and rupture, where the 'subject' of the volunteer is constantly becoming. We want to explore this phenomenon by considering how support people negotiate their various – often conflicting and overlapping – roles in relation to religion-based claims.

Our study is interested in the category work that volunteer support people use to make sense, navigate and diffuse moral tensions involved in their work. Categorizations are ubiquitous feature of culture, and they are formed, maintained and invoked in everyday life practices (Housley and Fitzgerald 2002). Systems of categorization and classification are fundamental elements in organizing our perception and knowledge of the world (Bowker and Star 2000). They are cultural resources that actors invoke to make sense of their surroundings. As Jayyusi (1991) points out, at the same time categorizations are tied to moral notions, values and normative order. The moral order involved articulates categorizations of actors with moral obligations, rights and conceptions of appropriate behaviour. In other words, it is used to make sense of who is responsible for what, which groups are deserving of certain rights and how different actors should behave (cf. Caglar and Ramsauer, Schlüter and Halonen in this book).

We analyse how the volunteer support persons utilize categorizations both in relation to themselves and to the other actors involved in their work. While we use the definition 'volunteer support people' to refer to our interviewees, we do not assume that this is a well-defined and fixed identity from which they view the world. Rather, we draw on ethnomethodology, which analyses the sense-making practices and practical reasoning that people use in mundane situations to create, assemble and reproduce the social structures that they orient to (Heritage 1987). From this ethnomethodological perspective identities and roles are seen as situated interactional achievements (Housley and Fitzgerald 2002). People can assume several identifications and speaker positions within a single interview. They can position themselves as 'volunteer support people' but they may as well take up the identification of, for example, 'a Finnish person', 'a religious person' or 'a mother'. Similarly, they can ascribe various identities and actor categorizations to other people. As identities shift, so do the normative obligations and rights ascribed to a person. As the same person can be described 'correctly' in a number of ways it raises the question what the criteria are by which a selection from this range of possibilities is made on different occasions and with what consequences (Jayyusi 1991). How are identities and categorizations of actors (Sacks 1992) ascribed to people involved in the asylum proceedings and how these categorizations are connected to an understanding of appropriate behaviour?

Data and methodology

The data for this study consists of seventeen semi-structured interviews conducted in 2022. The data is part of a bigger sociological research project led by Valtteri Vähä-Savo and funded by the Kone Foundation, which interrogates how experts and officials measure the 'inner truth' of individuals in different contexts. All the interviews used in this chapter were conducted by the second author Venla Koivuluhta.

All of the interviews except for one were individual interviews. One interview was conducted with two participants, and one participant was interviewed twice. The participants consisted of twelve women and five men. They were recruited through Christian congregations, one NGO and via personal contacts. The participants had assisted asylum seekers who had applied for asylum in Finland based on religious conversion. They had assisted them by virtue of their profession or during their free time as a form of voluntary work or activism. Some participants had assisted asylum seekers as both professionals and private individuals. Many of the interviewees had various professional or voluntary roles in their local Christian congregations. Some were (or had been) employed by a congregation while others worked in different fields but were active congregants in their free time.

The interviews were conducted in Finnish, either in-person or online. The interviews were recorded and then transcribed. The excerpts from the data have been translated from Finnish by the research group. To protect participants' anonymity, pseudonyms are used throughout the chapter. We identify the interviewees only by the letter I and a number (e.g. I-2, I-3). Additionally, any identifying information including the city of residence and the names of affiliated organizations has been removed.

The data is analysed by using membership categorization analysis (MCA), which has its origins in ethnomethodological scholarship and especially in the work of Harvey Sacks (see Garfinkel 1967; Sacks 1992). MCA offers a way of analysing and documenting how actors' senses of wider social structure and culture affect everyday social interaction (Housley and Fitzgerald 2002). To analyse the category work carried out by the support people, we combed through the transcriptions of the interviews to locate points where the interviewees talk about rights, obligations and proper behaviour. We then analysed what kinds of identifications the interviewees would take up in these instances. We examined how they articulated these moral notions with their own situational identifications and with categorizations of other people. In the following section we present our findings by discussing four strategies of category work that support persons use to deal with the moral conundrums involved in their work.

Navigating moral tension through category work and shifting identifications

In our data we found four discursive strategies the support persons use to handle the moral complexities involved in their work. They all offer different ways of shielding oneself from the image of failing to uphold one's own ethical principles and from the accusations of supporting potentially fraudulent asylum claims.

(A) Going formalist

The first strategy revolves around cultural differences and the art of telling a personal narrative. Almost all our interviewees told that they would advise asylum seekers on how to talk about their conversion during the asylum interview. Yet, they also felt it important to strictly condemn the idea of putting words into their mouths. This was something that we did not ask about, but the interviewees brought it up themselves as they were aware of this type of accusations being thrown at them. As one of our interviewees mentioned:

> They didn't have enough knowledge and initially they didn't receive proper legal counselling or nobody would advise them. And I am not saying that someone should tell them that you need to present these arguments so that you will receive asylum. That is not at all what I am saying.
>
> (I-4)

According to another interviewee:

> Many would ask even from us volunteers about what they should say in the interview, or they might not ask quite that directly, but I would always tell them that you need to tell your own story as well as possible.
>
> (I-5)

In both excerpts we can see that the interviewees were protecting themselves against the accusations of teaching to the test, which they in turn define as a morally reprehensible act. It is something unbecoming of a morally responsible volunteer. The latter interviewee goes so far as to shield even the asylum seekers from accusations of trying to find out how they could give good answers in the interview. The speaker corrects their statement in mid-sentence by clarifying that the asylum seekers would not ask advice too directly, implicating that even asking for this type of advice might be considered morally unacceptable. This goes to show how delicate this issue is for the support persons.

For many of our interviewees, the way to work around this moral pitfall was to go formalist. They emphasized that they were not teaching the asylum seekers how to give the 'right answers'. Instead, they were teaching them how to narrate one's personal experience in a way that is recognizable and, hence, convincing for a 'Westerner'. They were schooling them on how to tell a story of personal journey and spiritual change following the narrative conventions that are familiar to people from the Global North. Therefore, they were not dictating the content of the stories but instructing them on the basics of a genre of stories that might be called 'conversion narratives'. As one of our interviewees mentioned:

> Especially many Iranian women talked about dreams that they've had about Jesus. It can be an extremely significant Christian experience for them. But I really don't think that a Finnish public official will ever consider a dream about Jesus a genuine Christian experience. There's just, there's too wide a cultural difference. Also, it is not common for the Finnish people to take seriously

Christian or any religious experiences in that way. It may seem strange to them [immigration officials] that someone may actually be moved by an experience to the extent that it changes their whole life.

(I-7)

Our interviewees considered the art of telling a convincing narrative to be a culture-bound activity. According to them, it is very difficult for a person to convince Finnish officials if they do not know the right way to tell their story – the right way being the one that is familiar to Finnish people and to people from the Global North. This conception was connected to a way of speaking about the asylum seekers, the immigrations officials and the interviewees themselves through a heavy reliance on cultural categorizations. In these instances, the volunteers would position themselves as representatives of 'Western culture'. They did not define themselves so much by their specific religious faith or a specific congregation, as they did by their identity as 'Westerners', whose responsibility it is to explain local customs to their guests. According to one interviewee:

> Many asylum seekers are not familiar with this type of interview process. In Finland it is common for us to talk about our experiences, share our opinions and so on. Many of them are not familiar with this type of behaviour in their country of origin. First of all, you are not allowed to question religion at all, you cannot ask any questions. But in here it's more of a personal thing. So, you kind of have to, I've gradually encouraged them to talk about personal experiences and what are significant things for them in the Bible, how has it truly affected you. Not too broad themes, like love and all that, but how has it concretely affected your life.

(I-2)

Many interviewees also mentioned that due to their cultural background the asylum seekers might find it difficult to talk and to express themselves in an effective manner to the Finnish officials. Some thought that they were trying to be too friendly and speak very politely to a person who was making an important decision. Being friendly was presented as problematic cultural trait. In other accounts the asylum seekers were considered to be distrustful of public officials due to their culture:

> They have a hard time trusting that this person is trying to be neutral, or that maybe they even have your best interest at heart. There's always the fear that the officials are looking to blame you for something and to punish you. It so deep-rooted with these people.

(I-10)

Another interviewee said that the asylum seekers are customized to a culture where you do not chat with public officials and higher-ups. In their culture, according to the interviewee, it might be considered inappropriate, whereas in Finland avoiding eye contact with an official raises suspicions (I-5).

Cultural categorizations helped to navigate the moral tensions involved in coaching the asylum seekers. The volunteers saw themselves as guides that have a duty to educate foreigners in the genre of Western personal narratives and especially stories of personal change. Unlike 'putting words into people's mouths' teaching the form of the story could be considered a benign activity. And as one interviewee put it, 'if you are really good at talking about your fears and the threats that you are facing, the system will probably work in your favour, but otherwise it will fail you' (I-7).

While the volunteers found 'teaching the genre' a comfortable option, it was not without its drawbacks. On the one hand, asylum seekers might misunderstand some elements. For example, while the personal change narrative should involve dramatic personal experience it should not seem melodramatic or too 'over the top' (I-10). Hence, our interviewees considered stories of epiphanies, supernatural experiences and religious dreams as unfitting to the genre of 'Western conversion' narrative – at least when told to an immigration official. Quite surprisingly, these spiritual experiences were expected to be met with suspicion, and it was considered better to emphasize emotional everyday experiences. One must walk the tightrope between appearing deeply affected by a religious experience, while avoiding heavy-handed spiritual talk. Additionally, asylum seekers face the hurdle of following generic conventions without seeming too generic and impersonal. The story must be easily recognizable, but it cannot seem too much like a carbon copy of previous successful stories – a basic test for compelling stories in general (Bruner 1991), but a particularly challenging one when your life may be depend on convincing others. As on interviewee put it:

> The experience of inner peace, having love for others, and forgiveness are significant things. But when almost everyone mentions these same things, they are interpreted as a ready-made list that they have learnt and memorized. But we, who know these people, recognize that these are very profound experiences.
>
> (I-9)

Ironically, through their advice the volunteers may end up reinforcing specific forms of narration. This, in turn, may make certain types of stories appear more and more convincing, common and natural for the immigration officials. Stories that do not fit the genre may start to seem suspicious outliers. Then again, if too many asylum seekers tell similar stories, they might be accused of copying successful narratives in the hopes of receiving an asylum, leading to a catch-22 situation.

(B) Going psychological

Another strategy for handling moral tensions was to go psychological. This involves moving from cultural categorizations to focusing on individuals and their psychological factors. This is not about helping people to tell a convincing story of personal change or teaching facts about a religion, but about understanding, accepting and helping individuals living under extreme stress. This strategy is connected to how the interviewees categorize themselves as actors and how they define the asylum seekers. In these instances, the volunteers would not position themselves as representatives of Finnish or 'Western' culture. Instead, they would categorize themselves as empathetic individuals, friends or professional service providers helping individuals that are dealing with a variety of challenges. To quote one interviewee:

> Quite many of our Christians have been granted asylum. [...] Almost 90 per cent of them. But those that haven't, they all have some sort of learning disorder or they have never been to school and they don't know how to read. It's pretty hard to say that I'm studying the Bible if you are illiterate and can't remember things. Or you have severe mental health issues and aren't able to recall what you said yesterday, let alone four years ago in a previous asylum interview.
>
> (I-7)

The problems with the asylum interviews are not attributed to a lack of knowledge concerning cultural customs but to personal challenges and lack of resources. This also means that the asylum seekers are depicted as a heterogeneous group with varying skills and 'capitals'. Some individuals may be highly educated and capable of talking about themselves in a convincing manner, but others find themselves in a more difficult situation due to their individual backgrounds and abilities. Some interviewees would also bring up struggles with substance abuse. But there was also talk about less serious issues, as another interviewee mentioned:

> I was thinking that this fella, he's a very careful, polite, and considerate person. And that's why it has been difficult for him to talk about himself with more than a few words in the asylum interviews, even when the questions have been quite profound.
>
> (I-9)

In this case the interviewee is not talking about mental issues, but about personal characteristics that could in the right context be considered valued attributes. Again, we come across the view that politeness – and shyness, according to other interviewees – can be a significant vulnerability in asylum interviews. However, now these qualities are described as individual psychological traits and not features of a specific culture.

One of our interviewees (I-8) told that some asylum seekers would be heavily involved in the congregation until their application got approved and then they disappeared. According to the interviewee this might be simply due to practical matters such as being busy with finding an apartment and dealing with studies. However, some had said that after receiving asylum they felt like turning a new page and taking some distance from the people and surroundings that they associated with earlier feelings of fear, misery and disappointment. Some of them returned later, the interviewee mentioned. The interviewee also talked about an asylum seeker who had trouble convincing the immigration officials and became extremely calculating with their behaviour. The person tried to figure out how to act in a way that would finally sway the officials' opinion. The interviewee was a bit amused by the overtly religious behaviour of the person and their detailed calculations of how to perform convincing Christian faith. However, in the end the interviewee noted:

> Many of these people understand very well that they need to provide some proof. And in some ways, it is a good thing. But this whole thing has become so difficult that I cannot judge anyone, no matter how deeply Christian they really happen to be.
>
> (I-8)

This last point is what makes going psychological and focusing on individuals a feasible strategy for navigating moral tensions. The key is to avoid positioning oneself as someone whose responsibility is to morally judge people, while acknowledging that sometimes individuals may not appear as if they have gone through a profound conversion process. This strategy is based on a conception of two types of actors engaging with each other. There are the struggling individuals in need of help, who cannot be held completely responsible for their desperate actions. Alongside them are the volunteers, whose responsibility as support people is to understand the vulnerable individuals. Their obligation is to offer help, not to act as a gatekeeper either for the nation or for a religious community. Their work relies on knowledge concerning psychological factors and the immigration system, not on theological knowledge or on assessments of the asylum seekers' faith.

(C) Invoking a moral proxy

It was rare for the interviewees to take a strong stance concerning the 'authenticity' of people's conversion. If they did, it was usually done by emphasizing the cases where they felt that they could, as religious people themselves, clearly recognize the change in a person that was coming to faith. Mostly they seemed uncomfortable using this type of language. In fact, one interviewee said:

> That's why I've gone and provided support for those asylum applications, where I know that the person has gone through an authentic conversion, to use Migri's parlance [laughs].
>
> (I-6)

Here the interviewee takes up the theme of authenticity of conversion, but immediately attributes this type of deliberation and language as 'Migri's parlance'. This implies that it is not the way that the interviewee – and assumedly volunteer support persons in general – would think and talk. The foreignness is further marked by the laughter at the end of the sentence. It highlights how bizarre it is for a support person to assume the same perspective on religious conversion (or awakening) as an immigration official.

This was a common strategy of discussing cases where the volunteers felt uneasy about someone's sincerity in terms of conversion. To avoid positioning oneself as someone who judges others' faith, they would either momentarily position themselves as if they were immigration officials or refer to how the immigration officials have viewed or will likely view the case. In other words, they would invoke a discursive moral proxy. Moral proxies have been discussed in the context of medical decision-making. Scholars have examined the ethical dilemmas involved with human moral proxies (Wrigley 2015) and technological moral proxies (Millar 2015) that act as surrogate decision-makers for someone who is incapable of expressing their wish. Human moral proxy may be, for example, a relative who makes health care decisions on behalf of an incapacitated person. Technological moral proxies refer to design features of artefacts and software that automatically execute actions that would otherwise require human beings carrying out moral deliberation and decisions. By a discursive moral proxy we refer to speaker position that a person can assume when making a morally charged statement. By using the proxy a speaker can make moral statements as if they were talking for someone else or looking at the issue from someone else's perspective. Hence, the speaker does not have to make a stand concerning the issue. Consider the following quote from an interviewee who worked with asylum seekers both as volunteer and via their job:

> I said to this guy that I may be a Christian but in my work I deal with Muslims and Christians alike, and I don't care what you are, who you are, and what you believe in. But you need to understand that these questions I asked about your faith are a lot easier than the ones that the Immigration Service will ask you. There you will need to be sure about what you believe in and what kind of claims you make. But then he got offended and said that if you don't believe me maybe we should not meet again. And I said, it's not that. I believe that you are speaking the truth, but I still wish that you could explain this a little bit [laughs]. I tried saying that perhaps you should be able to tell about this a little more openly in in there, to explain the transformation you went through.
>
> (I-8)

Here the interviewee tries to handle a difficult situation where the other person feels like their faith and sincerity have been challenged by probing questions. The interviewee explains that it is not 'they' who are questioning the truthfulness of the story. They have not suddenly switched from being a supporting volunteer to interrogating the asylum seeker. They are merely saying the kind of things that an immigration official might say. Like in an above quote from another interviewee, the awkwardness of navigating between conflicting roles is again emphasized with laughter. The interviewee also noted that they were just 'testing' and in a way 'coaching' the asylum seeker with these types of questions.

Still another way of invoking a moral proxy is to stay as neutral as possible and lay the responsibility for 'gatekeeping' at the hands of the immigration officials and – in terms of faith – sometimes even on the feet of the God. In the following quote an interviewee explains how they managed a situation where they felt unsure about the conversion of a new member of their congregation:

> There was a guy that was a drug addict and a criminal. And another person would stick with us for years. It became difficult to come up with excuses not to baptize them, even though I was not completely convinced of their conversion. And it's also about egalitarianism, as the demands for Finnish people to be recognized as Christians are much lower. […] We believed him to be a Christian and have witnessed him practicing Christianity. […] But when I have my doubts, I will stretch the process as long as I can. […] But if they have been here more than a year, where do you draw the line. […] At some point I think it becomes a question between you and God.
>
> (I-7)

According to the interviewee, in cases like this, you try to juggle your obligations. On the one hand, you are a religious teacher who expects certain things from fellow congregants. On the other hand, you are a volunteer support person whose priority is the best interest of the asylum seekers. However, at some point you may have to position yourself as a neutral onlooker. As long as you stay as impartial as possible and do not give anyone an unfair disadvantage, you cannot be held accountable for discerning the true faith of an individual. It is the duty of others to make those calls. According to the interviewee, when navigating these kinds of difficult and delicate situations, one option is simply to do nothing. If the immigration officials are accustomed to you going out of your way to support asylum seekers, staying silent can speak volumes. This also emphasizes that it is the duty of the Immigration Service to act as a gatekeeper, which lets the volunteers off the hook.

(D) Evoking national interests

The fourth strategy is to evoke national interests. In these instances, the volunteers would position themselves as spokespersons for the Finnish society. This did not happen similarly as before, where volunteers positioned themselves as representatives of 'Western' culture and teachers of local customs. Talking about national interests in these instances meant drawing attention to the 'bigger picture' regarding the society in the long run. There were two ways of articulating national interests in relation to conversion-based asylum claims. One focused on the significance of religion from rather black and white perspective, as we can see in this quote:

> I can tell you that a Muslim that has converted into Christianity makes Finland more secure. If you think about religious wars and terrorist acts […] If a person becomes a Christian and embraces Christian values, it brings peace to this country. It's a huge deal. It's not just about one person's transformation. It's about, do we want the unrest and disturbances that are brought about by that religion, or do we give them a future, hope and new direction.
>
> (I-3)

Here the speaker assumes a strong religious identification as a Christian, an identification that is implied to extend to the Finnish people at large. Similarly, the asylum seekers are categorized through their religion by using negative stereotypes. However, the main point is not to pit one religion against the other, with the hope of the Christian ranks becoming more numerous with each convert. No matter what one thinks about acceptability of the statement, the argument concerns furthering religious conversion to strengthen the safety of Finnish society. Hence, we can see a different type of logic compared to the previous strategies. Here religion is emphasized as a defining feature of the volunteer(s) and the asylum seekers, but the value of faith is defined by its ability to integrate individuals into a society and to enhance national security. However, there is not much moral tension and ambivalence underlying the statement. The asylum seekers are expected to have truly converted, which is assumed to make them more peaceful residents.

Another way of evoking national interests to navigate moral tensions can be illustrated by the following quote:

> All those people that integrate into Finland make us richer and can bring with them a lot of blessings to Finland. I believe that is what we need, and it will also broaden our society. If we use terribly tight criteria, reject people, and drag things on endlessly, we will destroy all the benefits we could receive. People will get traumatized and become mentally ill. At that point they are only able to receive support from society, instead of being part of society and contributing to it.
>
> (I-6)

The point is that if the objective is to integrate asylum seekers into society, extremely stringent measures of assessing their conversion may defeat the whole purpose. According to the argument, whether they have truly converted or not, they may contribute to the society after gaining asylum. However, if they are put through a string of rigorous interrogations, treated with doubt and forced to wait for decisions, even the true converts can be so traumatized that they have difficulties in becoming functioning members of the society. The moral problematics involved in assessing people's faith are sidestepped by diminishing the importance of the evaluative process and focusing on the long-term results for societal well-being. We can observe the same logic in the following quote:

> It's the same as trying to prove that you're gay. It violates your privacy and identity. Here's a question that I'm not able to answer. Is the asylum process regarding Christians and sexually marginalized groups so long and damaging that we end up with a lot of traumatized people in our society? Should we ease the criteria a bit so that we could welcome into our society people who are healthy and doing well?
>
> (I-16)

This strategy defuses moral tensions by shifting the focus from the truth games involved in asylum interviews to challenges concerning integration. From this perspective the true faith of an individual may seem like a relatively insignificant question. It might even seem less risky to accept some fraudulent claims than to surely alienate people with traumatizing procedures. The speaker position in this case is not that of a cultural guide, a religious teacher or a gatekeeper in service of the state. It is that of someone trying to protect the nation's best interest, defined as a peaceful society. The asylum seekers are not viewed so much as people of faith or fellow congregants as they are future citizens of a complex society, whose functioning and well-being should be the main priority.

Conclusion

In this chapter we set out to analyse how the people that support and advise asylum seekers navigate conflicting demands and responsibilities. We found that volunteers are well-aware of the suspicions that have been advanced against them and they can easily find themselves dealing with conflicting moral demands. While they consider it their duty to support asylum seekers, they recognize that, for various reasons, not all of the asylum seekers come across as convincing converts. Many volunteers who advise asylum seekers in conversion cases are deeply religious people and active congregants. Hence, they do not take matters of religion lightly. We found that the volunteers rely on category work to defuse the moral tensions. This category work is carried out through four strategies: (1) going formalist, (2) going psychological, (3) invoking a moral proxy and (4) evoking national interests.

All of the strategies offer a way for the volunteers to avoid positioning themselves as judgemental evaluators and gatekeepers, while acknowledging the moral dilemmas involved. Maestri and Monforte (2020) have made similar findings by analysing how volunteers relate emotions of compassion with evaluations about the 'deservingness' of refugees. Their study found that it in order to keep themselves emotionally motivated, many volunteers will refrain from judging people's deservingness. They distinguished three coping mechanisms used by the volunteers: shifting the responsibility to make judgement to external agencies, actively avoiding situations in which they should produce a judgement and portraying the situation of the refugees as too complex to make a judgement. The first of these coping mechanisms comes very close to the strategy we call invoking a moral proxy. While our findings support the observations made by Maestri and Monforte, our analysis is focused on discursive strategies and category work, which makes it challenging to compare the results. However, both studies emphasize that moral tensions and dilemmas are common for volunteer work, and the volunteers use a variety of tools to either avoid moral judgements or defuse moral tensions.

Shifting between various speaker positions and identifications was common in our data and it was related to the way that the interviewees categorized other actors. The speakers easily switched back and forth between speaking as a representative of 'Western culture' and making sweeping cultural generalizations, to using psychological language to make sense of the asylum cases. Cultural categorizations were related to the strategy of going formalist, which made sense because, according to our interviewees, the Immigration Service had changed their approach from asking facts about Christianity to emphasizing stories of personal experience. This was considered a positive development and it was something that representatives of religious groups had advised the Immigration Service to do. According to many interviewees, most religious people, themselves included, would have had a hard time answering the formerly used questionnaires concerning Christian traditions. But this approach had its own challenges. Learning and recalling facts is demanding, but at the same time, there can be a shared understanding of the correct answers. With personal narratives this form of objectivity is lost and everything depends on the asylum seeker's ability to convince immigration officials. Telling one's story can be easier than recalling facts, but it is also easier for the official to disregard a story of personal experiences and deem it unconvincing. Hence, the art of storytelling and rhetorical skills became a key theme for the asylum seekers and their advisors.

Earlier studies have shown the importance of being able to tell culturally appropriate stories in asylum interviews (Vogl 2013; Hiitola and Vähä-Savo 2021; Rose and Given-Wilson 2021; see also Halonen in this book). While acknowledging this, our study looks at the issue from another perspective. We are interested in how the volunteer advisors handle moral tensions. Therefore, relying on cultural identifications and categorizations in relation to narrative skills is not something that is expected to be par for the course. From our viewpoint, it is not crucial whether culturally nuanced narratives of conversion really are more successful than others, but that this conception offers a logic for the volunteers to ease moral tensions in their work. It is a resource for sense-making. These categorizations can, of course, be stereotypical and contradictory. For example, by stating that being respectful of authorities causes problems for the asylum seekers, the interviewees were implying that this type of behaviour is foreign to Finnish culture. This is of course a coarse generalization but, additionally, the interviewees could also invoke a completely opposite stereotype of the Finns. For example, one person noted that the Finns – especially the men – would make the worst asylum seekers as they would be too quiet and unaccustomed to talk about their feelings. Nonetheless, cultural categorizations and conceptions of category-bound activities could be used to construct ad hoc explanations for making sense of the asylum proceedings. At the same time, this may lead to dismissing systemic problems caused by questionable procedures and asymmetrical power relations, while attributing blame on the asylum seekers' cultural background. It can also easily lead to projecting things on to 'other cultures' that could just as well be depicted as key features of one's own culture.

Going psychological avoids some of these issues as focus is sifted from assumedly homogeneous cultures to differences between individual skills and resources. Then again, it can also lead to problematic assumptions that the problems involved in the assessment of religious conversion are due to individual capabilities of the asylum seekers. A person with 'normal' capacities may be expected to pass the interview without major challenges while those who fail are probably dealing with personal problems. Nonetheless, it is a strategy that helps to explain the need for volunteer advisors to take part in the asylum proceedings, while avoiding moral evaluations of asylum seekers by drawing on psychological and individualistic discursive strategies.

The two remaining strategies, invoking moral proxies and evoking national interests, operate on different logics from the previous two. Instead of trying to defuse potential moral tensions, invoking a moral proxy simply allocates the responsibility for moral evaluation to another category of actors. It is the immigration officials whose obligation is to act as gatekeepers and assess the asylum seekers. Moral evaluation is accepted as a component of the asylum proceedings, but it is not something that the volunteers should or need to take part in. Invoking national interest, in turn, questions whether even the immigration officials should risk alienating future citizens by engaging in rigorous interrogations and moral assessments. The main rationale should be to ensure the well-being of asylum seekers in order to ease their integration into Finnish society.

Following recent studies (Doidge and Sandri 2018; Maestri and Monforte 2020), we consider it important to study the experiences, and rationales of volunteers working with asylum seekers and refugees. It is crucial to understand that the volunteers do not necessarily share the views professed by major NGOs in the field (Armbruster 2019). Nor do the volunteers form a homogeneous group with a shared perspective (cf. Välimaa et al. 2022). Even more importantly, individual volunteers can evoke several different identifications and logics of action while giving accounts of their work. As our study shows, shifting between identifications through category work can act as a way to handle conflicting emotions and moral pressures. Hence, category work offers significant tools for emotion management and sense-making in volunteer work. This category work is carried out by NGOs and other actors in public discussions to affect people's emotions and to mobilize them (Fassin 2012; Karakayali 2017; Ticktin 2017). However, it is also done on the ground level by the volunteers themselves, as Maestri and Monforte (2020) have also noted. We see the category work practised by the volunteers as a very significant and understudied topic. Especially the interrelations and articulations between emotions, moral judgements and categorizations in volunteer work offer a rich field for future studies.

Bibliography

Armbruster, Heidi (2019). '"It Was the Photograph of the Little Boy": Reflections on the Syrian Vulnerable Persons Resettlement Programme in the UK'. *Ethnic and Racial Studies*, 42 (15): 2680–99. https://doi.org/10.1080/01419870.2018.1554226.

Bowker, Geoffrey C. and Susan Leigh Star (2000). *Sorting Things Out*. Cambridge, MA: MIT Press.

Bruner, Jerome (1991). 'The Narrative Construction of Reality'. *Critical Inquiry*, 18 (1): 1–21. https://doi.org/10.1086/448619.

Doidge, Mark and Elisa Sandri (2018). '"Friends That Last a Lifetime": The Importance of Emotions amongst Volunteers Working with Refugees in Calais'. *British Journal of Sociology*, 70 (2): 463–80. https://doi.org/10.1111/1468-4446.12484.

Fassin, Didier (2012). *Humanitarian Reason. A Moral History of the Present*. Berkeley: University of California Press.

Fleischmann, Larissa and Elias Steinhilper (2017). 'The Myth of Apolitical Volunteering for Refugees: German Welcome Culture and a New Dispositif of Helping'. *Social Inclusion*, 5 (3): 17–27. https://doi.org/10.17645/si.v5i3.945.

Garfinkel, Harold (1967). *Studies in Ethnomethodology*. Cambridge: Polity Press.

Gibb, Robert and Anthony Good (2014). 'Interpretation, Translation and Intercultural Communication in Refugee Status Determination Procedures in the UK and France'. *Language and Intercultural Communication*, 14 (3): 385–99. https://doi.org/10.1080/14708477.2014.918314.

Heritage, John (1987). 'Ethnomethodology'. *Social Theory Today*, A. Giddens and J. Turner (eds.), 224–72. Cambridge: Polity Press.

Hiitola, Johanna and Valtteri Vähä-Savo (2021). 'Genres of Departure: Forced Migrants' Family Separation and Personal Narratives'. *Nordic Journal of Migration Research*, 11 (3): 235–49. http://doi.org/10.33134/njmr.372.

Hoppe-Seyler, Annika (2020). 'Arenas of Volunteering: Experiences, Practices and Conflicts of Voluntary Refugee Relief'. *Geographies of Asylum in Europe and the Role of European Localities*, B. Glorius and J. Doomernik (eds.), 225–44. Cham: Springer.

Housley, William and Richard Fitzgerald (2002). 'The Reconsidered Model of Membership Categorization Analysis'. *Qualitative Research*, 2 (1): 59–83. https://doi.org/10.1177/146879410200200104.

Huhtanen, Ann-Mari (2018). 'Strange Things Are Happening in Small Congregations as Large Numbers of Asylum Seekers Are Converting to Christianity [Villeissä pienseurakunnissa tapahtuu kummia, kun turvapaikanhakijat kääntyvät joukoittain kristinuskoon]'. *Helsingin Sanomat*, 4 March. https://www.hs.fi/paivanlehti/04032018/art-2000005590370.html.

Jayyusi, Lena (1991). 'Values and Moral Judgement: Communicative Praxis as Moral Order'. *Ethnomethodology and the Human Sciences*, G. Button (ed.), 227–51. Cambridge: Cambridge University Press.

Karakayali, Serhat (2017). 'Feeling the Scope of Solidarity: The Role of Emotions for Volunteers Supporting Refugees in Germany'. *Social Inclusion*, 5 (1): 7–16. https://doi.org/10.17645/si.v5i3.1008.

Kim, Jaeeun (2022). 'Between Sacred Gift and Profane Exchange: Identity Craft and Relational Work in Asylum Claims-Making on Religious Grounds'. *Theory and Society*, 51: 303–33. https://doi.org/10.1007/s11186-021-09468-8.

Laine, Sofia and Kirsti Salmi-Niklander (2017). 'Volunteer Work among Asylum Seekers and Refugees in Finland from 2015 to 2017'. *Gränsløs*, 8: 90–100.

Maestri, Gaja and Pierre Monforte (2020). 'Who Deserves Compassion? The Moral and Emotional Dilemmas of Volunteering in the "Refugee Crisis"'. *Sociology*, 54 (5): 920–35. https://doi.org/10.1177/0038038520928199.

Millar, Jason (2015). 'Technology as Moral Proxy: Autonomy and Paternalism by Design'. *IEEE technology and Society Magazine*, 34 (2): 47–55. https://doi.org/10.1109/MTS.2015.2425612.

Rose, Lena and Zoe Given-Wilson (2021). '"What Is Truth?" Negotiating Christian Convert Asylum Seekers' Credibility'. *The ANNALS of the American Academy of Political and Social Science*, 697 (1): 221–35. https://doi.org/10.1177/00027162211059454.

Sacks, Harvey (1992). *Lectures on Conversation, Vol 1 & 2*. Oxford: Basil Blackwell.

Ticktin, Miriam (2017). 'A World without Innocence'. *American Ethnologist*, 44 (4): 577–90. https://doi.org/10.1111/amet.12558.

Välimaa, Mira, Valtteri Vähä-Savo and Johanna Hiitola (2022). 'Enroling around – Reconfiguring Place and Space in the Wake of a New Reception Centre in a Small Rural Town'. *Population, Space and Place*, 29 (3): e2623. https://doi.org/10.1002/psp.2623.

Vandevoordt, Robin and Gert Verschraegen (2019). 'Subversive Humanitarianism and Its Challenges: Notes on the Political Ambiguities of Civil Refugee Support'. *Refugee Protection and Civil Society in Europe*, M. Feischmidt, L. Pries and C. Cantat (eds.), 101–28. London: Palgrave Macmillan.

Vogl, Anthea (2013). 'Telling Stories from Start to Finish: Exploring the Demand for Narrative in Refugee Testimony'. *Griffith Law Review*, 22 (1): 63–86. https://doi.org/10.1080/10383441.2013.10854767.

Wagner, Greta (2022). 'Helping Refugees in Rural Germany: Ambivalences of Compassion'. *Crisis under Critique: How People Assess, Transform, and Respond to Critical Situations*, D. Fassin and A. Honneth (eds.), 255–70. New York: Columbia University Press.

Wrigley, Anthony (2015). 'Moral Authority and Proxy Decision-Making'. *Ethical Theory and Moral Practice*, 18: 631–47. https://doi.org/10.1007/s10677-014-9548-2.

7

Tales of transformation: Conversion narratives of unaccompanied refugee minors in the Church of Sweden

Jonathan J. Morgan

Introduction

Between June 2020 and April 2023, I conducted fieldwork at a Bible study group in the Swedish county of Scania in southern Sweden.[1] The group was made up of asylum seekers who came to Sweden as unaccompanied refugee minors (URM). All but one of the group members converted from Shi'a Islam to Christianity since arriving in Sweden from Iran and Afghanistan and had been baptized in the Church of Sweden (CofS), Sweden's former state church.

While there is an abundance of literature on URM in Europe, little attention has been given to the phenomenon of religious conversion, or even the role of religion, among this group.[2] Where religion is mentioned in literature on this group, it is either identified as a psychological coping strategy,[3] dismissed as an attempt to accrue asylum capital[4] or used to attain a sense of solidarity.[5] While such analyses offer important perspectives, they are at times reductive, failing to take into account the complexity of identity processes in the midst of migration. As Leman contends, viewing conversion through the lens of the acquisition of asylum capital or mobility is problematic since conversion processes are 'too complex to reduce its totality to such functional logic'.[6] Thankfully, some recent ethnographic work on asylum and conversion has sought to offer more nuanced perspectives on this topic, acknowledging that while asylum seekers may initially be drawn to churches because of their social work activities or the chance of attaining asylum capital, they often maintain contact for a variety of additional reasons.[7] Within conversion theory, Jindra has offered a model which seeks to complicate our understanding of the causal mechanisms behind conversion processes. Instead of dismissing traditional deprivation or social network theories she combines them with other factors such as religious content and convert histories.[8] In the everyday discourse on asylum and conversion, the asylum capital explanation is regarded as the obvious explanation of the conversion of Muslim-background asylum seekers to Christianity. While I do not contest the validity of this analysis for describing some converts' motivations for conversion, one of my motivations for conducting long-term fieldwork with a group of converts to Swedish Lutheran Christianity is that it allows me to complicate our understanding of this phenomenon.

In this chapter, I draw on material collected through participant observation and narrative interviews with members of this group in order to describe a generalized process of conversion which is most common to all members of this group.[9] After describing and discussing this process, I examine the theme of authenticity which emerged from interviews and during the course of the fieldwork. Drawing on the work of philosopher Charles Taylor and learning theorists Lave and Wenger, I suggest that through experiences of belonging and legitimate peripheral participation[10] participants predispose themselves to experience a sense of authenticity when confronted with the possibility of embracing the truth claims of the church.

Between 2014 and 2016, 44,617 URM arrived and sought asylum in Sweden.[11] Since their arrival, the CofS has received hundreds of these young people seeking to join the church and be baptized as Christians. Although there are no official figures, it has been estimated that some 1,000–3,000 of these young people have converted to Christianity in a variety of churches in Sweden.[12] Since only 10 per cent of the URM that came were girls, and most of these have ended up living with families, rather than in care homes, they are less visible than their male counterparts.[13] The young men, due to the less personal institutional care which they receive, experience a greater sense of independence and more opportunity to explore for themselves what life in Sweden has to offer.

The Evangelical Lutheran Church of Sweden (*Svenska kyrkan*) is the largest religious denomination in Sweden.[14] It has an official membership of some 5.6 million, or 53.9 per cent of the population.[15] However, since it became disestablished in 2000, it has seen a steady attrition in membership, which in the last ten years has accelerated to a loss on average of 61,000 members per year. Sociologist of religion Grace Davie has characterized the Swedish approach to religion as 'belonging without believing' because, in spite of large membership numbers, active participation remains low.[16] It has been estimated that only around 80,000 (less than 1.3 per cent of the population) regularly attend Sunday services.[17] The CofS is not known for emphasizing evangelistic outreach, which makes conversion within its walls a particularly striking phenomenon.

The high influx of asylum seekers between 2014 and 2016 put the state's reception system under pressure and made a strong impact on Sweden's approach to migration.[18] Sweden's relationship with pluralism is relatively recent. It was not until the 1970s that the country began receiving non-European asylum seekers. However, it rapidly became the Nordic country with the biggest immigrant population, with today more than 20 per cent of the population boasting a history of migration.[19] The country maintained a warm approach to asylum seekers until the so-called 'crisis' of 2014–16 and its accompanying shift toward a more populist and nationalistic politics.[20] Acceptance rates of asylum applications dropped significantly between 2014 and 2017, including among URM.[21] Along with this, the majority of those who are granted asylum in Sweden no longer receive permanent residence, but are instead granted temporary protection.[22] This puts URM-background asylum seekers in a 'condition of social and civic limbo', not knowing if they will be permitted to remain in Sweden or face deportation to Afghanistan, along with the sense of precarity that this entails.[23]

Statist individualism and authenticity

Trägårdh uses the term 'statist individualism' to describe the combination of strong state and individual liberty which is emphasized in Swedish state policy.[24] According to this approach, as is common in classic Liberalism, the individual is the basic unit of society, and the social system is organized so as to minimize the individual's dependence on traditional support structures. While many states may make this claim, the Swedish example is particularly extreme because it extends to the idea that the less responsibility an individual has for spouse, children, ageing parents or significant others, the greater their potential to be who they wish to be.[25] Underpinning this statist individualism is what Taylor calls the ethics of authenticity, which he sums up like this: 'There is a certain way of being human that is my way. I am called upon to live my life in this way, and not in imitation of anyone else's.'[26] This ideal can be seen at play in the social provision of the Swedish welfare state and the conception of the good life which necessitates the freeing of individuals from that which encumbers them so that they might pursue that which most resonates with their inner selves. In *Culture and Authenticity*, Charles Lindholm describes this sense of authenticity and the cultural artefacts which underpin them through the lens of social construction.²⁷ It is, he argues, the destabilization caused by modern society which creates the need for authenticity projects:

> As taken-for-granted meaning systems have been challenged from within and without, human beings everywhere have sought to recapture a degree of significance and stability, often enough by inventing or affirming a form of authenticity they can claim for themselves and share with others.²⁸

In other words, the very processes of centralization, industrialization and workforce mobility that have shaped the modern nation state had a destabilizing effect on individual identity. An emphasis on one's inner sense of authenticity, the ethic of authenticity, has been the result. Those who migrate and seek asylum find themselves bereft of the institutions of their country of origin which previously provided a sense of stability and clarity of identity. In a recent article looking at Iranian converts to Pentecostalism in Stockholm, Ebru Öztürk describes the ontological insecurity experienced by refugees who become estranged from their primary institutions.²⁹ Such institutions, she argues, provide a sense of continuity and stability of identity, and the loss of such connection represents an inward crisis. What she calls 'secondary institutions' like the church provide an opportunity for these migrants to establish a firm grounding, a 'sense of home' in the face of change.³⁰

Method

I met these young men, all of whom arrived in Sweden in 2014 and 2015, in late 2019 when I began attending a Bible study group at the CofS congregation in which they participate. While three members of the group recently received residence permits, others are still awaiting a decision or going through the process of appealing a negative decision. All are Afghan, although only one – Amin – was actually born in Afghanistan. The others were born in Iran. All identify as members of the Hazara people group.³¹ Before I began talking to these young men, I sought and was granted ethical approval for the project by Sweden's Ethical Approval Authority.³² Although they arrived as minors, by the time I encountered them most were over the age of eighteen.

The study's participants were all part of the same Bible study group, recruited in-person. The priests and deacons (henceforth pastors) who led the group acted as gatekeepers, facilitating introductions and giving me the chance to explain my presence during the early gatherings which I attended. Since there is an uneven distribution of power between pastors and participants,[33] it was important for me to also take time to develop rapport and to establish my identity as distinct from the CofS, and to emphasize the voluntary nature of their involvement in this study. As a white male in my late thirties, I was already an outsider to their group and I reasoned that being understood to be representing the institution of the church could have its drawbacks, especially when conducting interviews. I sought to mediate this effect in a number of ways, including genuine participation in the group, choosing physical proximity to the participants rather than to the pastors, and by emphasizing my own status as an outsider in Swedish society.[34] I chose to capture data from this particular Bible study group in order to follow them over a longer period of time than I would if I had chosen multiple sites, or carried out interviews without participant observation.

The original research design took a standard ethnographic approach, with semi-structured interviews and participant observation, but with the onset of the Covid-19 pandemic I was forced to add certain digital methods for gathering data during the long months when I was unable to meet the participants face-to-face. During the pandemic, the church closed its doors for several months at a time. When it opened its doors again, the Mass was served in single-serving cups and the communion wafers provided in hermetically sealed packaging.[35] During the Mass, instead of greeting one another with a handshake, hands were placed over hearts as people nodded at each other from a distance. While this adjustment was underway, the pastors took the Bible study group online. They tried out a variety of video conferencing tools for this purpose but attendance was low, with just one or two participants joining myself and the pastors. After several weeks, they began using Facebook's Rooms feature, a tool which all members were familiar with, and this led to a more consistent turnout.

Anxious to gather data in spite of the pandemic, I started carrying out one-on-one interviews using Facebook Messenger's voice call feature. As teenagers and undocumented asylum seekers, the lives of these young men were often improvised and highly spontaneous in nature. During the pandemic, when their language schools were closed, the everyday activities which had been structuring their lives were no longer there, which only added to this spontaneity. Because of this, I realized that there was no use planning interviews a week or more in advance and instead began contacting the participants the day before I wanted to interview them. Sometimes I was even asked if I would like to interview them immediately and so I hurriedly set up my recording app in order to make the most of the opportunity.

The interview data I gathered during this time surprised me. I had expected that building rapport with these young men would be more difficult online. I instead found that they were even more prepared to discuss the intimate details of their lives and conversion processes online than they had been in person. This may have been due to the amount of time they had known me, but I am inclined to believe that it had something to do with the levelling effect of social media. I think that, somehow, using Messenger and talking using just voices, reduced the power of distance between us and therefore made it easier to confide. Added to this, I was essentially interviewing them in their homes, since that is where they sat while speaking to me. The familiarity and privacy of this environment no doubt contributed to their candour. Of course, conducting interviews in this way also involved certain drawbacks. For example, I could not make eye contact or read their body language as I could in person.

I took a narrative interview approach[36] in which I asked the interviewees to tell me about their lives, beginning with family and where they grew up, and then followed up with questions hoping to refine the narrative. While the participants were aware that I was studying them because they represent the intersection of migration and religious transformation, focussing on their biographies more broadly gave them the opportunity to cover the ground that they wanted to cover, rather than limiting them just to their conversion stories.

There is a difference between interviewing URM in the CofS and those in more evangelical churches where the practice of giving testimony or 'witnessing', as Susan Harding calls it, is more established.[37] The liturgy of the CofS does not generally allocate space for the sharing of 'personal testimonies' or accounts of how one has been changed or transformed by a relationship with God. There is no particular tradition of encouraging church members to tell their personal stories to each other or to those outside the church.[38] However, just because the church does not make witnessing a key practice does not mean that the participants are unschooled in telling their stories. Indeed, their asylum processes necessitate it. Migration officials ask URM not only how they came into contact with the church, but also detailed questions about their theologies. This requires not only that the individual asylum seeker demonstrate the plausibility of their faith, but also a level of discursive competence.[39] A similar trend can be seen in Halonen's study of asylum decisions by the Finnish board of migration. Regarding the questions that are asked of applicants, she notes that 'More than the sincerity of a claimant's faith, these questions end up measuring their eloquence and capacity for abstract self-reflection'.[40] While priests and pastors do not train these new converts to witness, they do help them to prepare for meetings with the office for migration. They help them to think about the credibility of their stories, and to answer theological questions that may arise. And sometimes the shape of the Bible studies is adjusted to include questions that the state will ask these young men about their faith.[41] Although all of the participants in this study were clear that they were not involved with the Farsi-speaking congregations in the city, images and videos posted on their Facebook profiles that they were exposed to 'Persian-language Christian discourse' described by Römer.[42]

Findings and discussion

In the next section I draw on fieldwork data to look at the process by which Hazara unaccompanied refugee minors leave Islam and become baptized members of the CofS.

A process of transformation

Figure 1 offers a generalized overview of the conversion processes which the participants in this study have followed.[43] In what follows, I describe the figure from left to right in order to give clarity to each stage of the process. Before I do, it should be pointed out that although I believe that such models offer a worthwhile insight into the shape that these processes take, the processes themselves are, like all social phenomena, far more complex, and the steps within them far less distinct than such an illustration might imply.

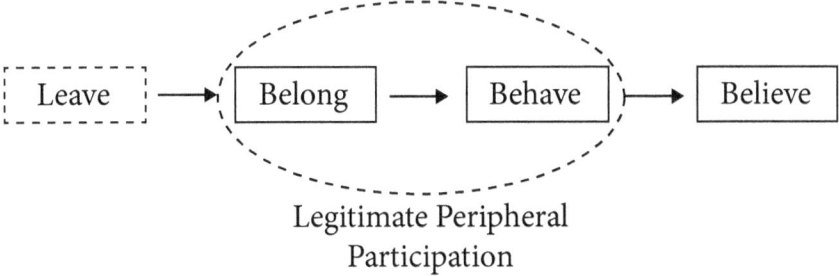

Figure 1 The general process of conversion that the participants in this study followed.

1 Leave

Beginning on the left, with the dotted border, we have the word *Leave*. I include this because, as Kraft has pointed out, converts to a new religion usually go through a process of leaving Islam and enter a period of avoiding religious engagement before they begin any other religious practice.[44] According to the accounts of participants in this study, they either became disillusioned with, and left, Islam prior to engaging with the church, or, although they still considered themselves Muslims, were somewhat ambivalent towards the faith of their parents. In his later chapter, Benedikt Römer seeks to add nuance to the somewhat monolithic way in which Iran is understood by many in the West, and to suggest that the conversion of Iranians to Christianity in Europe is also reflective of 'an ongoing religious transformation of Iran'.[45] Although this may be true in the case of Iranian converts, my data indicates that the participants in this study were somewhat sheltered from the religious pluralism that Römer portrays. This is perhaps because of their precarious social status and marginalization that Hazaras are subject to in Iran.[46]

For most of the participants, early contact with the church occurred because of curiosity, either their own or that of their friends and, according to the interview data, was preceded by a season of disillusionment with the religion of their birth. Islam is routinely described in negative terms, for example, Amin compared the church with his religious experience in Iran:

> we had lots of pictures at home: of Imams, and prophets, lines from the Quran. And my mum told me the whole time: 'they're watching you when you are home. You must be careful to do your best, otherwise God will punish you.' And so I was afraid. I was afraid of Islam and I was afraid of God.[47]

While the presence of Shia 'saints' was ubiquitous in his home, the overarching impact was to create a sense of social control and surveillance. A similar sense of being surveilled was described by Shaheed in relation to the permissability of speaking about God: 'I remember when I was little [...] I asked my friend "who is God? Can you tell me?" And he said to me "no, no! We are not allowed to think about God. Maybe we would doubt and then we would go to hell."'[48]

According to these participants, in this context, religious conversation was carefully regulated by specific knowledgeable figures. Most of the participants knew little about Christians prior to leaving Iran. Those who had knowledge had been warned against mixing with them:

> If I mentioned anything to my uncle he would say 'Oh yes those are the enemies of Islam.' [...] I learned that Jews are the biggest enemy of Islam and

that Christians are second. When I went with my parents to Muslim important celebrations, we would always pray good things for Islam and Muslims and bad for Jews, Buddhists, Christians[49]

This exclusivist approach, highly critical of Christianity and Judaism, led the participants to view Christians as their enemies. This was relatively unproblematic when they did not have contact with Christians, but when they entered a more pluralistic setting, they discovered that their experiences contradicted what they had been told. Jeremiah described his first encounter with Christians as follows:

> In Bulgaria I met all kinds of groups. And that's where I first met Christians. And I saw how they were on fire for people. They were passionate about refugees. And we were mostly from Muslim lands. They did everything to help us. [...] And when I saw that one of them was wearing a cross I asked them about it and someone told me, 'Oh yes they are Christians from Poland.' I thought, 'Christians? Should I receive help from them? They're supposed to be our enemies. But they're here and they're helping Muslims. And Muslims are not helping us. Why is that?'[50]

Such apparent contradictions produced a degree of cognitive dissonance in the participants. They were forced to question which was right – their parents, or their experiences? For some, discovering these 'cracks' in the story which they had been told was the beginning of a loss of trust in their preconceived notions about the world and an accompanying openness toward those who they had previously been taught to judge. This effect is like that experienced by Öztürk's Iranian participants whose loss of trust in the institutions of their homeland brought with it a destabilizing effect on their identities.[51]

It is important to contextualize the criticism of Islam above. While these participants are using rather generic language to talk about a seemingly monolithic 'Islam', it is clear from their comments that they are referring to the particular expression of Shi'a Islam that they were socialized to in the home. While some describe being treated harshly by imams, the majority of commentary on the subject of Islam is localized around the home setting. Added to this, it is to be expected that converts portray their past experiences in negative terms and juxtapose these negative experiences with their new positive experiences of transformed faith.[52]

2 Belong

This stage in the process is described by the next box in Figure 1: *Belong*. The participants in this study came into contact with the church usually after being invited by a friend or, less commonly, independently seeking it out following a period of intense curiosity about Christianity. They began attending services there long before they decided to become Christian and get baptized.[53] Indeed, participants reported arriving at the church with a high degree of scepticism about its truth claims. In spite of this, they described being offered a warm and non-judgemental welcome and the space to be present without having to account for their presence or indicate commitment to a particular creed.

One of the most common themes that emerged from the data was that, according to the participants, the church views everyone as equal. This is communicated in words, but also in the welcome that participants reported receiving when they made contact with the church. This is particularly important for the participants because of their status in society and the contrast it makes with the exclusivity of what they experienced at home. Jeremiah recounts arriving at the church for the first time and being welcomed but not asked questions about his background. After finding a seat at the back of the sanctuary, he was invited by the pastor to come and sit closer to the front, again without any sign of concern about his background or status. He described this experience:

> I sat far back from the others because in Islam I had seen that when you go to the mosque, those who are rich get to sit around the imam, but those who were poor were always furthest back, or somewhere else. [...] So I arrived at the church and sat far back from the other Swedes who were there. And the priest came forward to me and invited me to sit at the front with the others. When they said this to me, I thought this was really nice. They respected me as a person. They didn't ask who I was or about my background. They just asked if I would like to sit with the others.[54]

Rather than being categorized by social status or nationality, Jeremiah was included as any other person in the Mass. This positive impression was reinforced by the topics raised during the prayer time:

> she started the prayer time by praying for everyone in the world, in different countries, for Muslims in Muslim countries like Yemen, Syria, Afghanistan. I thought 'wow this is so good'. It sat well in my heart. And I thought 'this is how we should treat strangers!' I really liked it.

The church did not just refrain from criticizing Muslims, but prayed for their wellbeing. This was the opposite of the hostility that Jeremiah had anticipated from Christians when he came to Europe. He told me that this warm and non-judgemental welcome increased his curiosity about Christianity:

Because of this experience I had of Christianity, of protestantism, I became curious. I said 'okay, I know this is a risk, I know that I might get attacked if someone finds out that I go to Church' but I continued going to church because I was interested in how they lived.[55]

3 Behave

After this, they *Behave*. They participate in the Mass, sing hymns, read a scripture passage out loud during a service, light candles in prayer, and volunteer serving coffee and tea after these gatherings. This is what Halonen identifies in Finnish asylum decisions as the notion of *active religion*: 'a discourse of religion as something a claimant is expected to actively practice, often in particular conventional ways such as praying, studying the Bible, or attending church'.[56] In this stage, the participants are able to rehearse membership without the commitment of calling themselves Christian. In their work on communities of practice, Lave and Wenger introduce the concept of *legitimate peripheral participation*.[57] The involvement of URM in the life of the church is peripheral in the sense that it is a somewhat lessened form of full involvement, while still allowing them to build competence and progress towards full participation.[58] This can be seen in the exclusion of participants from certain rites available to full members, such as full participation in the communion meal.[59] But it should be noted that as a folk church the CofS has a tradition of offering close to full participation to anyone who wants to. Full membership is indicated by baptism, a ritual by which water is poured over the head of the person being baptized and that individual is welcomed into the family of the church. According to Wenger, 'legitimacy can take many forms: being useful, being sponsored, being feared, being the right kind of person … '[60] For the participants in this study, legitimacy is offered by the pastors who engage them in activities such as Bible readings, joining the entry procession, or serving food. This kind of participation embraces the 'relational character of knowledge and learning', which implies 'emphasis on comprehensive understanding involving the whole person rather than "receiving" a body of factual knowledge about the world'.[61] Viewing the context of the church as a site of situated learning, and the Bible study as a community of practice allows us to consider learning as it relates to practice rather than simply the communication of facts or ideas.

These two stages, belonging and behaving, have less to do with cognitive understanding than they do with precognitive learning. They are not about thinking about ideology and creating an argument for why they should or should not believe but are instead more focussed on experiencing or embodying the practices of the church. Even the second stage in this model, belonging, is an embodied practice – one puts oneself in a space and experiences the belonging through feelings, sights, smells, handshakes, smiles and a general sense of the disposition of others towards one's embodied self. This is not about an encounter of a disembodied mind with a disembodied ideology, but of flesh and bones embodiment. I reflected on this in my field notes after attending a Taizé mass at the church:

> Then comes an extended time of silence and the shell of the sanctuary is filled with an other worldly peace. This is the calm that my participants speak of in their interviews as one of the first factors that attracted them to the church. With lives that are often chaotic and fraught with challenges, this space of peace holds great meaning and allows the kind of spiritual centring that the world outside does not.[62]

During my time at the church, I got into the habit of asking the participants not only why they came to the church, but why they stayed. The responses rarely involved some kind of 'theological' answer, but usually revolved around the sense of peace, the silence, and its accompanying calm that they find at the church. Stark and Finke are well known for emphasizing the non-ideological aspect of conversion. They have suggested that conversion has less to do with being ideologically persuaded and more to do with becoming like those you are close to.[63] Kraft paraphrases their theory this way, 'when attachments to members become stronger than attachments to nonmembers, it becomes more socially expedient to join the group'.[64] Such a theory offers insight into the importance of embodiment to conversion; that even though most conversions also involve ideological change, there is usually a strong social aspect to the process.[65] As Stark and Finke put it, 'social networks make religious beliefs plausible'.[66] Jeremiah said it like this:

> It was through the church that God changed my life. It has had a big role in my life. It's a place I can really feel that I am secure. I can really feel that I am like everyone else. Sometimes I think when I go to church on Sunday or another day, that it's a whole other world. There's no difference between people. And when I come from Church for a while, I see that there's injustice, evil, wrong, together with light. But in the church, I feel that there is no injustice, there is no difference between people, everyone is equal. That means a lot to me.[67]

While this description of the church is somewhat rosy, it serves to illustrate the importance with which Jeremiah regards the behaviour of those who call themselves Christians. Having experienced disillusionment with Islam after his Muslim friends failed to help him when he needed them, he looks to the church to embody the message that it preaches. This is perhaps a lot to ask consistently of any community of people, but for now this congregation has sufficiently met that expectation for his engagement to remain high.

4 Believe

The final stage in this figure, *Believe*, is what is often, in the post-Enlightenment West, understood primarily as a rational decision; it is a decision in which all the facts have been weighed using one's cognitive faculties, and the outcome is a mental assent to particular ideological claims. This model of belief is affirmed by migration officials who ask their interviewees to, for example, explain the trinity. Halonen characterizes this view of conversion as *internal religion*: 'By internal religion, I mean discourses that treat religion as an individual cognitive or emotional matter, a question of knowing, believing, or decision-making.'[68] She points out that this take on religion is at odds with the way in which religiosity is embodied in Finnish society. Leaning on Charles Taylor and James K.A. Smith, and in agreement with Halonen, I would offer some resistance to this reductionistic account of belief vis-a-vis practice. There is certainly consideration involved in making the decision to be baptized, however I would suggest that this stage also involves what philosopher Charles Taylor calls one's 'social imaginary':

> I adopt the term imaginary (i) because my focus is on the way ordinary people 'imagine' their social surroundings, and this is often not expressed in theoretical terms, but is carried in images, stories, and legends. It is also the case that (ii) theory is often the possession of a small minority, whereas what is interesting in the social imaginary is that it is shared by large groups of people, if not the whole society. Which leads to a third difference: (iii) the social imaginary is that common understanding that makes possible common practices and a widely shared sense of legitimacy.[69]

Smith adds to this explanation: 'To call this an "imaginary" is already to shift the center of gravity from the cognitive region of ideas to the more affective region, which is "closer" to the body, as it were – since the imagination runs off the fuel of the body.'[70] During the stages of belonging and behaving, the participants learn through legitimate peripheral participation what it means to be a Christian in the CofS. In this process, I would argue, their imaginaries – the ways they pre-cognitively understand their social setting are being shaped through practice, as well as through embodying the social imaginary which is carried by the liturgy. Although the welcoming nature of the church gives the sense that participation is a low-stakes activity, such participation is by no means value-neutral. Instead, engaging in such practice, while weighted towards the embodied rather than the cognitive, predisposes the participants to experience a sense of resonance[71] or authenticity[72] when they encounter the truth claims of the church.

When Jeremiah first visited the congregation, he was in a state of dissonance, confused by the experience of being told to believe one thing (that Christians are his enemies) and then experiencing its opposite (receiving their help). When he heard the priest praying for Muslims in different countries, he did not navigate this clash of information by resorting to theological debate, pitting the claims of Islam against the claims of Christianity. This process took place on a more intuitive level. He told me, 'it sat well in my heart.'

As we saw earlier, perhaps because they are crafted under the gaze of migration officials, the narratives of participants often portray a long-term dissatisfaction with the religion of their birth. According to his account, Amin lost interest in Islam when his father died and he heard an Imam describe the trials that a person goes through after death. He told me, 'my Dad was a good man, a kind man. Even if I wanted I could not be religious like my Dad for God, for Allah. But why, when he died, did that Mullah say those scary things?'[73] Amin could not believe that God would punish his father in spite of his devotion and good character. Shortly after that, his mother enrolled him at an Islamic school:

> I started at the Islamic school and I had to learn things I didn't like, for my family's sake. And when I started at the Islamic school I only had a negative perspective. I only saw bad things. When I was that age, 8 years old, it was too early for me to start with this. [At] that age, kids play, they are totally free, they don't think about these things. But for me, because I had lost the most important person in my family, I had begun [thinking about these things] that year. And then I didn't want to learn about the Qu'ran.[74]

Amin is clear that, after this point, there was a rupture between the self that he presented to the world, and his authentic inner self. According to his account, living as a Muslim did not make him Muslim since his thinking had already begun to diverge from the norms around him. His view of the world was different from that of his society and so, in order to protect his family, he behaved in one way, while thinking and feeling another. In the quote above, he remarks on the discomfort this caused him at a time in life when he felt that he really should have been just enjoying being a child. After leaving Iran, Amin is able to resolve this sense of division in his identity and begins to admit to others that he is no longer Muslim. He tells the story of an encounter with a priest in a refugee camp in Germany who had come to visit his Afghan neighbours and asked them if they were Muslim:

> I raised my hand and said 'no, I'm not Muslim.' Because by then I could say that in front of people. And the priest was a bit surprised – he looked at me in a way that showed me he was surprised. I realise it was maybe a bit strange – a guy who was young, who came from Afghanistan, who isn't Muslim – how could this be? In the end, about two hours later, they were going to leave and he said to me first of all 'do you know that what you said could be dangerous for you? It might be better not to say it so directly.' I told him, 'no, I'm not afraid.'[75]

This part of his narrative illustrates a crucial moment for Amin – a point at which, by aligning his public description of himself with the reality he feels within, he resolves a tension he has carried with him for a long time.[76]

In *The Ethics of Authenticity,* Taylor makes the case that the modern age is permeated by the morally grounded ethic that 'there is a certain way of being human that is my way'.[77] Being true to this authentic self is not just a nice-to-have, but a moral imperative. Amin's story seems to be marked by traces of this ethic. He narrates his story as though becoming Christian enabled the fulfilment of this underlying inner identity, a way of remaining a believer while escaping religiosity that he had experienced as troublesome. At one point during the interview, he emphasized the individuality of his faith by contrasting it with Shaheed's: 'We have different, different experiences or feelings. But the most important is that feeling that can warm the heart.'[78] While his previous environment stressed the importance of outward activity, the current one has to do with finding his own way of being with God. This is highlighted as he contrasts his own relationship with God with Shaheed's. Rather than framing Shaheed's views as wrong in contrast with his own, he argues that this divergence demonstrates the importance of knowing God in your own way.

Since conversion narratives cannot be understood as purely factual accounts, but also as meaning-making performances, it is difficult to know if the perspectives that these participants claim to have had when they lived in Iran – including thoughts about no longer being Muslim – really represent their state of mind at that time, or are simply an attempt to understand their process of transformation as long-term and predating their contact with Christians. If it is a new perspective that is being inscribed on old events, this could be understood as evidence of value acquisition. Evidence that the ethic of authenticity has left its mark on these young men during the seven years that they have lived in Sweden.

Conclusion

Unaccompanied refugee minor converts to Christianity are an understudied group. Little is know of how their conversion processes affect their identity processes and value acquisition in Sweden. As mentioned earlier, too often their processes are explained away using theories which tend to portray them one dimensionally, and their conversions as having overly simplistic explanations.

In this chapter, I have sought to complicate our understanding of the phenomenon of conversion among this group. By framing the process of URM conversion in the CofS as belonging-behaving-believing, I have described the general pattern by which these young people become members in the church, a process which culminates in baptism. It is my hope that by using learning theory – for example that of Lave and Wenger – it is possible to move beyond reductionistic accounts of motivation and to look toward formation, that is, how these young people are formed through their legitimate peripheral participation (and eventually full participation) in the life of the church.

More work is needed to understand the long-term impact of conversion on this group, to understand if they remain engaged in the activities of the CofS over an extended period after receiving a permit to reside in Sweden. There are also those who are deported to Afghanistan: do they continue to self-identify as Christians outside of the Swedish context and in spite of the threat of persecution? As mentioned earlier, URM girls have been largely absent from much of the public discourse and academic research surrounding URM.[79] Further work is needed to illuminate the experience of female URMs and to understand their post-migration relationship with religion.

Notes

1. As part of my doctoral research project.
2. One exception is Elin Ekström, whose Licentiate dissertation described the innovative religious practices of URM girls. Cf. Ekström 2019.
3. Raghallaigh 2011: 539–56; Völkl-Kernstock et al. 2014: 6–11.
4. Cf. Skodo 2018.
5. Herz and Lalander 2021: 110.
6. Leman 2007: 101–14, 3.
7. Ringgaard Lorensen and Buch-Hansen 2018: 29–41; Öztürk 2022: 224–39.
8. Jindra 2014.

9. I carried out two or three in-depth interviews with ten participants in the study. All names used in this chapter are pseudonyms.
10. Lave and Wenger 1991: 1.
11. Morgan 2020.
12. Miller and Johnstone note that, due to underreporting and over-reporting of conversion figures by various parties, it is notoriously difficult to establish accurate figures on Muslim-to-Christian conversion (Miller and Johnstone 2015: 3–19). However, from conversations within the CofS, free churches and members of the group behind the 2019 report on decision making on cases where conversion to Christianity was a factor (Bergström et al. 2019), I synthesized this figure as a best estimate. It should be noted that the figures suggested by some were higher than this.
13. Ekström, Bülow and Wilinska 2019: 9.
14. Berntson 2022: 94.
15. Kyrkan 2023.
16. Davie 2007: 6.
17. Ekenberg 2016: 23–45, 31. This contrasts with Sweden's so-called 'free churches', 'those Protestant Churches that are not a branch of the state', which historically have a more engaged, albeit smaller, membership. Halldorf and Wenell 2014: 1–12, 6; Ekenberg 2016: 31.
18. Gustafsson Lundberg 2018: 123–43.
19. Gustafsson Lundberg 2018: 125.
20. Gustafsson Lundberg 2018: 125. Today in Sweden, questions of migration continue to dominate the public debate, and the loss of dominance of the left-of-centre *Socialdemokraterna* (Social Democrats) to the right-of-centre *Moderaterna* (the Moderates) and *Kristdemokraterna* (Christian Democrats) and the anti-immigration *Sverigedemokraterna* (the Sweden Democrats) has been largely attributed to those parties commitments to reduce immigration. Gustafsson Lundberg 2018: 33.
21. Garvik and Valenta 2021: 15, 11–13.
22. Granting of residence is the means by which the Swedish state grants asylum.
23. Garvik and Valenta 2021: 14.
24. Trägårdh 2014: 13–38, 22.
25. He comments, 'an overarching ambition in the Nordic countries [is] not to socialize the economy, but to liberate the individual citizen from all forms of subordination and dependency within the family and in civil society'. Trägårdh 2014: 22.
26. Taylor 1992: 28–9.
27. Lindholm 2008.
28. Lindholm 2008: 144–5.
29. Öztürk 2022.

30 Öztürk 2022.
31 As Shi'a Muslims in predominantly Sunni Afghanistan, Hazaras have long faced religious persecution. Cf. Crews 2015: 82–3.
32 Application number 2019-04246, approval date 10 December 2019.
33 Particularly because of the asylum assistance and help with sustenance grant applications which pastors offer participants outside of the Bible studies.
34 Since I was born and grew up in Wales.
35 Usually, wafers are handed out by the priest ('Body of Christ Broken for You') and then dipped into a communal cup of wine ('Blood of Christ Shed for You').
36 What Wengraf calls the 'Semi-Structured Depth Interview', Wengraf 2001: xxv.
37 Harding 2001: 37.
38 Indeed, my fieldwork data suggests that there is some ambivalence about the very idea of personal spiritual formation among priests, apparently somewhat influenced by a particular interpretation of Luther's *Simul Justus et Peccator* and its implications for the sinner's relation to sin.
39 As can perhaps be expected, those participants who received residency during the course of this study were those most competent in speaking Swedish.
40 Halonen, this volume.
41 This was particularly common until the release of the *Konvertitutredningen* report in 2019, along with Micael Grenholm's viral quiz *'Klarar du Migrationsverkets kristendomsfrågor?'* ('Can you answer the Migration Office's questions on Christianity?') (Grenholm 2019).
42 Römer, this volume.
43 Although the word 'Behave' has some unfortunate connotations, I use the 'Three Bs' of belonging, believing, and behaving for this model since they are such a common (and, I think, useful) trope for describing Christian social identity in both missiological and sociological literature, cf. Weyers 2012; Friesen and Wagner 2012: 224–52.
44 Kraft 2013: 6–7.
45 Römer, this volume.
46 Monsutti 2007: 167–85, 171; Glazebrook and Abbasi-Shavazi 2007: 187–201, 191–2.
47 Interview with Amin 10 November 2021.
48 Interview with Shaheed 25 June 2020.
49 Interview with Jeremiah 5 March 2021.
50 Interview with Jeremiah 15 October 2020.
51 Öztürk 2022: 227–8.
52 Stene 2020: 210–19, 212.
53 In order to establish a genuine interest and understanding of Christianity in the participants, priests require that these young men spend one year participating in the life of the church before they can be baptized.

54 Interview with Jeremiah 5 March 2021.
55 Interview with Jeremiah 5 March 2021.
56 Halonen, this volume.
57 Lave and Wenger 1991; Wenger 1999.
58 Wenger 1999: 100.
59 Those who are not yet baptized are encouraged to come forward when the bread and wine are served, but to place a hand across their chest so as to indicate that they will receive a blessing instead of the bread and wine.
60 Wenger 1999: 101.
61 Lave and Wenger 1991: 33.
62 Extract of author's field note 17 September 2020.
63 Stark and Finke 2000: 117.
64 Kraft 2013: 7.
65 Kraft 2013: 9.
66 Stark and Finke 2000: 117.
67 Interview with Jeremiah 5 March 2021.
68 Halonen, this volume.
69 Taylor 2004: 23.
70 Smith 2009: 65.
71 Rosa 2019.
72 Taylor 2004.
73 Interview with Amin 10 November 2021.
74 Interview with Amin 10 November 2021.
75 Interview with Amin 10 November 2021.
76 In writing this, I am drawing on Peter Stromberg, who argues that conversion narratives are performative acts which resolve psychological conflicts by converting the unspeakable into a socially acceptable codified language. See Stromberg 2008.
77 Taylor 1992: 28–9.
78 Interview with Amin 10 November 2021.
79 Ekström 2019.

Bibliography

Bergström, Maria Gustin, Ulrik Josefsson, Maria Lindqvist, Ruth Nordström, Rebecca Ahlstrand and Jakob Svensson (2019). 'Konvertitutredningen: Rapport Om Migrationsverkets Hantering Av Konvertiters Asylprocess'. https://www.pingst.se/wp-content/uploads/2021/06/konvertitutredningen.pdf.

Berntson, M. (2022). *Kyrko – Och Samfundskunskap: En Introduktion*. Stockholm: Verbum.

Crews, Robert D. (2015). *Afghan Modern: The History of a Global Nation.* Cambridge, MA: The Belknap Press of Harvard University Press.

Davie, Grace (2007). 'Vicarious Religion: A Methodological Challenge'. *Everyday Religion: Observing Modern Religious Lives*, Nancy T. Ammerman (ed.), 21–36. Oxford: Oxford University Press. https://doi.org/10.1093/acprof:o so/9780195305418.001.0001.

Ekenberg, Anders (2016). 'The Church in Sweden. Secularisation and Ecumenism as Challenges'. *Polonia Sacra*, 20 (2): 23–45. https://doi.org/10.15633/ps.1686.

Ekström, Elin (2019). *From a Place without Speech: Negotiations of Othering among Unaccompanied Female Minors in Sweden.* Jönköping: Jönköping University, School of Health and Welfare.

Ekström, Elin, Pia H. Bülow and Monika Wilinska (2019). '"I Don't Think You Will Understand Me Because Really, I Believe" Unaccompanied Female Minors Re-Negotiating Religion'. *Qualitative Social Work*, 19 (4): 719–35. https://doi.org/10.1177/1473325019848481.

Friesen, Amanda and Michael W. Wagner (2012). 'Beyond the "Three Bs": How American Christians Approach Faith and Politics'. *Politics and Religion*, 5 (2): 224–52. https://doi.org/10.1017/S1755048312000028.

Garvik, Marianne and Marko Valenta (2021). 'Seeking Asylum in Scandinavia: A Comparative Analysis of Recent Restrictive Policy Responses towards Unaccompanied Afghan Minors in Denmark, Sweden and Norway'. *Comparative Migration Studies*, 9 (1): 15. https://doi.org/10.1186/s40878-020-00221-1.

Glazebrook, Diana and Mohammad Jalal Abbasi-Shavazi (2007). 'Being Neighbors to Imam Reza: Pilgrimage Practices and Return Intentions of Hazara Afghans Living in Mashhad, Iran'. *Iranian Studies*, 40 (2): 187–201. https://doi.org/10.1080/00210860701269535.

Grenholm, Micael (2019). 'Klarar Du Migrationsverkets Kristendomsfrågor?' https://www.arjagkristen.nu/.

Gustafsson Lundberg, Johanna (2018). 'Christianity in a Post-Christian Context: Immigration, Church Identity, and the Role of Religion in Public Debates'. *Religion in the European Refugee Crisis*, Ulrich Schmiedel and Graeme Smith (eds.), 123–43. Cham: Springer. https://doi.org/10.1007/978-3-319-67961-7_7.

Halldorf, Joel and Fredrik Wenell (2014). 'Introduction'. *Between the State and the Eucharist: Free Church Theology in Conversation with William T. Cavanaugh*, Joel Halldorf and Fredrik Wenell (eds.), 1–12. Eugene: Pickwick Publications.

Harding, Susan Friend (2001). *The Book of Jerry Falwell: Fundamentalist Language and Politics.* Princeton, NJ: Princeton University Press.

Herz, Marcus and Philip Lalander (2021). *Social Work, Young Migrants and the Act of Listening: Becoming an Unaccompanied Child.* Routledge Advances in Social Work. 1st ed. Abingdon, Oxon; New York: Routledge. https://doi.org/10.4324/9781003088837.

Jindra, Ines W. (2014). *A New Model of Religious Conversion.* Leiden: Brill.

Kraft, Kathryn (2013). *Searching for Heaven in the Real World*. Eugene, OR: Regnum.
Kyrkan, Svenska (January 2023). 'Svenska kyrkan i siffror'. https://www.svenskakyrkan.se/statistik.
Lave, Jean and Etienne Wenger (1991). *Situated Learning: Legitimate Peripheral Participation*. Cambridge: Cambridge University Press.
Leman, Johan (2007). 'A "Lucan Effect" in the Commitment of Iranian Converts in Transit. The Case of the Pentecostal Iranian Enclave in Istanbul'. *Revue Des Mondes Musulmans Et de La Méditerranée*, 119–20: 101–14. https://doi.org/10.4000/remmm.4323.
Lindholm, Charles (2008). *Culture and Authenticity*. Malden, MA; Oxford: Blackwell.
Miller, Duane Alexander and Patrick Johnstone (2015). 'Believers in Christ from a Muslim Background: A Global Census'. *Interdisciplinary Journal of Research on Religion*, 11 (10): 3–19.
Monsutti, Alessandro (2007). 'Migration as a Rite of Passage: Young Afghans Building Masculinity and Adulthood in Iran'. *Iranian Studies*, 40 (2): 167–85. https://doi.org/10.1080/00210860701276183.
Morgan, Jonathan (2020). 'Finding Belonging, Finding Agency: Unaccompanied Refugee Minors Converting to Christianity in the Church of Sweden'. *Review of Faith and International Affairs*, 18 (3): 40–52. https://doi.org/10.1080/15570274.2020.1795410.
Östman, Caroline (2019). *Unaccompanied Refugee Minors and Political Responses in Sweden: Challenges for Social Work*. Sundsvall: Mid Sweden University.
Öztürk, Ebru (2022). 'Finding a New Home through Conversion: The Ontological Security of Iranians Converting to Christianity in Sweden'. *Religion, State and Society*, 50 (2): 224–39. https://doi.org/10.1080/09637494.2022.2061828.
Raghallaigh, Muireann Ni. (2011). 'Religion in the Lives of Unaccompanied Minors: An Available and Compelling Coping Resource'. *British Journal of Social Work*, 41 (3): 539–56. https://doi.org/10.1093/bjsw/bcq136.
Ringgaard Lorensen, Marlene and Gitte Buch-Hansen (2018). 'Listening to the Voices: Refugees as Co-Authors of Practical Theology'. *Practical Theology*, 11 (1): 29–41. https://doi.org/10.1080/1756073X.2017.1415577.
Rosa, Hartmut (2019). *Resonance: A Sociology of the Relationship to the World*. Medford, MA: Polity Press.
Skodo, Admir (2018). 'Migrant Smuggling, Reasons for Fleeing, and Uses of Asylum Capital among Afghan Asylum Seekers in Sweden'. *Nidaba*, 3 (1): 1–11.
Smith, James K. A. (2009). *Desiring the Kingdom: Worship, Worldview, and Cultural Formation*. Grand Rapids: Baker Academic.
Stark, Rodney and Roger Finke (2000). *Acts of Faith: Explaining the Human Side of Religion*. Berkeley: University of California Press.
Stene, Nora (2020). 'Leaving Islam for Christianity: Aylum Seeker Converts'. *Handbook of Leaving Religion*, Daniel Enstedt, Göran Larsson and Teemu T. Mantsinen (eds.), 210–19. Leiden: Brill.

Stromberg, Peter G. (2008). *Language and Self-Transformation*. Cambridge: Cambridge University Press.
Taylor, Charles (2004). *Modern Social Imaginaries*. Durham: Duke University Press.
Taylor, Charles (1992). *The Ethics of Authenticity*. Cambridge, MA: Harvard University Press.
Trägårdh, Lars (2014). 'Statist Individualism'. *Between the State and the Eucharist: Free Church Theology in Conversation with William T. Cavanaugh*, Joel Halldorf and Fredrik Wenell (eds.), 13–38. Eugene Oregon: Pickwick Publications.
Völkl-Kernstock, Sabine, Niranjan Karnik, Michaela Mitterer-Asadi, Elisabeth Granditsch, Hans Steiner, Max H. Friedrich and Julia Huemer (2014). 'Responses to Conflict, Family Loss and Flight: Posttraumatic Stress Disorder among Unaccompanied Refugee Minors from Africa'. *Neuropsychiatrie*, 28 (1): 6–11. https://doi.org/10.1007/s40211-013-0094-2.
Wenger, Etienne (1999). *Communities of Practice: Learning, Meaning, and Identity*. Cambridge: Cambridge University Press.
Wengraf, Tom (2001). *Qualitative Research Interviewing: Biographic Narrative and Semi-Structured Methods*. London; Thousand Oaks, CA: SAGE.
Weyers, Mario (2012). 'The Nature of the Church in Some Post-Christendom Models and According to Some Authors in the New Testament'. Ph.D. Dissertation, University of South Africa.

8

Becoming Christian, remaining Iranian: The salience of national identity in Iranian evangelical exile churches

Benedikt Römer

Introduction

Among the different cases in which religious conversion has become the subject of asylum trials, conversions of Shi'ite Muslim-born Iranians to evangelical Christianity appear to be very common. Endeavours to contextualize such conversions come from different fields, including anthropology (Spellman 2004), sociology (Akcapar 2006, 2010, 2019; Öztürk 2022; Stene 2020), the study of religions (Darwish 2018; Stadlbauer 2019), history (Hopkins 2020; Rzepka 2017), psychology (Kéri and Sleiman 2017) and theology (Krannich 2020; Leman 2007; Miller 2012, 2015). This chapter adds expertise from Iranian studies to scholarly perspectives on Iranian Shi'ite Muslim conversions to evangelical Christianity. By shifting the view to an area studies perspective, two previous shortcomings in research can be addressed: firstly, scholars in the field have so far refrained from drawing upon relevant Persian-language primary material from the Iranian evangelical milieu. While some have pointed to these sources in passing remarks,[1] none of the existing works have analysed them in detail.

Secondly, scholars have tended to approach conversions of Muslim-born Iranians to evangelical Christianity as de-territorialized and detached from structural socio-cultural developments in contemporary Iran. Previous analyses have characterized such conversions as results of religious individualism (cf. Darwish 2018; cf. Kéri and Sleiman 2017)[2] and a migration strategy (cf. Akcapar 2006, 2010, 2019). Öztürk, who contextualizes Muslim-born Iranians' conversions to Evangelicalism as a salient source of ontological security in their post-migratory lives, acknowledges the general religious disillusionment of Iranians with political religion in post-revolutionary Iran as a relevant factor (Öztürk 2022: 225; cf. Gholami 2016). In this chapter, I would like to further this argument by situating Iranian conversions to Evangelicalism in the context of a wider religious transformation occurring in contemporary Iran. To take this approach does not mean to reject other contributing factors, among them a general quest for spiritual fulfilment or of strategical considerations in migration. Rather, the present approach aims to caution the observer, both academic and non-academic, to be wary of reductionisms. An assessment of conversions that disregards current events inside Iran and focuses solely on post-migratory conversion narratives runs the risk of being flawed.

While the official population census of Iran creates the image of a religiously homogeneous country with a Muslim population of 99.6 per cent (Markaz-e Āmār-e Irān 2018 [1397]), a recent quantitative study by Netherlands-based scholars Maleki and Tamimi Arab finds that only around 40 per cent of Iranians self-identify as Muslims of different streams (Maleki and Tamimi Arab 2020: 6). A striking 22.2 per cent indicated that they did not feel close to any religion, and almost 16 per cent identified as either atheist or agnostic. These figures ought to be taken with a pinch of salt, considering that religious identities can be complex and carry diverse meanings. An illustrative example for this complexity is the striking 7.7 per cent of the respondents who identified as Zoroastrian. Although qualitative research would be needed to explore the exact motives of the respondents, one may safely assume that to identify as Zoroastrian for them did not mean to practice Zoroastrianism in the traditional sense.[3] Rather, they may feel alienated from Islam and consider Zoroastrianism the original religion of Iranians (cf. Gholami 2016; Marashi 2020; Zia-Ebrahimi 2016).

Alongside documenting the ongoing religious transformation of Iranian society, Maleki and Tamimi Arab's study thus, albeit implicitly, foregrounds another core aspect helping to better understand Iranian conversions to Evangelicalism: the salience of national identity. In this chapter, I will draw upon recordings of Persian-language sermons from Iranian Christian exile churches as well as Iranian Christian exile magazines to illustrate the vibrant negotiations of Iranian national identity among Iranian Christians. Three concrete examples will serve to underline this argument: (1) Iranian-Christian readings of the figure of King Cyrus the Great, (2) the commemoration of the 'Martyrs of the Iranian Church' and (3) critical engagement with Islam. Through an analysis of these examples, it will become apparent how Iranian Evangelicals in exile present Christianity as a religious alternative to Islam that is well-suited for Iranians and their 'national dispositions'. Before entering the main discussion, however, I will provide a short historical overview on the Persian-speaking evangelical Christian movement in Iran.

The emergence of a Persian-speaking Christianity in Iran

Research on Iranian Christians, especially Iranian Protestants/Evangelicals, has often adopted an overtly theological or even missionary perspective. The latter is particularly true for the books by Mark Bradley (Bradley 2008, 2014) which nevertheless contain valuable accounts of the developments of the recent decades.[4] Regarding the different Western Protestant missions which commenced in the nineteenth century, Thomas S. Flynn has recently put forward a truly meticulous work (Flynn 2017). Although slightly outdated, the book *Christians in Persia* by the late Anglican missionary Robin E. Waterfield offers an illustrative introduction to the history of the different churches in Iran (Waterfield 1973). Other notable works include Christian Van Gorder's *Christianity in Persia* (van Gorder 2010), Marcin Rzepka's *Prayer and Protest* (Rzepka 2017) and Philip O. Hopkins' *American Missionaries in Iran* (Hopkins 2020).

For many centuries, Iran has been home to both an Armenian and an Assyrian Christian ethno-religious minority. In the mid-1990s, their communities comprised around 150,000–200,000 and 16,000–18,000 individuals respectively (cf. Sanasarian 2004: 36). Although Armenians and Assyrians, who usually belong to Eastern Orthodox churches, enjoy a degree of legal recognition in the Islamic Republic of Iran, they continue to emigrate at a high rate.[5] Since the arrival of Western Protestant missions in Iran, some Armenians and Assyrians have converted to different Protestant churches. Remaining in ethnically homogeneous parishes, they continued to use their native languages Armenian and Neo-Aramaic. Until the mid-twentieth century, there were very few converts from a Muslim background. One prominent exception is Hassan Dehqāni-Tafti who in 1961 was consecrated as the first native Iranian Anglican Bishop and became a pioneer of a Persian-language Christianity (cf. Dehqani-Tafti 2000).

By the mid-twentieth century, a group of Armenian and Assyrian Pentecostal Christians from Iran began to consciously use the Persian language for their services and missionary activities. Alongside serving as a mutual language for Armenians and Assyrians, the use of Persian also enabled them to preach to the Iranian Muslim population with the aim of attracting converts. As recounted by an Iranian Assyrian pastor, he and his Iranian Armenian colleague during one of their early ventures in the Urmia region, a historical stronghold of Iranian Assyrians in North West Iran, were confronted with a lack of understanding by local Assyrians who expected them to preach in Neo-Aramaic (cf. Thomas and Dibāj 2010). Until today, some Armenians and Assyrians oppose the use of the Persian language in a Christian context because they consider it subversive to traditional ethno-religious boundaries and a potential vehicle for assimilation.

Their opposition, however, does not measure up to the violent state-sanctioned oppression levelled against Persian-language Christian communities in Iran since the 1979 Islamic Revolution. Between 1979 and 1996, seven leading members of different Persian-speaking Protestant churches in Iran were killed.[6] While six of the seven cases were extrajudicial killings – allegedly instructed or, at least, condoned by Iranian governmental forces[7] – one pastor, the Mashhad-based Hoseyn Sudmand, was executed on the grounds of 'apostasy' (*ertedād*). Sudmand until today remains the only Iranian Christian against whom the death penalty for 'apostasy' was implemented. Applicable through clerical rulings but not specified in the Iranian Penal Code, the verdict of 'apostasy' in the Islamic Republic of Iran has more commonly been used against *Muslim* critics of the government than to persecute converts to other religions (cf. IHRDC 2014).

Following the 1990 killings, many leading members of Protestant churches, especially the Pentecostal *Jamā'at-e Rabbāni* Church, decided to emigrate from Iran and continue their activities in exile. At the same time, there seems to have been a considerable increase in the number of Muslim-born Iranians interested in attending Persian-language evangelical services. Some began to gather in so-called 'house churches' in the private homes of fellow Persian-speaking Christians while others attended the few existing public Persian-language churches that continued to operate. However, until the year 2013, the Iranian government shut down all remaining public churches offering Christian services in Persian (cf. ICHRI 2013; IHRDC 2021).

As of today, the Iranian authorities consider any Christian activity carried out in the Persian language a missionizing endeavour and persecute Persian-speaking Christians (both Muslim-born converts and Armenians/Assyrians) in different ways, including detainment and legal trials, refusal of employment or enrolment at educational institutions, and travel bans. House church leaders are put on trial for 'acting against national security', 'espionage' or 'promoting Zionist Christianity', among other accusations;[8] while these accusations generally do not usher in death sentences, they are used to justify lengthy imprisonment under harsh conditions. As a result, the number of Iranian evangelical exile churches has increased drastically during the past two decades. In 2004, sociologist

Kathryn Spellman estimated that 20,000 Iranian evangelical and Pentecostal Christians were living outside their home country (Spellman 2004: 169). This number is likely to have grown markedly since then. Especially in Turkey, Germany, the Netherlands, Scandinavia, the UK and North America, Persian-speaking Christian churches can be found in virtually all major cities.[9]

Given that the use of the Persian language has historically emerged as the main defining feature of their movement, Iranian Evangelical Christians in exile primarily identify through the label 'Persian-speaking' (*Fārsi-zabān*) and their Iranian nationality, rather than through denomination or affiliation with a particular church. This should be kept in mind during the following presentation of major narratives drawing a connection between the religious and national identities of Iranian Christians. Secondly, Iranian evangelical exile communities today in their vast majority comprise first-generation emigrants of a nominally Muslim background, although Iranian Armenians[10] and Assyrians still play an important role in the movement, given that they often hold leading positions in churches.

It bears mentioning that not all attendants of Iranian Evangelical exile churches have been active in Persian-speaking churches inside Iran already. Spellman offers a threefold model distinguishing between converts inside Iran, converts in transit (especially in Turkey) and converts in the destination country (Spellman 2004: 181). Moreover, not all Iranian Christians living abroad attend Persian-speaking churches as some prefer to join churches using the language of their country of residence. Even then, however, they may take part in Persian-language Christian discourse by additionally listening to sermons from Persian-speaking churches online or reading Persian-language Christian material.

Narratives of an Iranian-Christian national-religious identity

The primary material used in this chapter consists of recordings of Persian-language sermons delivered in Iranian evangelical exile churches and articles written in Persian-language Christian exile magazines. Iranian evangelical Christians in the diaspora are very active online with the aim of connecting the dispersed communities and reaching potential converts inside Iran. This is why, in the words of Marcin Rzepka, 'research on Iranian Christian cyberspace seems to be unavoidable today' (Rzepka 2017: 205). Comprising 'archives with very rich and diverse sources: audio-visual, visual, oral, and written, containing the personal testimonies of converts, pictures, films, and recorded sermons' (Rzepka

2017: 205–6), researchers find themselves challenged to decide which material to include and which to omit.

In this chapter, I am drawing upon a set of sources I archived for a different research project.[11] This archive comprises 70 hours of sermons, services and Iranian Christian Online TV programmes which were recorded on the Iranian national festivals of Nowruz and Yaldā, mainly during the 2010s. Given my interest in negotiations of Iranian national identity among Iranian Christians, I picked these occasions assuming that main relevant aspects would come up here. After an initial qualitative content analysis, I more specifically searched for relevant material, for instance, sermons on King Cyrus the Great. Partially necessitated by the Covid-19 pandemic, my methodology favours churches that have an online presence; that said, it seems to be the norm that Iranian Christian exile churches upload recordings of their services or at least sermons and make them publicly available. As the scope of the present chapter is limited, I have picked episodes well-illustrative of the broader trends discernible in my set of sources regarding the three topics of Cyrus the Great, Iranian Christian martyrs and critical engagement with Islam.

This also applies to the second source used, namely Iranian Christian exile magazines. Such magazines can be viewed as a sequel to Persian-language magazines that, in the past, were published by different Protestant Churches in Iran.[12] Noteworthy publications are: *Kalameh* ('The Word'), 1995–2012, London/UK; *Tabdil* ('Transformation'), c. 2005–2013, Los Angeles/US; *Rāh-e Salib* ('The Path of the Cross'), 2012–22, Doorn/The Netherlands; *Shāgerd* ('The Disciple'), 2015–18, London/UK; and *Smyrna* (Ancient Greek name of the Turkish city İzmir), 2016–ongoing, İzmir/Turkey. For the present chapter, I am confining myself to articles appearing in *Kalameh* which was published by *Elam Ministries*, until today the main and arguably most influential publisher of Persian-language evangelical material. Based in the UK, many contributors to *Elam Ministries* are exiled Iranian pastors formerly active in the Pentecostal *Jamā'at-e Rabbāni* Churches inside Iran. Many of them are also regular guests on Iranian Christian Online TV channels.

Iranian-Christian readings of King Cyrus the Great

Historical documents accounting for details of the life of King Cyrus the Great (600–530 BCE), founder of the Achaemenid Persian Empire, are scarce (cf. Dandamayev 1993). Despite this, a 'cult of Cyrus the Great' (Ansari

2012: 166–78) that discovered the ancient king as the supposed father of the Iranian nation and a primary icon of Iranian-ness emerged during the twentieth century and especially under the rule of the second Pahlavi Shah, Mohammad Rezā Pahlavi (Marashi 2017; Steele 2021). One key narrative among admirers of Cyrus is that the inscription found on the historic Cyrus Cylinder rendered the ancient Persian king a global pioneer of human rights (Steele 2021: 1).

In recent years, the figure of King Cyrus the Great has evolved as a symbol of resistance against the Islamic Republic of Iran. Protestors use slogans like 'Iran is our homeland, Cyrus is our father' (cf. Mohammadi 2018); occasionally, such slogans also feature anti-Arab chants, thus reflecting what historian Reza Zia-Ebrahimi has termed 'dislocative nationalism' (Zia-Ebrahimi 2016).[13] Every year on 29 October, swathes of overwhelmingly young Iranians gather at Cyrus's tomb at the remnants of ancient Persepolis to celebrate 'Cyrus the Great Day' and voice their discontent with the Iranian government. In 2022, after weeks of anti-governmental protests following the killing of 22-year-old Mahsā Amini, the Iranian authorities closed the site surrounding the tomb of Cyrus in late October, officially citing concerns for the personal safety of visitors (Radio Farda 2022). Prominent figures in the Iranian opposition have nevertheless issued statements on the occasion of 'Cyrus Day', including musician Shāhin Najafi, former footballer and political activist ʿAli Karimi, and the son of the late Mohammad Rezā Shah, Rezā Pahlavi Jr. The latter published a video message in which he proudly explained that Iran, through Cyrus the Great, had been the cradle of human rights and contrasted Cyrus's supposed legacy with the human rights breaches of the current Iranian government (Pahlavi 2022).

King Cyrus the Great is referred to several times in the Old Testament of the Bible.[14] His prominence in the biblical tradition and positive role as liberator of the Jews from their Babylonian exile are causes of deep pride for Iranian Evangelicals. A Persian-speaking church in Apeldoorn/Netherlands is even named after Cyrus ('*Kelisā-ye Korush*'/'*Kores Kerk*');[15] moreover, one finds references to Cyrus in Persian-language worship songs (cf. Shariʿat 2020, m. 36:05). Pastors preaching in Persian-speaking churches in the diaspora often proudly refer to the number of times Cyrus was mentioned in the Bible (Shabānlāri 2017, m. 15:25). Thus, they may also be able to speak to Iranians who have not yet converted to Christianity and positively surprise them to find the 'father of their nation' in the seemingly unrelated context of a Christian sermon.

That biblical texts refer to Cyrus as an 'anointed one', or 'messiah', prompts Iranian evangelical Christians to ascribe a certain chosenness to the Iranian nation. This notion, occasionally, goes hand in hand with the observation that

Iran, according to Iranian Evangelicals, is subject to a tremendous 'spiritual awakening'. In a sermon entitled 'The Anointment of Cyrus for Iran', Dallas-based televangelist Hormoz Shariʿat[16] states:

> God is working in a peculiar way among Iranians. It is not just me who is saying this, it is the whole world. Do you know what they say? Again and again they are telling me: 'The Iranians are different! We have travelled to all the countries, especially Islamic countries. In Islamic countries, Muslims don't dare to question their religion, their faith, their [holy] book and their political leaders. But the Iranians are free, they are investigating, they are comparing, they are asking questions!' God has liberated us. All this is from God, let's not think that this is because we Iranians are particularly clever or something! It is the grace of God. (…) God has opened the door for Cyrus and now opens it for us.[17]
>
> (Shariʿat 2018, m. 1:25:31–1:26:45)

Shariʿat's statement draws an immediate connection between the Iranian opposition to their Islamist government and the biblical role of Cyrus as an anointed liberator. That Cyrus has become an icon of anti-governmental resistance offers Iranian evangelical Christians the opportunity to speak to the sensibilities of many Iranians, both inside Iran and abroad, and promote their very own reading of the famed Persian king. Christianity then appears as a religious alternative that, different from Islam, is well-suited to Iranians fed up with the current government.

The commemoration of the 'Martyrs of the Church of Iran'

Notions of martyrdom are central to Shi'ite Islam and find their culmination in the Kerbela episode during which Hussein, the grandson of the Prophet Muhammad, was killed at the hands of his antagonists. Some scholars have pointed to the re-activation of the Kerbela narrative in modern political contexts (cf. Fischer 1980); in post-revolutionary Iran, politicians and clerics have postulated a continuity from the martyrs of Kerbela to protestors killed against the Pahlavi monarchy and Iranians killed during the Iran-Iraq War in the 1980s (cf. Aghaie 2004). The grateful commemoration of the martyrs who died fighting for the Islamic Republic is part and parcel of Iranian state discourse. Stories of the heroic martyrs also feature in school curricula and are therefore well-known to Iranians who went to school in post-revolutionary Iran.

The category 'martyr' (*shahid*), however, is a contested one. Shahla Talebi has spoken about 'state martyrs' and 'dissident martyrs', the latter of which suffer from a 'discriminatory invisibility and lack of recognition' (Talebi 2012: 122). While Talebi is primarily concerned with leftist victims of the Islamic Republic's anti-oppositional violence, the Iranian Protestant pastors killed shortly after the 1979 Revolution and during the 1990s likewise constitute 'dissident martyrs'.[18] Their commemoration as 'Martyrs of the Church of Iran' ('*Shohadā-ye Kelisā-ye Irān*') is a recurring element in Persian-language Christian exile magazines. Referring to a series introducing the biographies of the martyred pastors, a reader of the UK-published magazine *Kalameh* ('The Word') explains in a letter to the editors:

> By reading 'The Lives of the Martyrs of [the Church of] Iran', I have understood that, although these people were normal humans, they even under difficult conditions remained steadfast in their faith and have demonstrated that his [God's] grace is enough. Seeing this kind of people increases the belief and self-confidence of us Christian Iranians, for we comprehend that we have role models among ourselves and do not need to search for them anywhere else. Role models that, like us, were Iranian and come from a similar cultural background, so we can establish a connection with them.
>
> (Kalameh 2005: 14)

For the writer of the letter, the biographies of the murdered Iranian pastors serve as an assurance of his Iranian-Christian identity. Through their biographies, they become relatable role models to other Iranian Christians, especially to those who have experienced discrimination by the Iranian government. Similar to the figure of Cyrus the Great, the fate of the 'Martyrs of the Church of Iran' as well as ongoing persecution are read as indicators of the success of the Christian movement, or a 'spiritual awakening'. 'Isā Dibāj, son of Iranian Pentecostal Pastor Mehdi Dibāj who was extrajudicially killed in 1994, writes in the magazine *Kalameh*:

> Throughout the history of Christianity, the persecution and discrimination of Christians has always resulted in the further growth of the Church. Our dear country Iran is by no means an exception to this principle. In the words of Tertullian, the outstanding thinker of the church: 'The blood of the martyrs is the seed of the Church.'
>
> (Dibāj 2004)

The 'Martyrs of the Church of Iran' thus constitute an alternative catalogue of martyrs that is subversive to the state-promoted narrative of martyrdom in the Islamic Republic. In light of the injustices occurring in Iran, many Iranians cast doubt on the prerogative of their government to determine who ought to be revered as a 'martyr' and who shunned as a 'traitor'. Moreover, the killings of the Protestant pastors in the 1990s coincided with the serial killings of prominent Iranians in the political opposition.[19] Thus, there is an immediate connection between the 'Martyrs of the Church of Iran' and other 'dissident martyrs'.

Critical discourses on Islam

Alongside other aspects mentioned in the introduction, the 2020 quantitative study by Maleki and Tamimi Arab highlights one key trait of the religious landscape in contemporary Iran: the disillusionment with Islam. As early as 2008, the late Michael Axworthy noted in his history of post-revolutionary Iran that Iran 'is an Islamic republic, but one in which only 1.4 percent of the population attends Friday prayers' (Axworthy 2008: xiii). Similarly, Shahram Khosravi in his ethnography of youth culture in Teheran has pointed to the phenomenon of *din-gorizi*, the widespread 'escaping from religion', as a concern to clerics and politicians in Iran (Khosravi 2008: 126). For many Iranians, the dissatisfaction with the Islamist government translates to a dissatisfaction with the religion of Islam *as a whole*. Especially those who deem Islam a foreign element to Iran and advocate what sociologist Reza Gholami has termed 'non-islamiosity' tend to regard the Islamic Republic as 'an inevitable outcome of the "misguided" religion of Islam' (Gholami 2016: 8).[20]

Conversions to evangelical Christianity can be viewed as one result of the image crisis of Islam in Iran. In the words of Marcin Rzepka, 'in a country that called itself the Islamic Republic (...) [c]onversion is a means of protest' (Rzepka 2017: 188). Since the vast majority of members in Persian-speaking churches outside of Iran today are Muslim-born converts, it seems reasonable to assume that references to Islam can be found in sermons and the written material produced by the communities. Such discourses, however, are often subtle and generally refrain from direct attacks on Islam and Muslims. An example is the following excerpt from a 2019 sermon by Netherlands-based Iranian Armenian pastor Verzh Bābākhāni:

> God wants us to have a joyful life, in high spirits, full of freshness, did you know this? This is the desire and wish of God! His wish is not for us to be depressed, in grief and sadness or that we cry and constantly beat our chests – none of these things.
>
> (Bābākhāni 2019, m. 0:32–0:49)

Bābākhāni here contrasts his perception of the Christian God with the sadness supposedly inherent to Shi'ite Islam. By mentioning 'chest-beating', the pastor makes an indirect reference to a key mourning practice of Shi'ism and avers that Christianity, much different from Islam, endorsed a joyful lifestyle. This is a recurring trope in Iranian evangelical apologetics that has also come to the attention of other researchers (cf. Spellman 2004: 184). In a 2013 TV-series on the Persian-language evangelical channel *Mohabat TV*, theologian and pastor Sāsān Tavassoli remarked that many Iranian Muslims, upon entering a church for the first time, were struck by the cheerful atmosphere (Keshish-Ābnus and Tavassoli 2013b, m. 5:58). In a mosque, conversely, 'no one sings joyful worship songs'. Both Bābākhāni and Tavassoli suggested that Christianity thus was close to the Iranian cultural spirit that, like Christianity, appreciated joyfulness and celebrations.

A second major trope through which Iranian Evangelicals differentiate Christianity from Islam is the notion that Christianity, unlike Islam, was *not* a legalist religion (*mazhab*).[21] Again, this trope chimes well with the sensibilities of many Iranians who are fed up with the strict moral code implemented by the Islamic Republic's governmental forces in the public sphere. Tavassoli contrasts the relationship between humans and God in Islam and Christianity: while, he suggests, this relationship in Islam was that of 'a master and his servant' (*arbāb o bandeh*), in Christianity the same relationship could be likened to that of a father and his child, of a husband and his wife, or that of a shepherd and his sheep (Keshish-Ābnus and Tavassoli 2013a, m. 9:37). This characterization has strong reverberations with evangelical readings of Christianity as 'a personal relationship'.

Critical discourses on Islam in Iranian evangelical exile churches, then, present Christianity as a liberating force available to Iranians frustrated with Islam, particularly in the way it is propagated by the Iranian state. Secondly, Iranian Evangelicals, like in the previous two sections, present Christianity as being in harmony with the Iranian national spirit. Occasionally, Iranian pastors and ministers supplement this claim by portraying Islam as an 'Arab religion' that forced non-Arab Muslims to deliver their prayers in a language they did not understand (Bāghestāni 2016, m. 33:36). Christianity, much differently, as they argue, was a religion embracing cultural diversity, including and especially the culture of Iranians. Accordingly, a convert, by no means, had to give up their native culture but could continue to be fully immersed in it (Dibāj 2003: 36).

Conclusion and notes on the asylum conundrum

Previous analyses of Muslim-born Iranians' conversions to evangelical Christianity characterized these as results of religious individualism (cf. Darwish 2018; cf. Kéri and Sleiman 2017), a 'migration strategy' (Akcapar 2006) and a source of ontological security (Öztürk 2022). Criticizing these approaches for their tendency to remain detached from socio-cultural developments in contemporary Iran, I have situated Iranian conversions to Evangelicalism in the context of an ongoing religious transformation of Iran and pointed to the saliency of national identity in the religious discourse of Iranian evangelical Christians. Using the examples of notions of King Cyrus the Great, the commemoration of Iranian Christian 'dissident martyrs' and critical discourses on Islam, I have illustrated how Iranian evangelical Christians represent Christianity as a religion well-suited for Iranians.

There are further interesting examples of how Iranian Christians in exile connect their Christian faith with elements of their national culture. A most striking context is Iranian Christian celebrations of Nowruz and Yaldā, and the re-interpretation of these occasions as bearing Christian symbolism. Most noteworthy is, moreover, the usage of Persian poetry in Iranian evangelical services, both classical poetry and self-composed poetry by Iranian Christian artists. Iranian Evangelicals regularly claim that the famed heroes of the Persian poetic tradition, among them Hāfez and Rumi, had a particular predilection for the figure of Jesus Christ in their works. Sporadically, this claim goes so far as to portray these poets as pseudo-Christians (Zargari and Zargari 2014, m. 10:24). I will treat the construction of a distinct Iranian-Christian national identity in greater detail in a forthcoming book (Römer, forthcoming).

An area studies perspective on Muslim-born Iranians' conversions to evangelical Christianity can also yield illustrative insights relevant to the conundrum posed by asylum adjudications on the basis of religious conversion.

Firstly, the present approach foregrounds the importance of localized knowledge regarding the claimants' countries of origin. No doubt, decision-makers are generally aware of this importance; that said, it is not always transparent what sources decision-makers use to stay informed. Regarding the cases of Iranian Christians, the present chapter has foregrounded how the use of the Persian language in a Christian context is heavily penalized in the Islamic Republic of Iran. Accordingly, the issue at stake, at least on the surface, is not so much apostasy as is the accusation of engagement in 'subversive acts' through the promotion of a Persian Christianity.

This accusation can be held against both Muslim-born converts to Christianity and members of Armenian and Assyrian ethno-religious communities who have chosen to leave their traditional Orthodox Churches and join a Persian-speaking Christian community. On a similar note, members of other religious minorities, among them Jews and Zoroastrians, may equally become subject to legal persecution if joining Persian-speaking Christian communities. Like Armenians and Assyrians, they can hardly be accused of 'apostasy'. Overall, the religious freedom of Persian-speaking Christians inside Iran is drastically curtailed. Whether they actively proselytize or not, their *mere usage* of Persian is considered a measure of (illegitimate) evangelism by the Iranian state. While the death penalty today is rather unlikely to be applied for such cases – though this would not be without historical precedents – there are other harsh measures of persecution.

A second relevant issue pointed to in this chapter is the salience of national identity which may caution decision-makers to not reduce conversions of Muslim-born Iranians to being a 'matter of faith and spirituality'. As the body of scholarly literature on such conversions is growing, decision-makers are enabled to recognize the *multiple* contextual factors playing a role. The relevance of national identity and the idea of Christianity reconciling Iranians with their own national cultures being one of them, decision-makers may miss out on important aspects if they approach conversions through their individual preconception of what issues, conventionally, play a role in religious conversions (cf. Halonen, this volume).

This point, finally, brings me to another contextualizing factor that has not been mentioned yet: the global spread of evangelical and Pentecostal Christianity. Especially in Central and Northern Europe, or any other context in which Catholicism and mainline Protestantism constitute the normative variant of Christianity, decision-makers may be unfamiliar with theological concepts and vocabulary stemming from the evangelical milieu. Accordingly, descriptions of a 'second birth', 'testimonies of faith', 'worship sessions', alongside many other examples, may be concepts appearing odd to decision-makers who do not have personal connections with the evangelical milieu. This problem likewise applies to interpreters who, in the context of Iran, may be equally unfamiliar with such concepts and their, often very recently coined, Persian translations. Thus, a combination of academic expertise in the study of global evangelicalism and area studies knowledge about Iran could prove most fruitful, both for scholarly purposes and for the introduction of new perspectives to decision-makers in the asylum conundrum.

Notes

1 Rzepka mentions a Persian-language article by Ārmān Roshdi from *Kalameh* magazine but does not further engage with Persian-language material; Rzepka 2017: 56.
2 Darwish, for example, highlights a 'religious quest for personal spiritual fulfilment, a universal expression of human spirituality'; Darwish 2018: 5. Kéri and Sleiman, who also took into account conversions outside the Iranian case, speak of an 'intraindividual processes dominated either by intellectual-experimental orientation or emotion-driven mystical experiences'; Kéri and Sleiman 2017: 12.
3 There is a legally recognized Zoroastrian ethno-religious community in Iran that today may comprise no more than several thousand individuals; cf. Sanasarian 2004: 37. Conversion to Zoroastrianism is not foreseen in conventional interpretations of the religion and there is no religious infrastructure inside Iran that could accommodate potential converts. Such conversions, moreover, would be at odds with the governmental approach to religious belonging and would be likely to be legally persecuted.
4 Bradley's 2008 book, for instance, begins with the following statement: 'Early on I noticed that Iranians were willing not to just give Christians a hearing, but some were ready to actually become Christians. As someone who wants people to respond to the Christian Gospel this was of course encouraging'; Bradley 2008: ix. He is therefore accused by Hopkins of not being 'an unbiased observer accounting the facts of a movement; he [Bradley] is a Christian who desires Iranians to convert to Christianity'; Hopkins 2020: 22.
5 By the mid-2010s, no more than around 30,000 Armenians were likely to have remained in Iran, Barry 2020: 248.
6 For the detailed circumstances of the killings, see: Bradley 2008: 164–74; Dehqani-Tafti 1981; Rzepka 2017: 137–41; Sanasarian 2004: 123–7; van Gorder 2010: 180–2, 219–36. The murdered pastors were Arastu Sayyāh (1928–79; Anglican), Bahrām Dehqāni-Tafti (1955–80; Anglican), Hoseyn Sudmand (1951–90; Pentecostal), Mehdi Dibāj (1935–94; Pentecostal), Hāyk Hovsepiān (1945–94; Pentecostal), Tateos Mikāʾeliān (1932–94; Presbyterian) and Mohammad Bāqer 'Ravānbakhsh' Yusefi (1964–96; Pentecostal). More recent accounts also list the Iranian Turkmen house church leader Qorbān Turāni (1952–2005).

7   The Iranian government blamed the killings on three young women accused of being affiliated with the Islamist-Marxist group *Mojāhedin-e Khalq* which, shortly after the 1979 Revolution, had fallen out with the followers of revolutionary leader Ruhollah Khomeini.
8   A recently updated list on Iranian Christians legally persecuted by the Iranian government is provided by the UK-based NGO Article18: https://articleeighteen.com/prisoners-list/; last accessed 13 March 2023.
9   In the larger cities of the countries mentioned here, one can even find more than just one Persian-speaking church. To the best of my knowledge, there currently are at least three Persian-language churches in London, Berlin, and Istanbul, respectively. The umbrella organization Persian Christian Community Church on its website lists member churches in Germany, Austria, Armenia, Belgium, Turkey, Sweden, Finland and the Netherlands, see: https://kelisayejame.org/%d8%b4%d8%b9%d8%a8-%d9%85%d8%a7/; last accessed 30 October 2022.
10 As discussed by Barry, the label 'Iranian Armenian' appears to be most plausible in English, corresponding with the Armenian self-designation *Iranahay*; Barry 2020: 8. For heuristic purposes, I analogously speak of 'Iranian Assyrians' in this chapter.
11 This research project formed the foundation of my PhD thesis at the University of Bayreuth, and will be published by I.B. Tauris (forthcoming) under the title *The Iranian Christian Diaspora: Religion and Nationhood in Exile*.
12 Examples are the magazines *Māhnāmeh-ye Kelisā* ('Church Monthly') and *Payām-e Kelisā* ('Message of the Church'), published by the *Jamāʿat-e Rabbāni* churches, as well as *Nāmeh-ye Mohabat* ('Love Letter') and *Nur-e ʿĀlam* ('Light of the World') by the Anglican Diocese. It is difficult to acquire copies of these magazines today.
13 Zia-Ebrahimi describes a strand of Iranian nationalism that considers the Arab conquest of Persia a corrupting intrusion of pure Iranian nationhood. Proponents of the 'dislocative' narrative insist on Iran's characterization as an 'Aryan' nation and argue that Iran's geographical location in the Middle East did not reflect its true national spirit which was closer to Europe. They glorify the pre-Islamic era in Iranian history as a supposedly golden age of freedom and progress. According to Zia-Ebrahimi, dislocative nationalism since the 1980s has become 'the most conventional form of secular opposition to the Islamic Republic'; Zia-Ebrahimi 2016: 3.
14 Most importantly, Isaiah 45.1-13 mentions God choosing Cyrus to forge an alliance with him. Further mentions include 2 Chronicles 22–3 and Ezra 1, both of which are concerned with Cyrus' permission for the Jews in Babylonian Exile to return to the Land of Israel. In the book of Daniel, Cyrus is passingly mentioned several times, mainly as a calendric reference ('In the third year of King Cyrus … ').
15 As of November 2022, the church continued to be highly active on YouTube, posting recordings of its services: https://www.youtube.com/channel/UC_KSxY4d5aalBLumGfurHUg; last accessed 1 November 2022.

16 Shari'at is senior pastor at the Persian-language Christian online TV channel *Shabakeh 7*. In 1979, he left Iran to pursue his PhD studies in the United States where he, shortly after, converted to Evangelical Christianity. Starting in the early 2000s, Shari'at became a pioneer in the usage of satellite TV to missionize in Persian. In 2020, he published an English-language autobiographical book entitled 'Iran's Great Awakening: How God's Using a Muslim Convert to Spark Revival', cf. Shariat 2020.

17 Translations, both of audiovisual and written sources, are my own.

18 Among other aspects, Talebi refers to the spatial separation governmental clerks implement on public graveyards between 'dissident martyrs' and others; Talebi 2012: 131. This separation is also implemented for some of the murdered Iranian pastors of the 1990s, for instance Hoseyn Sudmand, whose burial place additionally was vandalized by unknown perpetrators in late 2019; cf. Article18 2019.

19 Between 1988 to 1998, several outspoken opponents of the Islamic Republic's government, among them the last prime minister of Pahlavi Iran Shāpur Bakhtiār, the nationalist politician Dāriush Foruhar and the Iranian Kurdish activist 'Abdorrahmān Qāsemlu, were assassinated. Their killings were finally blamed on 'rogue elements' in the Iranian Ministry of Intelligence; cf. Ansari 2019: 361–2; Axworthy 2013: 344–8. Whether the extrajudicial killings of Iranian Protestant pastors were committed in the same context remains a matter of speculation, as do much of the serial killings' details.

20 In his enlightening 2015 book, Gholami has studied a particular mode of the secular prevalent in the London Iranian diaspora that is rooted in 'dislocative nationalism' (Zia-Ebrahimi) as introduced earlier in this chapter. 'Non-Islamiosity' often entails overt anti-Arab racism and surfaces in multiple narratives and practices, among them the usage of a supposedly 'pure' form of Modern Persian which refrains from the usage of Arabic loanwords, the usage of Old Persian cuneiform in Iranian restaurants or cultural institutions, and satirical stage performances portraying the Muslim faith of an Iranian villager as a disease requiring cure; cf. Gholami 2016.

21 To avoid misunderstandings, it should be mentioned that the word *mazhab* in Persian can generally describe a 'religion' and does not necessarily mean a 'denomination' or a 'legal school of thought' as suggested by its Arabic root.

Bibliography

Aghaie, Kamran Scot (2004). *The Martyrs of Karbala. Shi'i Symbols and Rituals in Modern Iran*. Seattle, WA: University of Washington Press.

Akcapar, Sebnem Koser (2006). 'Conversion as a Migration Strategy in a Transit Country. Iranian Shiites Becoming Christians in Turkey'. *International Migration Review*, 40 (4): 817–53.

Akcapar, Sebnem Koser (2010). 'Re-thinking Migrants' Networks and Social Capital. A Case Study of Iranians in Turkey'. *International Migration*, 48 (2): 161–96.

Akcapar, Sebnem Koser (2019). 'Religious Conversions in Forced Migration. Comparative Cases of Afghans in India and Iranians in Turkey'. *Journal of Eurasian Studies*, 10 (1): 61–74.

Ansari, Ali M. (2012). *The Politics of Nationalism in Modern Iran*. Cambridge; New York: Cambridge University Press.

Ansari, Ali M. (2019). *Modern Iran since 1797. Reform and Revolution*. New York: Routledge.

Article18 (2019). 'Takhrib-e Mahall-e Dafn-e Hoseyn Sudmand; Keshishi keh beh Ettehām-e Ertedād Eʿdām shod'. Available online at https://articleeighteen.com/fa/news/2167/ (last accessed 14 March 2023).

Axworthy, Michael (2008). *Iran. Empire of the Mind: a History from Zoroaster to the Present Day*. London: Penguin.

Axworthy, Michael (2013). *Revolutionary Iran. A History of the Islamic Republic*. New York: Oxford University Press.

Bābākhāni, Verzh (2019). 'Payām-e Nowruzi-ye Sāl-e 1398: Zendegi-ye Shādāb-tar va Tāzeh va Sabz. Almere: Kelisā-ye 222 Ālmireh'. Available online at https://www.youtube.com/watch?v=3L9f5sGfl3Q (last accessed 5 December 2019).

Bāghestāni, Elnātān (2016). 'Jashn-e Nowruz-e Kelisā-ye Safirān-e Masih 1391. Los Angeles: Kelisā-ye Safirān-e Masih'. Available online at https://www.youtube.com/watch?v=2E4Fkrq_ksQ (last accessed 2 September 2019).

Barry, James (2020). *Armenian Christians in Iran. Ethnicity, Religion, and Identity in the Islamic Republic*. Cambridge: Cambridge University Press.

Bradley, Mark (2008). *Iran and Christianity. Historical Identity and Present Relevance*. London; New York: Continuum.

Bradley, Mark (2014). *Too Many to Jail: The Story of Iran's New Christians*. Oxford, MI: Monarch Books.

Dandamayev, Muhammad A. (1993). 'CYRUS iii. Cyrus II The Great. Encyclopaedia Iranica'. Available online at https://iranicaonline.org/articles/cyrus-iiI (last accessed 5 May 2021).

Darwish, Linda (2018). '"When Your Heart Is Touched, It's Not a Decision". A Narrative Analysis of Iranian Muslim Conversion to Christianity'. *Studies in Religion/Sciences Religieuses*, 47 (1): 1–33.

Dehqani-Tafti, Hassan (1981). *The Hard Awakening*. New York: Seabury Press.

Dehqani-Tafti, Hassan (2000). *The Unfolding Design of My World. A Pilgrim in Exile*. Norwich: Canterbury Press.

Dibāj, ʿIsā (2003). 'Masihiyyat va Nowruz-e Bāstān'. *Kalameh: Majalleh-ye Imān o Farhang-e Masihi-ye Irāni*, 9 (33): 14, 36.

Dibāj, ʿIsā (2004). 'Moruri bar Zendegi-ye Shohadā-ye Kelisā-ye Irān. Bakhsh-e Avval'. *Kalameh: Majalleh-ye Imān o Farhang-e Masihi-ye Irāni*, 10 (40). https://www.kalameh.com/article/%D9%85%D8%B1%D9%88%D8%B1%DB%

8C-%D8%A8%D8%B1-%D8%B2%D9%86%D8%AF%DA%AF%DB%8C-
%D8%B4%D9%87%D8%AF%D8%A7%DB%8C-
%DA%A9%D9%84%DB%8C%D8%B3%D8%A7%DB%8C-%D8%A7%DB%8C%D8
%B1%D8%A7%D9%86 (last accessed 12 November 2021).

Fischer, Michael M. J. (1980). *Iran. From Religious Dispute to Revolution*. Wisconsin: The University of Wisconsin Press.

Flynn, Thomas S. (2017). *The Western Christian Presence in the Russias and Qajar Persia, c.1760–c.1870*. Leiden: Brill.

Gholami, Reza (2016). *Secularism and Identity. Non-Islamiosity in the Iranian Diaspora*. London: Taylor and Francis.

Hopkins, Philip O. (2020). *American Missionaries in Iran during the 1960s and 1970s*. Cham: Springer.

ICHRI (2013). *The Cost of Faith: Persecution of Christian Protestants and Converts in Iran*. New York: International Campaign for Human Rights in Iran.

IHRDC (2014). *Apostasy in the Islamic Republic of Iran*. New Haven: Iran Human Rights Documentation Center.

IHRDC (2021). *Living in the Shadows of Oppression: The Situation of Christian Converts in Iran*. New Haven: Iran Human Rights Documentation Center.

Kalameh (2005). 'Āshti-ye Masihiyyat va Farhang-e Irāni'. *Kalameh: Majalleh-ye Imān o Farhang-e Masihi-ye Irāni*, 11 (41): 14.

Kéri, Szabolcs and Christina Sleiman (2017). 'Religious Conversion to Christianity in Muslim Refugees in Europe'. *Archive for the Psychology of Religion/Archiv für Religionspychologie*, 39 (1).

Keshish-Ābnus, Edvin and Sāsān Tavassoli (2013a). 'Moqāyeseh-ye Elāhiyāt-e Eslām va Masihiyyat. Southern California: Mohabat TV'. Available online at https://www.youtube.com/watch?v=NUu_EX4w7Y4 (last accessed 8 June 2021).

Keshish-Ābnus, Edvin and Sāsān Tavassoli (2013b). 'Moqāyeseh-ye Elāhiyāt-e Eslām va Masihiyyat. Southern California: Mohabat TV'. Available online at https://www.youtube.com/watch?v=xaunUeuaCIo&t=11s (last accessed 8 June 2021).

Khosravi, Shahram (2008). *Young and Defiant in Tehran*. Philadelphia: University of Pennsylvania Press.

Krannich, Conrad (2020). *Recht Macht Religion. Eine Untersuchung über Taufe und Asylverfahren*. Göttingen: V&R unipress.

Leman, John (2007). 'A "Lucan Effect" in the Commitment of Iranian Converts in Transit. The Case of the Pentecostal Iranian Enclave in Istanbul'. *Revue des mondes musulmans et de la Mediterranee*, 119–20: 101–14.

Maleki, Ammar and Pooyan Tamimi Arab (2020). *Iranians' Attitudes toward Religion: A 2020 Survey Report*. Tilburg: GAMAAN.

Marashi, Afshin (2017). 'Return of the King: Cyrus the Great and the Iranian National Imagination. Oklahoma: University of Oklahoma'. Available online at https://www.youtube.com/watch?v=P1gqPULW1AI (last accessed 5 May 2021).

Marashi, Afshin (2020). *Exile and the Nation. The Parsi Community of India and the Making of Modern Iran*. Austin: University of Texas Press.

Markaz-e Āmār-e Irān (2018 [1397]). *Natāyej-e Kolli-ye Sarshomāri-ye ʿOmumi-ye Nofus o Maskan-e 1395-e Koll-e Keshvar*. Tehran: Nashriyyāt-e Markaz-e Āmār-e Irān.

Miller, Duane Alexander (2012). 'Iranian Diaspora Christians in the American Midwest and Scotland. Historical Background, Present Realities and Future Challenges'. *Global Missiology*, 9 (2): 1–9.

Miller, Duane Alexander (2015). 'Power, Personalities and Politics'. *Mission Studies*, 32 (1): 66–86.

Mohammadi, Majid (2018). 'Tahlil-e Shoʿār-hā-ye Harekat-e Eʿterāzi-ye Dey-Māh 1396-e Irān'. *BBC Persian*. Available online at https://www.bbc.com/persian/blog-viewpoints-42620668 (last accessed 7 May 2021).

Öztürk, Ebru (2022). 'Finding a New Home through Conversion: The Ontological Security of Iranians Converting to Christianity in Sweden'. *Religion, State and Society*, 50 (2): 224–39.

Pahlavi, Rezā (2022). 'Beh Monāsebat-e Haftomine Ābān, Ruz-e Kurush'. Edited by Instagram. Available online at https://www.instagram.com/reel/CkOglBwIcBS/?utm_source=ig_web_copy_link (last accessed 31 October 2022).

Radio Farda (2022) 'Ruz-e Kurush: Haml-e Namād-e Derafsh-e Kāviāni dar Irān va Gardehamāyi-ye Irāniān dar Khārej az Keshvar'. Available online at https://www.radiofarda.com/a/cyrus-the-great-pasargadae-day-protests/32107552.html (last accessed 31 October 2022).

Römer, Benedikt (forthcoming). *The Iranian Christian Diaspora: Religion and Nationhood in Exile*. London: I.B. Tauris.

Rzepka, Marcin (2017). *Prayer and Protest. The Protestant Communities in Revolutionary Iran*. Krakow: Unum Press.

Sanasarian, Eliz (2004). *Religious Minorities in Iran*. Cambridge; New York; Melbourne: Cambridge University Press.

Shabānlāri, Peymān (2017). 'Payām-e Nowruz-e Kelisā-ye Navid-e Rahāyi: Sokhani bā To Hamvatan. Amsterdam: Kelisā-ye Navid-e Rahāyi'. Available online at https://www.youtube.com/watch?v=ZS-blfbnCcg (last accessed 9 February 2019).

Shariat, Hormoz (2020). *Iran's Great Awakening. How God Is Using a Muslim Convert to Spark Revival*. Melissa, TX: Iran Alive Ministries.

Shariʿat, Hormoz (2018). 'Mash-e Kurosh bar Irān. Dallas: Shabakeh 7'. Available online at https://www.youtube.com/watch?v=53pJAYWNtpk (last accessed 16 September 2019).

Shariʿat, Hormoz (2020). 'Vizheh Barnāmeh-ye Nowruzi-ye Kelisā-ye Haft. Dallas: Shabakeh 7'. Available online at https://www.youtube.com/watch?v=ldM_SjZZIpM (last accessed 22 March 2020).

Spellman, Kathryn (2004). *Religion and Nation. Iranian Local and Transnational Networks in Britain*. New York: Berghahn Books.

Stadlbauer, Susanne (2019). 'Between Secrecy and Transparency': Conversions to Protestantism among Iranian Refugees in Germany'. *Entangled Religions*, 8.

Steele, Robert (2021). *The Shah's Imperial Celebrations of 1971. Nationalism, Culture and Politics in Late Pahlavi Iran*. London; New York: I.B. Tauris.

Stene, Nora (2020). 'Leaving Islam for Christianity: Asylum Seeker Converts'. *Handbook of Leaving Religion*, Daniel Enstedt, Göran Larsson and Teemu T. Mantsinen (eds.), 210–29. Leiden: Brill.

Talebi, Shahla (2012). 'From the Light of the Eyes to the Eyes of the Power: State and Dissident Martyrs in Post-Revolutionary Iran'. *Visual Anthropology*, 25 (1–2): 120–47.

Thomas, Dāvud and ʿIsā Dibāj (2010). 'Pā-ye Sohbat-e Chehreh-hā-ye Barjasteh-ye Kelisā-ye Irān: Mosāhebeh bā Keshish Dāvud Thomas'. *Kalameh: Majalleh-ye Imān o Farhang-e Masihi-ye Irāni*, 16 (63): 10–13.

van Gorder, A. Christian (2010). *Christianity in Persia and the Status of Non-Muslims in Iran*. Lanham, MD: Lexington Books.

Waterfield, Robin Everard (1973). *Christians in Persia. Assyrians, Armenians, Roman Catholics and Protestants*. London: Allen and Unwin.

Zargari, Siāmak and Rozitā Zargari (2014). 'Mowʿezeh-ye Nowruz-e 93: Kurosh keh beh Imān Dāsht?' Essen: Elam Alive Ministries. Available online at https://www.youtube.com/watch?v=ECdIUIP3N3g (last accessed 2 April 2020).

Zia-Ebrahimi, Reza (2016). *The Emergence of Iranian Nationalism. Race and the Politics of Dislocation*. New York; Chichester, WS: Columbia University Press.

9

'She lacks a "male network" in her home country': Gendering the credibility assessment and the discursive space of intersectionality in migration courts in Sweden

Ebru Öztürk

Introduction

In a courtroom, every person accused of a crime is presumed innocent until proven guilty, but at the migration courts, appellants are presumed bogus until proven otherwise. Since they were not found credible by the respective migration agency (for many reasons, including unproven identity, documents, etc.), they appeal to a migration court and the court assesses whether there is a reasonable basis for changing the migration agency's decision. Migration courts have been places where truth is thought to be produced through asylum determinations. In that text-world (Gavins 2007), the truth is discursively constructed, and it is nothing more than what judges decide to be true. In the shade of this precarious truth (Fassin 2013), this chapter seeks to understand how those asylum seekers who have converted from Islam to Christianity in Sweden and have taken religion as a grounds for asylum application have become a discursive space (Dunn 2003) through legal texts onto which several actors have impelled meanings with the ambition to demarcate their conversion process. Credibility assessment regarding religious conviction, which remains at the heart of this discursive space, includes determining whether the claimant is genuinely religious. While some actors, such as judges and lay judges, try to separate the ones who are telling 'the truth' from the 'ones who are lying' (see also Affolter 2021: 162; Fassin and Kobelinsky 2012: 446; Kobelinsky 2015: 67), other actors, such as lawyers, interpreters and volunteers from churches and human rights organizations help converts (professionally or voluntarily) attempt to prove their plausibility to the court. These converts rarely have agency in court rooms.

The definition of conversion is contingent on the person who defines it. According to Lewis Rambo (1993), while the convert feels that their conversion is genuine and profound, it is conceivable that the advocate who tries to find the 'pure convert' (5) may see it as inadequate. Rambo (1993), who sees the conversion as a dynamic, multilayered process of transformation, deems that 'conversion is what a group or person says it is' (7).

Rambo's (1993) eminent, interdisciplinary, process-oriented conversion model has seven stages,[1] but this chapter accords more weight to the last stage, known as the 'consequences' (22). It contributes to the argument that conversion as a cumulative phenomenon (148) may, together with other consequences[2] that Rambo mentions, involve significant 'juridical consequences' that are matter of life and death to the converts.

Legal arguments are accounts that link the power domains and structural power relations that refer to legal institutions. This chapter will analyse the power relations constructed in the judgements, which are interrelated and mutually shape one another during the formation of the discursive space through the process of 'credibility'. I am mostly interested in understanding how the imbalanced juridical process shapes ongoing power inequalities between asylum seeking cultural/ethnic/religious others and judicial actors.

The literature on religious conversion is expansive and covers many disciplines, such as sociology, anthropology, theology, psychology, history and interdisciplinary scholarships (e.g. socio-legal studies) that combine integrated methods and perspectives.

The administrative migration courts in many European countries that oversee the asylum cases that have been rejected by the respective countries' migration agencies have been studied by scholars through various methods, including those in which courtroom ethnographies are prominent. Scholars have observed the social and institutional setting while interacting with subjects they have studied through interviews and archives in several settings, including Germany (see Rose and Given-Wilson 2021[3] and Anne Schlüter in this volume[4]), Sweden (see Johannesson 2022),[5] Austria (see Ramsauer and Caglar in this volume),[6] France (Kobelinsky 2019),[7] the UK (Hambly 2019)[8] and Norway (Fossdal in this volume).[9]

Knowledge about the structures and the mechanisms of law are an important part of our life, which has been organized according to them. The fundamental categories of 'modern law' and structures of 'modern society' and 'modern culture' are both interconnected and interdependent (Kaarlo 2002: 188). While exploring the relationship between legal narratives and power that relate to conversion, my research questions have been sociologically informed. I believe that the sociological interpretation of legal narratives is indispensable because, initially, social categories that are created by law become a subject of focus for sociology (Cottorell 1998). To reinterpret law systematically as a social phenomenon requires a sociological understanding of legal ideas with a 'transdisciplinary understanding' (183). This will 'situate the richness of the unique in a broader theoretical context and so provide orientation for its interpretation' (183). And then, as has been argued by legal scholars (see Dobinson and Johns 2007; Epstein and King 2002), many scholars in the field of law are untrained and lacking in experience when it comes to empirical research and the general rules applicable to such research (Cottorell 1998: 17). Epstein and King (2002) analysed published legal articles with the reference 'empirical' in the title and found that they are purely theoretical and not empirical: 'As a result, readers learn considerably less accurate information about the empirical world than the studies' stridently stated, but overly confident, conclusions suggest' (18).

Materials and methods

In order to answer the research questions, text-based data (judgements) obtained from the Migration Court in Stockholm were used. I received and reviewed approximately 35,000[10] asylum application judgements made between 2015 and 2021. Among them, approximately 1,500 named conversion as grounds for their asylum claim. Of these 1,500, 1,304[11] judgements of relevance were considered in the study, as they were specifically about conversion from Islam to Christianity.

Law as a powerful social institution has been an area of interest for qualitative researchers for a long time, but legal text analysis specifically regarding religious conversion cases is rare in legal, sociological and socio-legal scholarship. To expand the engagement on the conversion cases, I will deploy qualitative text analysis to analyse the judgements of the Migration Court in Sweden.

Mitchell (2023) distinguishes between two dominant strands of legal scholarship: 'doctrinal' (otherwise known as 'internal') legal research and 'non-doctrinal' (otherwise known as 'external') legal research (103). Doctrinal (internal) legal research is a field where legal scholars analyse the law itself (its nature, principles, etc.) and non-doctrinal (external) legal research, which is theoretically and empirically driven, analyses the law's 'social, cultural, political, or practical dimensions' (104) and 'the characteristics of existing systems of law, including the state and development, the causes and effects, and the functions and objectives of the institution and practices of law' (Deflem 2008, cited in Mitchell 2023: 5).

A qualitative approach, different from the positivist approach to legal interpretation, draws on critical and constructivist ontologies and holds that 'social[ly] and historical[ly] constituted power relations affect and mediate all ideas and thinking, values and facts can never be separated; facts always contain an ideological dimension; [and] ideas and objects are mediated through social relations' (Howel 2013: 80, cited in Mitchell 2023: 105).

As there is no 'pure' or 'true' law, and there are only the meanings that socially situated actors attribute to texts when reading the legal texts as a part of qualitative research, where the truth is not absolute but contextual, the goal would be to examine how truth, credibility and power regimes are constructed through the law and the exercises of power in those constructions (Mitchell 2022: 106).

Legal judgements, as a means of legal power, have 'a determinative status and are a primary source of legal principle in legal system', so looking into the articulations of power may produce valuable insights when judgements related to conversion cases are analysed (107).

Mitchell (2022) suggested three significant points that qualitative researchers should consider when approaching legal texts. The first is that legal texts have performative character; law does things with words (Austin 1975) and has the power to create realities. Legal texts 'make things true simply by saying them' (Terdiman, cited in Bourdieu 1987: 809). They privilege certain realities over others. The second is that judgements have rhetorical character. They are the court's 'argument for the validity of the decision it has reached' (Mitchell 2023: 109). So, both the structure of the truth claimed by the court and the process of how these decisions in the judgements have been justified and explained (109) are present in the judgements. The third and final consideration is about 'voice and authorship' (109). Judgements are not an individual judge's own decision or voice; they speak for the court and they are institutional decisions. The 'many-voicedness' that appears through the judgements as a 'monologic voice' (110) must be considered while analysing the legal texts.

The existing literature on conversion studies does not look at the topic from this approach, so I think that analysing the judgements on conversion through a qualitative perspective with a sociologically informed approach will challenge the hegemony of doctrinal legal research regarding the judgements in a novel way and shed light on the juridical consequences that converts experience.

Legal background

The 1951 Refugee Convention[12] that 'exclusively pertained to Europeans who were the victims of World War II' (Fassin 2013: 6) generalized protection to everyone with the 1967 Protocol of New York. It has been by far the most important instrument in refugee protection. Article 1 of the Convention states that anyone who is outside their country of origin as a result of a well-founded fear of persecution due to their race, religion, nationality or membership of a certain social group or political opinion must be considered a refugee. To be considered a refugee, the person seeking asylum must therefore have a well-founded fear of persecution. As 'well-founded fear' may be subjective, it is further required that the fear must be to some extent objective; that is, based on 'real conditions'. *Sur place* grounds are expressly not mentioned in the Refugee Convention. However, since the Convention requires that a person be outside their country of origin, it does not matter whether the fear of persecution arose before or after the person crossed the border. The common view is thus that *sur place* reasons are equal to reasons that arose before the refugee left his or her country of origin (Hathaway and Foster 2014: 75).

At the end of the 1970s, UNHCR prepared a manual called the Handbook on Procedures and Criteria for Determining Refugee Status.[13] With regard to the concept of a refugee, the Handbook states that since fear is a subjective[14] element, determinations of refugee status 'therefore primarily require an evaluation of the claimant's statements rather than a judgement on the situation prevailing in his country of origin' (19). A decision-maker who would take a position on an asylum application must understand the claimant's origin, characteristics and experiences in light of reliable information about the situation in their country of origin. UNHCR has also issued guidelines for the assessment of religious grounds for asylum (Guidelines: Religion-Based Refugee Claims),[15] which is considered a complement to the above-mentioned Handbook and describes in greater detail how credibility assessments regarding religious refugee claims should be carried out. Conversions *sur place* are treated specifically.

Credibility is of central importance when it comes to deciding religious refugee claims. The Guidelines speak of the 'narrative' as an important form of credibility assessment in such situations. Through open-ended questions, the claimant has the opportunity to explain their religious beliefs and actions. In this way, information extracted can form the basis of the credibility assessment. According to the Guidelines, knowledge of the religion is a factor in the credibility assessment. However, the requirements that can be placed on the claimant's knowledge vary depending on the circumstances of the individual situation.

The right to asylum is regulated in Sweden in chapter 4 §§ 1 and 2 of the Aliens Act (*utlänningslagen*) (2005: 716), and in Sweden, as in most Western countries, the bureaucracy of asylum comprises two levels and two institutions. A first step in the procedure is administrative, in the Migration Board (*Migrationsverket*). On the basis of an examination of the application, usually complemented by an interview of the applicant, officers decide whether asylum should be granted.

The second step is juridical, consisting of an appeal to the Migration Court. The adjudicating board in most asylum cases at the Migration Court of Stockholm consists of one professional judge and three lay judges. Lay judges, who are not trained judges, are nominated by the political parties in proportion to the votes for the county council and serve for a period of four years. Every Swedish citizen above the age of eighteen is eligible. The purpose of lay judges in the Swedish administrative court system is to bring citizen's direct representation into judicial reasoning in administrative courts (Sverige 1998).[16]

Theoretical framework

As this research aims to understand how converts became a discursive space through legal texts, it would be useful to see what lays the ground for this development. The general objective of discourse-theoretical empirical research is the production of novel and plausible interpretations of selected cases and problems (Howarth 2000: 142). Understanding and interpreting the constructed objects of inquiry is the overall aim of the social and political analysis from a discursive perspective (139). What is implied by 'discursive' is that all objects are objects of discourse, in that a condition of their meaning depends upon a socially constructed system of rules and significant differences (Laclau and Mouffe 1985: 107). To put it simply, discursive practices are synonymous with systems of social relations (Howarth 2000: 8). Discursive practice, according to Hall (1996), is the practice of producing meaning, and because all social practices involve meaning, 'all practices have a discursive aspect' (204). Discourses produce knowledge, too. It is a system of representation and a 'regime of truth'; 'therefore, it has consequences for both those who employ it and those who are "subjected" to it' (225).

As a significant part of this theoretical and methodological approach, the problematization of the phenomenon of concern, in this specific research, is done through the transformation of the research questions, which are raised from the limitations of existing interpretations on adjudications (specifically the conversion-based asylum claims). The interrelated and mutually shaping constructions of different power relations in these narratives together form the discursive space in which converts cannot locate themselves. These constructed discourses involve intersections in terms of power, which I will outline in the following section.

Gendering the credibility assessment: 'Lack of male network'

Establishing or failing to establish credibility in migration court can literally be a matter of life and death.

The UNHCR Eligibility Guideline for Assessing the International Protection Needs of Asylum Seekers from Afghanistan[17] mentions that in Afghanistan, 'unaccompanied women or women lacking a male "guardian" (*mahram*), including divorced women, unmarried women who are not virgins, and women whose marriage engagements have been broken, continue to face social stigma and general discrimination' (23).

In a case widely known as *N. v. Sweden*,[18] a female asylum seeker from Afghanistan applied for asylum (together with her husband), and her application was rejected by the Migration Board (*Migrationsverket*) in 2007. She later appealed the Migration Board's decision after her divorce from her husband, claiming that this separation and her extramarital relationship with a man in Sweden may have particularly painful consequences, such as social exclusion and possibly death, if she returned to Afghanistan. Her appeal was rejected by the Migration Court, too. The justification for the rejection by the court was that the fact that the spouses were separated does not show that N. runs a concrete and individual risk of persecution for having violated Afghan traditions. N. did not show that the alleged rumours had reached the Afghan authorities, nor did she show that her family had displaced her and that she thus lacked a network in her home country. Later, the ECHR found that if N. were deported to Afghanistan, Sweden would violate Article 3[19] of the European Convention.

ECHR, among many other reasonings, stated that 'an extramarital relationship, adultery is a crime under the Afghan Penal Code', 'abuse or honour crimes upon return were often committed with impunity' and that 'she had had no contact with her family for almost five years and therefore no longer had a social network or adequate protection in Afghanistan'.

Both in the UNHCR's above-mentioned guide for asylum assessment for asylum seekers from Afghanistan and in precedents of ECHR concerning similar cases, the condition of not having a network in Afghanistan is called lacking a 'social network' because of 'no contact with the family' and subsequently 'no adequate protection'. In Sweden, in the judgements of the Migration Court in Stockholm that I reviewed, this notion of 'social network' is remarkably being employed as '*Manligt Nätverk*', which can be translated into English as 'male network' or 'network of men'. 'Male network' (I will use this one from now on) has been mentioned in 977 judgements between 2015 and 2021, of which forty-one have religious conversion listed as the grounds for asylum application. It was used more intensively in 2018 when compared to other years. It has been used both as a part of the 'motive for decision'[20] (for instance, 'lack of male network in the country' and 'threat scenario due to lack of male network'[21]) and within the body of the rulings' texts.

For instance, in an application made in 2020, the court rejected the claimant's appeal on the grounds of religious conversion but accepted it as 'she lacks a male network' in Afghanistan: 'In an overall assessment, the migration Court thus finds that L.M. has not made it likely that her conversion from Islam to Christianity is based on a genuine conviction. The Migration Court is also of the opinion that she has therefore not made it likely that, after a return to Afghanistan, she intends to live as a convert and thereby risk incurring interest from the Afghan authorities or individuals. The appeal must therefore be rejected in this part.' In the following section, it mentioned that 'There is no reason to question what L.M.[22] has stated that she has divorced, that her father is no longer alive and that her brother lives in Sweden. The Migration Court also finds no reason to question what L.M. has stated that she only has an elderly aunt left in her home country who, receives help from a man in her livelihood, but she does not want to have anything to do with L.M. Against this background, the Migration Court considers that L.M. has made it likely that she now lacks a male network in Afghanistan and that her situation in her home country is such that the circumstances are extremely painful.'[23]

On the one hand, L.M.'s conversion to Christianity and its subsequent consequences if she returned did not appear plausible to the Migration Court, but, on the other hand, she was deemed credible in terms of not having a male network. Wikström and Johansson (2013) argued that regarding the statements made by institutional actors in the court about 'victimhood due to patriarchal cultures' (94), gender in relation to credibility plays an important role in the assessment of female asylum seekers. The legal discourse favours treating women asylum seeking converts as victims of patriarchal structures but does not find them credible in relation to conversion narratives. The possible status of asylum seeking male converts as victims of the patriarchal structure is not considered by the court. Joorman (2019) examined the Swedish Migration Court of Appeal's precedents and similarly argued that being 'young' (age), a 'man' (gender) and 'healthy' (health) is correlated negatively with the legal term 'need for protection' (144).

The Swedish Migration Agency's database of 'country information'[24] is an important part of the asylum process and an important document to the Migration Court as well: 'Country information shows, among other things, that women in Afghanistan are generally very vulnerable, their freedom is severely restricted and that in many respects they lack basic human rights in the strongly patriarchal country. Women risk various forms of violence and abuse without access to official protection and are completely dependent on a male network' (UM 6481-16:9).

According to McKinnon (2009), one of the primary challenges for women asylum seekers who make their applications on the basis of gender is that the political subjectivity of women during the legal process changes hands, and 'women claimants are often interpreted as private subjects who have experienced personal forms of persecution, not out of political motivation, but because of sexual desire, male dominance, or repressive cultural norms' (212).

The legal reasoning of the court can be construed to indicate that the presence of a sufficient male network – it does not seem important whether they reinforce the patriarchal system – that will protect women asylum seekers make it safe and legal to send them back to Afghanistan. The highly 'politicized rescue narrative' (Hurd 2013), where sovereignty and therefore the protection of national borders and its members are at stake, can turn into a 'sacrificing' narrative, not metaphorically but substantially, in migration courts.

Dauvergne (2004) showed the way that migration law spells out who is accepted into the nation. Most of the claimants' applications were accepted by the Migration Court in Stockholm, not with a refugee status but for being in 'need for protection' or for humanitarian reasons. Humanitarian admissions, stated Dauvergne, confirm the nation itself as good and generous (590). Fassin

(2012) argued that lives in modern society – a society of humanitarian reason and humanitarian government – are defined in relation to those who have power over them (4). Humanitarian government, according to Fassin, discredits the political refugees' agency and is indeed a politics of precarious lives.

Hurd (2013) in the context of religious and secular categories argued that 'women's rights and bodies are critical sites for the social and legal mobilization of the categories of the secular and religious in nationalist discourse in Europe and North America' (177). The above-mentioned excerpt from the judgement demonstrates that through the legal texts, with the means of asylum seeking convert women's rights and bodies, men, and the masculinity within the discourse of 'male network', are being constructed as the provider of security. This has been naturalized at the institutional level. Legal discourses can be seen as political constructions involving the exercise of power, and while they are shaped by social practices, they also shape social relations and institutions (Foucault 1980). In another judgement, the court expressed that 'She (F. H.[25]) lacks a male head of the family'. The idea of men as the head of the family is secured in legal narrative.

Rather than overcoming the gendered constructions on an institutional level, the Migration Court has expanded its reconstruction in relation to the 'non-Westerners' as well. The same assessment criterion, 'lacking a male network', is being used for the credibility assessment of asylum seeking converts coming from Turkey, Kazakhstan, Iraq and Jordan. Although the UNHCR's guide for the protection of asylum seekers, for instance, coming from Iraq[26] mentions 'traditional support networks' and states that households are headed by women, especially in urban areas, in the Migration Court's judgements, the 'male network' is still used: 'S.S.W.W.[27] states that she lacks a male network in Iraq. In light of the unclear information provided in these parts, the court finds that there is a great uncertainty about which family exists or has existed in Iraq. The Court considers that this uncertainty means that S.S.W.W. cannot be considered to have made it likely that she lacks a male network in Iraq.'

(Re)construction of the truth

Making a bad story worse[28] does not make an asylum seeker a liar and as Dauvergne (2004) also claimed, 'telling a lie does not mean one is not a refugee …. In an atmosphere where the incentives to lie are being increased for non-refugees, credibility is ever harder to establish, and suspicion abounds' (602).

In migration courts, judges (both professional and lay) decide on the validity of the appellants' claims in the shade of a public discourse that often stigmatizes and blames asylum seekers for economically, or illegally, exploiting the system. Discursive spaces are made possible through the intertwining discussions of migration law and sovereignty (Lynch 2013: 598).

Caplow (2008) claimed that for a story to be found credible by a migration judge, 'the facts need to be detailed, plausible, and consistent, and the applicant must relate them convincingly in writing and orally' (5). But the discourse that is believed to lay the essential grounds for credibility assessment has a history, too. While Rose and Given-Wilsen (2021) suggested that credibility indicators are bound by cultural beliefs and expectations (233), Holland (2018) argued that the understanding of a 'true story' is shaped by Western literary standards and 'this conflation of *literary* storytelling and *truthful* storytelling in the context of asylum proceedings can result in the failure to recognize "true" stories told by asylum seekers' (86).

Court judgements have a single voice: that of the court. The conversations between judges and appellants and the replies of asylum seeking converts are absent here. But when the following quote, which is prevalent, clichéd and exists in almost every judgement, is declaimed, it appears that the way asylum seeking converts answer – naturally, in the way they understand rather than the way the court requires – is seldomly sufficient:

> However, the Court still considers that the information, especially regarding his[29] own religious beliefs, is general and vague. He has shown that he has some knowledge of Christianity, but there is a lack of more concrete reflections and thoughts about what it is within the Christian faith that appeals to him, and which has been decisive for his choice to convert to Christianity. He has not been able to explain in detail what questions he has had and discussed with his friend or the meetings or other contexts he has participated in. Nor has he reflected to any great extent on the risks of converting.

Holland (2018), in her research on credibility in the United States' political asylum application, indicated that 'commonly applicants from countries with less focus on calendar time tell their stories on what sound to American audiences like faulty timelines' (90). This can also be seen in the judgements of the Migration Court in Stockholm as well. When A.K.[30] appealed to the Migration Court, he stated the following: 'He was born on the 30th day of month nine in 1387. This corresponds to November/December 2000. The information was noted in the family's Coran. He remembers starting school in Iran when he was 7 years old in 1386.' The story develops as follows:

A.K. stated during the Migration Agency's asylum investigation that he was born on 1379-09-20 according to the *Afghan calendar*,[31] which was converted to 2000-12-10 according to the *Western calendar*.[32] He has further stated that his mother told him that he was seven years old when he started school and that he was 11 years old when there were presidential elections in 1392. The Migration Court finds that A.K. was only able to provide vague information when he received age – and identity-related questions.

When the court decides on appeals, the decisions of the Migration Board play a substantial role. The Migration Board's decision consists of narratives constructed through leading and suggestive prompts by immigration officers (Keselman 2009) and interpreters. During the asylum screening process, case officers question minors in an extensive manner, so that the minor asylum seeker's humanitarian claim is reduced to specific and exact details, and they construct their legally legitimate arguments about the credibility of these minors (Hedlund 2017: 157). During the initial stages of the asylum process, so-called 'lies', 'liars' and elements of non-credibility are produced through the questioning techniques used in asylum interviews themselves (Affolter 2021: 191). On the inherently politicized question of whether the asylum screening process is based on a legal framework or a social, cultural and political context, Jubany (2021: 74) used a four-year-long ethnography in Spain and the UK to demonstrate that the initial asylum screening process (which is often accepted simply as a bureaucratic stage and a routine for implementing legal regulations) is unaffected by legal regulations. Instead, it is derived from officers' own categorizations, rules and values, which are derived from ambiguous stereotypes nurtured by their experiences and social prejudices (74).

A proven identity with confirmation of chronological age is fundamentally important in European countries' asylum system since age determines how the individual will be treated by the state. Article 7[33] of the UN Convention on the Rights of the Child, states that 'the child shall be registered immediately after birth and shall have the right from birth to a name'; this is taken to be synonymous with birth registration. So, the convention – which was ratified by Sweden in 1990, making it legally binding, and was incorporated into Swedish law in 2020[34] in a bid to further improve children's rights in the country – suggests that children without birth registration are being deprived of that right. Without taking this into consideration, producing facts for non-credibility, during the imbalanced encounter between the court and the (legally unproved) minor asylum seeking convert provides the court a hegemonic power where the responsibility for the outcome of the decision is shifted to the asylum seeker

(Affolter 2021: 194). The 'Afghan calendar', also called the Hijri calendar[35] and known in English as the Islamic calendar, is pitted against the alleged 'Western calendar', which is actually called the Gregorian calendar[36] and is also known as the Christian calendar, as something Western and thus modern and more reliable. This is a part of the above-mentioned fact production for non-credibility. While both calendars have their roots in religion – within which they have had important roles in regulating religious rituals, fasts and feasts – the latter is, through the religious–secular binary being employed, used to construct the otherness of the Eastern asylum seeking convert.

While meeting the converts with disbelief, the court, through legal discourse, constructs them as 'knowable' to avoid the possibility that being 'unknown' in the asylum court may turn to a resistant strategy for the asylum seeker convert to maintain their agency (Johnson 2013). While A.K. tries to prove his (under)age, and therefore his credibility, through his stories that are 'unknown' to the court, the court, although intellectually uninformed about the context of the convert's narrative, judges it as 'vague' and adds: 'A.K. did not make it likely that he converted to Christianity because of genuine conviction. Rather, it appears to the court that he wants to live according to Western customs and norms.'

In the context of his ethnography on the Congo, Dunn (2003) argued that 'many Westerners are intellectually uninformed about the Congo but are so inundated by stereotypical images that they feel they have a defined cognitive framework'. In light of his argument, we can argue that the discourse on the conversion-based asylum claims is inundated by normatively constructed narratives and stereotypical images about refugees that have allowed the court to see the others as 'knowable'. The discourses enable the court to 'know' the converts and to act upon what they 'know'. As Hall (1996) has argued, discourses in which Europe describes the encounter between itself and the 'others' it reinforce its identity. Within the legal discourse of the court, asylum seeking converts from Afghanistan are presented as the antithesis of the West. Therefore, they are presented as unmodern people who want to conform to Western norms.

Foucault establishes a relationship between discourse, knowledge and power. The power that has been exercised over the 'known' makes them subject to it (Foucault 1980, cited in Hall 1996: 201). The discourse produced by the court has the power to make something true and 'power operates so as to enforce the "truth" of any set of statements, then such a discursive formation produces a "regime of truth"' (204).

Due to the need to restrict and limit 'the access to the labour market for non-European foreigners, the refugee question was redefined by the economic needs and asylum was subsumed under the logics of immigration control' (Fassin 2013: 10). Judges, for almost three decades, constructed refugee status as an unattainable goal, so it became normal to exclude 'unworthy' claimants from the process. As a result, mistrust replaces trust, and to justify suspicion, one must overestimate the value of asylum (10). The lack of confidence in asylum seeking converts necessitates an idealized construction of the truth of asylum.

Stock stories portrayed as the 'truth'

All legal processes begin with, develop around and end with a story. The stories 'which are accepted by the dominant power groups as representing "the way the world is"' (Scheppele 1989: 2073) are acknowledged as 'stock stories'. Arguments constructed in these stories became identifiable and thereafter interpreted by judges again within these stories. These stock stories are portrayed by judges as truth. The legal texts that claim to be objective have a voice behind them, whether personal or institutional. Contrary to the voices of the dominant power groups are the voices and stories of 'outsiders, [which,] even if they are told, are rarely received as authoritative, as "the way the world is" but are perceived as being aberrant' (Matsuda 1987: 323). Espinoza (1997) argued that the legal system 'freezes the story', so that it becomes the 'official story' (901), but that in the freezing, the broader socio-political narrative of oppression is lost (Chiarella 2000: 191) because 'language as a product of a hierarchical society often renders mute the language of oppression' (Espinoza 1997: 901).

Delgado (1989) describes a stock story as 'the one the institution collectively forms and tells about itself. The story picks and chooses from among the available facts to present a picture of what happened: an account that justifies the world as it is' (2421). One of these stock stories, which can be found in several forms in numerous judgements and which constructs and portrays the argument of the court by the court as truth, is the following: 'Converting to another religion can generally be considered as an upheaval change in a person's life, especially for a person who was born and raised in a Muslim country where the religion is compulsory and leaving Islam can be associated with danger to life.'

In accordance with the above-mentioned 'stock story', which serves to reinforce the dominant discourse, the court asks the convert[37] to explain 'why she changed her religion and the importance of Christianity to her' (6). The answer that was received from her (an illiterate person according to the judgement) is quoted as follows:

She has stated that she had many questions and when she received answers to these questions, she decided to convert. However, she has not expressed any deeper reflections on the decision to leave Islam and has not been able to explain how she reasoned about the risks the conversion was associated with. She refers in general terms to Christianity's message of love and rights for women. Furthermore, the lack of personal thoughts and reflections in A's story speaks against her conversion being based on genuine religious conviction. This is because it must be assumed that such a conversion is an extremely important decision in the life of an Afghan person.

Matsuda (1990) specifies that the difficulty for outsiders is that this acceptance of the stock story as truth becomes a further way of establishing and reinforcing their subordination: 'Power at its peak becomes so quiet and obvious in its place of seized truth that it becomes, simply, truth rather than power' (1763). Asylum-seeking converts, as seen in the judgements, take the stock stories constructed by the court as 'the way the world is' and to prove that they are aware of the risks, however, their belief weighs more than the risks and danger, they expose themselves to greater risks, such as publishing their conversion testimonies, baptism ceremonies and other activities on their social media accounts. But the court does not pay attention to the risks that the convert is exposed to but assesses their credibility of her, this time through a film published on social media. Power, through the stock story, enabled the subordination of outsiders and quietly took truth's place: 'The film also cannot show that A[38] confesses Christianity in a genuine and personal way' (6); 'Regarding the Christian images and messages that A[39] published on her open Facebook account, the court has made the assessment that A has not made her identity probable, which is why her account on Facebook cannot be linked to her personally'; 'The court also considers that the evidence A[40] has submitted in the form of screenshots of the posts is evidence that can be easily falsified.'

Chiarella (2000: 193) argues that as an antidote to stock stories, storytelling by outsiders can break down a prevailing ideology by demonstrating that it is biased, stupid, selfish or cruel (Delgado 1989). For asylum seeking converts, their 'story' is their life. They carry their past in their story. It is that story that links their past and future. Their story which would be a vehicle for breaking down the oppression of the stories of the dominant discourse can only be conveyed by an interpreter. The process of credibility assessment, for them, has been turned into a default judgement – in their presence. The counter discourse, which may have the power to create a counter reality, has not yet appeared.

Conclusion

The analysis, through the unique and rich data presented in this article, clearly demonstrates that the asylum seeking converts' credibility is being gendered throughout the legal texts. In the judgements of the Migration Court of Stockholm, the notion of 'social network', as it is expressed by ECHR, is being translated as '*Manligt Nätverk*' ('male network', i.e. male relatives), and women's asylum applications are assessed on whether they have a 'male network' in their country of origin. The legal discourse favours treating women asylum seeking converts as victims of patriarchal structures that need a 'male network' in the country of origin. However, the possibility of asylum seeking male convert's status as victims of patriarchal structures has not been an issue of discussion for the court. Men, through the discourse of 'male network' and women's protection, are constructed as providers of security. This has been naturalized on an institutional level. As argued throughout the chapter, having a sufficient 'male network' is perceived as an adequate protection for the female asylum seekers, so it is, for the court, safe and legal to send women back to Afghanistan. The highly 'politicized rescue narrative' (Hurd 2013), where sovereignty and, therefore, the protection of national borders and the members in it are at stake, can turn into a 'sacrificing narrative', not metaphorically but substantially, in migration courts.

While discourse constructed in the judgements has intersections in terms of power, the asylum seeking converts, through the religious-secular binary, are being presented as the antithesis of the West and, therefore, non-modern religious and ethnic 'others' who want to conform to Western norms.

Even while meeting the converts with disbelief and being intellectually uninformed about the context of asylum seekers' backgrounds, the court, through the legal discourse, constructs them as 'knowable'. This chapter argues that the discourse on the conversion-based asylum claims is inundated by normatively constructed narratives and stereotypical images about refugees that cause the court to sense that the others are 'knowable'. The discourses enable the court to 'know' the converts and to act upon what they 'know'.

Legal arguments during the imbalanced juridical process of credibility assessment create a discursive space in which many actors, except asylum-seeking converts, articulate. Court judgements have a single voice: that of the court. Analysing the stock stories 'which are accepted by the dominant power groups as representing "the way the world is"' (Scheppele 1989: 2073) showed that they are portrayed by judges as truth. The discourse produced by the Migration Court has formed a discursive space, in which the credibility assessment process of asylum seeking converts has been turned into a default judgement – in their presence – and this discursive formation has produced a 'regime of truth'.

The 'juridical consequences', which are a matter of life and death to the converts, are produced and constructed through these legal processes that pervade into their existence.

Notes

1   Context, crisis, quest, encounter, interaction, commitment, consequences (Rambo 1993: 16–8, 165–70).
2   'Sociocultural and historical consequences, psychological consequences, and theological consequences of conversion' (Rambo 1993: 142).
3   On negotiating truth and credibility in the process of assessing religious conversion in asylum applications in German Administrative Courts.
4   On how individual judges vary in terms of how they make use of and weigh the results of the various state tests in their final decisions on refugee status, which leads to highly divergent recognition rates.
5   On the relationship between symbolic communication in the Swedish Migration Courts and perceived legitimacy in credibility assessment.
6   On how the space for the voice of the converts in Austrian Federal Administration Courts is constituted and negotiated by various actors.
7   On how the in-time conviction (inner belief) that the court's actors talk about is fabricated and on how it has an impact on legitimizing their decision when legal elements lack in asylum decision-making.
8   On asylum lawyers at tribunals arguing legal values of fairness and justice in refugee determination procedures and how they are subsumed by political, administrative and economic concerns to control migration.
9   On the roles of objects in conversion narratives from the perspective of materiality in Norwegian courts.
10 As the grounds (religious, political, sexual orientation, etc.) for asylum applications are not openly mentioned while registering the cases, I had to go through all 35,000 cases to discover which ones name conversion as grounds for the application.
11 A complete list of the Migration Court judgements included in this study is not included for reasons of limited space in this chapter but is available upon request from the author.
12 It can be found here: https://www.unhcr.org/3b66c2aa10.

13 Handbook on Procedures and Criteria for Determining Refugee Status under the 1951 Convention and the 1967 Protocol relating to the Status of Refugees. The Handbook was first published in 1979 and was re-issued in 1992 and 2019.
14 According to the Handbook, the term 'well-founded fear' contains a subjective and an objective element, and in determining whether well-founded fear exists, both elements must be taken into consideration (19).
15 Guidelines on International Protection: Religion-Based Refugee Claims under Article 1A(2) of the 1951 Convention and/or the 1967 Protocol relating to the Status of Refugees.
16 https://www.government.se/contentassets/a1be9e99a5c64d1bb93a96ce5d517e9c/the-swedish-code-of-judicial-procedure-ds-1998_65.pdf.
17 United Nations High Commissioner for Refugees (UNHCR), 17 December 2010, HCR/EG/AFG/10/04.
18 *N. v. Sweden* – 23505/09. Judgement 20 July 2010 [Section III].
19 'No one shall be subjected to torture or to inhuman or degrading treatment or punishment.'
20 *Skälen för avgörandet* in Swedish.
21 UM 2700-20 (translation from Swedish to English is mine).
22 Although the full name is openly mentioned in the judgement, I anonymized the name.
23 UM 6481-16.
24 Lifos is the Swedish Migration Agency's database for country information and legal governance.
25 UM 16510–17.
26 https://www.refworld.org/docid/4fc77d522.html.
27 UM2763-18.
28 See the *New Yorker* story by Sukhetu Mehta, entitled 'The Asylum Seeker' with the following heading: 'For a Chance at a Better Life, It Helps to Make Your Bad Story Worse': https://www.newyorker.com/magazine/2011/08/01/the-asylum-seeker.
29 UM 88-19.
30 UM 101–18.
31 Italics are mine.
32 Same as above.
33 https://www.ohchr.org/en/instruments-mechanisms/instruments/convention-rights-child.
34 https://ec.europa.eu/newsroom/just/items/672546.
35 That counts the years from the date of the flight of the prophet Muhammad from Mecca to Medina.
36 That counts the years from the presumed birth of Christ.
37 UM 209-18.

38 UM 210-18.
39 UM 210-18.
40 UM 4249-18.

Bibliography

Affolter, Laura (2021). 'The Normalisation of Disbelief'. *Asylum Matters*, 187–200. Cham: Palgrave Macmillan. https://link.springer.com/book/10.1007/978-3-030-61512-3#toc.

The Aliens Act [Utlänningslagen] SFS (2005): 716, available in English at http://www.sweden.gov.se/sb/d/5805/a/66122.

Austin, Johan Langshaw (1975). *How to Do Things with Words*. Cambridge, MA: Harvard University Press. https://doi.org/10.1093/acprof:oso/9780198245537.001.0001.

Bourdieu, Pierre (1987). 'The Force of Law: Toward a Sociology of the Juridical Field'. Translated by R. Terdiman. *The Hastings Law Journal*, 38: 805–53.

Caplow, Stacy (2008). 'Putting the "I" in Writing: Drafting an A/Effective Personal Statement to Tell a Winning Refugee Story'. Brooklyn Law School, Legal Studies Paper No. 94. Available at SSRN: https://ssrn.com/abstract=1104535 or http://dx.doi.org/10.2139/ssrn.1104535.

Chiarella, Mary (2000). 'Silence in Court: The Devaluation of the Stories of Nurses in the Narratives of Health Law'. *Nursing Inquiry*, 7: 191–9. https://doi.org/10.1046/j.1440-1800.2000.00068.x.

Cotterrell, Roger (1998). 'Why Must Legal Ideas Be Interpreted Sociologically?' *Journal of Law and Society*, 25 (2): 171–92. http://www.jstor.org/stable/1410686.

Dauvergne, Catherine (2004). 'Sovereignty, Migration and the Rule of Law in Global Times'. *Modern Law Review*, 67: 588–615. http://www.jstor.org/stable/3699155.

Deflem, M. (2008). *Sociology of Law: Visions of a Scholarly Tradition*. Cambridge: Cambridge University Press. https://doi.org/10.1017/CBO9780511815546.

Delgado, Richard (1989). 'Storytelling for Oppositionists and Others: A Plea for Narrative'. *Michigan Law Review*, 87: 2411.

Dobinson, Ian and Francis Johns (2007). 'Qualitative Legal Research'. *Research Methods for Law*, M. McConville and W. H. Chui (eds.), 18–48. Edinburgh: Edinburgh University Press. https://doi.org/10.1515/9781474404259-005.

Dunn, Kevin C. (2003). *Imagining the Congo: The International Relations of Identity*. New York: Palgrave Macmillan. https://doi.org/10.1057/9781403979261.

Epstein, Lee and Garry King (2002). 'Empirical Research and the Goals of Legal Scholarship: The Rules of Inference'. *University of Chicago Law Review*, 69 (1): 1–133.

Espinoza, Leslie (1997). 'Legal Narratives, Therapeutic Narratives: The Invisibility and Omnipresence of Race and Gender'. *Michigan Law Review*, 95: 901.

Fassin, Didier (2013). 'The Precarious Truth of Asylum'. *Public Culture*, 25 (1): 39–63. https://doi.org/10.1215/08992363-1890459.

Fassin, Didier and Caroline Kobelinsky (2012). 'How Asylum Claims Are Adjudicated: The Institution as a Moral Agent'. *Revue Francaise De Sociologie*, 53 (4): 657–88.

Foucault, Michel (1980). *Power/Knowledge: Selected Interviews and Other Writings, 1972-77*. Brighton: Harvester Press.

Gavins, Joanna (2007). *Text World Theory: An Introduction*. Edinburgh: Edinburgh University Press. http://www.jstor.org/stable/10.3366/j.ctt1r285f.

Hall, Stuart (1996). 'The West and the Rest: Discourse and Power'. *Modernity: An Introduction to Modern Societies*, S. Hall, D. Held, D. Hubert and K. Thompson (eds.), 184–227. Oxford: Blackwell.

Hall, Stuart (2011). 'Introduction: Who Needs "Identity"?' *Questions of Cultural Identity*, S. Hall and P. du Gay (eds.), 1–17. London: SAGE. https://www.doi.org/10.4135/9781446221907.n1.

Hambly, Jessica (2019). 'Interactions and Identities in UK Asylum Appeals: Lawyers and Law in a Quasi-Legal Setting'. *Asylum Determination in Europe. Palgrave Socio-Legal Studies*, N. Gill and A. Good (eds.), 195–218. Cham: Palgrave Macmillan. https://doi.org/10.1007/978-3-319-94749-5_10.

Hathaway, James C. and Michelle Foster (2014). *The Law of Refugee Status*. 2nd ed. Cambridge: Cambridge University Press.

Hathaway, James C. and Michelle Foster (2015). 'The Law of Refugee Status'. *European Journal of International Law*, 26 (2): 564–67.

Hedlund, Daniel (2017). 'Constructions of Credibility in Decisions Concerning Unaccompanied Minors'. *International Journal of Migration, Health and Social Care*, 13: 157–72.

Holland, Madeline (2018). 'Stories for Asylum: Narrative and Credibility in the United States' Political Asylum Application'. *Refuge: Canada's Journal on Refugees*, 34 (2): 85–93. https://doi.org/10.7202/1055579ar.

Howarth, David (2000). *Discourse*. Buckingham, PA: McGraw-Hill Education.

Howell, K. E. (2013). *An Introduction to the Philosophy of Methodology*. London: SAGE.

Hurd, Elizabeth Shakman (2013). 'Rescued by Law?: Gender and the Global Politics of Secularism'. *Religion, the Secular, and the Politics of Sexual Difference*, Linell E. Cady and Tracy Fessenden (eds.), 211–28. New York: Columbia University Press.

Hurd, Elizabeth Shakman (2015). *Beyond Religious Freedom: The New Global Politics of Religion*. Princeton: Princeton University Press.

Johannesson, Livia (2022). 'The Symbolic Life of Courts: How Judicial Language, Actions, and Objects Legitimize Credibility Assessments of Asylum Appeals'. *International Migration and Integration*, 24: 791–809. https://doi.org/10.1007/s12134-022-00989-4.

Johnson, Toni A. M. (2013). 'Reading the Stranger of Asylum Law: Legacies of Communication and Ethics'. *Feminist Legal Studies*, 21: 119–39. https://doi.org/10.1007/s10691-013-9237-x.

Joormann, Martin (2019). 'Legitimized Refugees: A Critical Investigation of Legitimacy Claims within the Precedents of Swedish Asylum Law'. PhD diss., Lund University.

Jubany, Olga (2011). 'Constructing Truths in a Culture of Disbelief: Understanding Asylum Screening from Within'. *International Sociology*, 26 (1): 74–94. https://doi.org/10.1177/0268580910380978.

Keselman, Olga (2009). *Restricting participation: Unaccompanied children in interpreter-mediated asylum hearings in Sweden*. Linköping: Linköping University Electronic Press.

Kobelinsky, Caroline (2015). 'Judging Intimacies at the French Court of Asylum'. *PoLAR*, 38: 338–55. https://doi.org/10.1111/plar.12114.

Kobelinsky, C. (2019). 'The "Inner Belief" of French Asylum Judges'. *Asylum Determination in Europe. Palgrave Socio-Legal Studies,* N. Gill and A. Good (eds.), 53–68. Cham: Palgrave Macmillan. https://doi.org/10.1007/978-3-319-94749-5_3.

Laclau, Ernesto and Chantal Mouffe (1985). *Hegemony and Socialist Strategy: Towards a Radical Democratic Politics*. London: Verso.

Latour, Bruno (2010). *The Making of Law: An Ethnography of the Conseil D'etat*. Cambridge: Polity.

Lynch, C. (2013). *Interpreting International Politics* (1st ed.). New York, NY: Routledge. https://doi.org/10.4324/9780203801086.

Matsuda, Mari (1987). 'Looking to the Bottom: Critical Legal Studies and Reparation'. *Harvard Civil Rights–Civil Liberties Law Review*, 22: 323.

McKinnon, Sara L. (2009). 'Citizenship and the Performance of Credibility: Audiencing Gender-based Asylum Seekers in U.S. Immigration Courts'. *Text and Performance Quarterly*, 29 (3): 205–21. https://doi.org/10.1080/10462930903017182.

Mitchell, Matthew (2023). 'Analyzing the Law Qualitatively'. *Qualitative Research Journal*, 23 (1): 102–13. https://doi.org/10.1108/QRJ-04-2022-0061.

Noonan, John T., Jr. (1976). *Persons and Masks of the Law: Cardozo, Holmes, Jefferson, and Wythe as Makers of the Masks*. New York: Farrar, Straus and Giroux.

Öztürk, Ebru (2022). 'Finding a New Home through Conversion: The Ontological Security of Iranians Converting to Christianity in Sweden'. *Religion, State and Society*, 50 (2): 224–39. https://doi.org/10.1080/09637494.2022.2061828.

Rambo, Lewis R. (1993). *Understanding Religious Conversion*. New Haven, CT: Yale University Press.

Rose, Lena and Zoe Given-Wilson (2021). 'What Is Truth? Negotiating Christian Convert Asylum Seekers' Credibility'. *The ANNALS of the American Academy of Political and Social Science*, 697 (1): 221–35. https://doi.org/10.1177/00027162211059454.

Scheppele, Kim (1989). 'Foreword: Telling Stories'. *Michigan Law Review*, 87: 2073.

Segenstedt, Alexandra and Rebecca Stern (2011). *Vad krävs för att få skydd?* Stockholm: Svenska Röda Korset.

Sverige (1998). *The Swedish Code of Judicial Procedure* [New, enl. ed.] Stockholm: Fritzes offentliga publikationer.

Tuori, Kaarlo (2002). *Critical Legal Positivism*. London: Routledge. https://doi.org/10.4324/9781315258867.

Wikström, H. and T. Johansson (2013). 'Credibility Assessments as "Normative Leakage": Asylum Applications, Gender and Class'. *Social Inclusion*, 1 (2): s. 92–101. https://doi.org/10.17645/si.v1i2.115.

Afterword: In the eye of the inquisitor: The politics of religious asylum

Elizabeth Shakman Hurd

'Be aware that, even if the applicant has detailed theoretical knowledge of their religion, this does not necessarily mean that their belief is sincere.'
'There are limits to the extent to which beliefs and convictions can be established as genuine.'
– 'Interviewing Applicants with Religion-Based Asylum Claims', European Union Agency for Asylum, November 2022, pp. 38, 45

In November 2022, the European Union Agency for Asylum (EUAA) issued a long-winded and somewhat tortured document offering guidance to employees whose job it is to assess religion-based asylum claims by interviewing claimants about their religious beliefs and practices.[1] At a whopping eighty-seven pages, the length of the document attests to the authors' sense that they had broached an unwieldy topic. Some handwringing may have been involved. This is understandable. The quotes above and in the notes below (see notes 3 and 4) attest to the wariness and suspicion that hover over these high-stakes interviews. The pressure is palpable, and clarity and certainty are elusive. I do not envy those whose job it is to make these asylum determinations.

The editors of this volume joined forces with the intention of exploring religion-based asylum claiming in northern Europe countries in response to a substantial uptick in such applications beginning in 2015 in response to war, violence, and insecurity in the Middle East, North Africa and Central Asia that forced and continues to impel desperate individuals and families to flee their homes in search of safe harbour. The reasons for flight are complex and varied. Rarely can they be distilled to a single cause. As one can glean from the excerpts from the EEAA guidance, even more rarely, if ever, can asylum adjudicators who make these potentially life and death decisions peer into the soul of the applicant and definitively confirm the sincerity or lack thereof of their conversion. Yet it is clear in reading the guidance that the agency and others like it are committed to doing just that. Why the imperative?

Despite the nagging doubts that permeate this document and others like it,[2] despite its colourful graphics quixotically breaking down 'religion' into three components (belief, identity, way of life) and optimistic flow charts explaining the stages of religious conversion, despite the uncertainty that demands such elaborate and detailed descriptions of which questions to ask and exactly how to ask them,[3] despite all of this, the dogged adjudicator *must* find a way through to the truth, or a good enough approximation of it, for every claim that presents itself for consideration. It is exhausting to think about.

One answer to the question of why many remain attached to the religious asylum regime is that the law requires it. To some extent we are stuck with it. International refugee and asylum law is written such that if a person can convincingly prove to the relevant authorities that they were persecuted or have a credible fear of persecution on account of religion (and/or other factors including race, nationality, membership in a particular social group and political opinion) upon return to their home country then they qualify for protection. The category of religion bears a heavy load in many cases. It appears simultaneously as a stable and knowable, but also complex and elusive, quantity or attribute that is continually threatening to escape the adjudicators' grasp while also somehow existing (or not) in the petitioner independently of and prior to the asylum-seeking process. It can be verified by the proper authorities. It is something one has, or doesn't have, as may be the case. You're in or you're out. You cannot have more than one religion. You need to know something about your (non)-religion in terms that make sense to the people tasked with deciding your case. 'What made you love Jesus?'[4]

I have expressed reservations about the modern category of religion as an object of governance elsewhere.[5] Several contributors to this volume express their own. In 'Making the Convert Speak', Markus Elias Ramsauer and Ayşe Çağlar observe that religion-based asylum claims 'operate outside the secular state's "comfort zone" of objective facts'. The unease is noticeable. Yet a raft of critical scholarship has established that the secular state has never operated in a cleanly-demarcated 'comfort zone'. There has never been a final break between religious and secular forms of public order, even in what is vaguely referred to as 'the West'. To adapt Nandini Chatterjee's formulation, secularism does not and never has implied the withdrawal of the governing authorities from religious matters, but on the contrary consists of (in the case at hand) the asylum adjudicator assuming the role of the ultimate regulator of religious affiliations and arbiter of religious claims.[6]

This perspective on how secular authority works allows us to see religious asylum adjudication differently. It is not neutral and above the fray. It cannot operate in a comfort zone of objective facts. The implications of this perspective are among the yet-to-be-fully-unpacked insights on religion and politics that emerge as a result of what Nilüfer Göle has described as 'an unpacking of secularity as a religion-free, neutral, and universal development of European modernity'.[7]

Combining these insights with the provincialization of Europe along the lines suggested by Dipesh Chakrabarty in his landmark volume *Provincializing Europe*[8] suggests yet another perspective on the religious asylum regime. It suggests a different answer to the question of why we persist in attempting to locate the 'truth' of religious conversion in the adjudication of such claims although we know it is impossible. To the extent that the asylum regimes continues to rely on religion as a category of protection it will be difficult to escape a secularist regime of religious authentication, suspicion, verification and doubt. Uncertainty is endemic to the process. This equivocation about the demarcation between the religious and the political is at the heart of secularist authority.[9] To move past it will require de-exceptionalizing religion as a category of governance,[10] releasing 'the space of the political from the grasp of the secularization doctrine'.[11]

Until and unless we do so, we are likely to continue to see a series of recognizable patterns, failures and frustrations in attempts to govern religion as a coherent object of law, whether nationally or transnationally. Variations on these patterns of secular governance appear in the contributions to this volume, all of which bring into sharper relief interesting specificities of the asylum regime.

One example is the role of expertise in the regime of religious asylum seeking and claiming, particularly in cases that hinge on the authenticity of religious conversion. This is not surprising given the ambiguities surrounding the category of religion. The authors of Chapters 4, 5 and 6 all point to the significant role played by experts in these proceedings. As Ramsauer and Çağlar explain:

> One peculiarity of asylum cases based on conversion is the increased role the expert witnesses play in the decision-making process. The crucial role the witnesses play in the decision-making processes marks a distinction from other asylum cases for which witnesses are rarely available; ... in addition to the expert knowledge about Christianity, a witness contributes to the truth-finding process in conversion claims by drawing on knowledge about his/ her acquaintanceship with the asylum seeker and the latter's beliefs.

These experts range from religious authorities, judges, authors of Country of Origin Information (COI) fact sheets and briefings, employees of national asylum agencies, volunteers who support asylum seekers, to the authors of the handbook published by the EEAA discussed above.

There is also an attempt among several contributors to this volume to make the system work better. In his chapter on the material aspects of asylum seekers' conversion narratives to Christianity in Norway, Olav Børreson Fossdal 'offers a guide to authorities that aims towards a more nuanced and accurate assessment of asylum seeker claimants' credibility'. Børreson Fossdal's chapter speaks to an interesting tension that emerges in these pages between those contributors who have one foot outside the process, such as Ramsauer and Çağlar, who express scepticism about the role of expertise and expert witnesses in asylum decision-making, and those with both feet in the process, as in Børreson Fossdal's attempt to enrich adjudicators' understanding of the significance of materiality and material religion in the conversion process and Valtteri Vähä-Savo, Venla Koivuluhta, and Johanna Hiitola's discussion of the roles of volunteer support persons assisting asylum seekers in Finland. One of the strengths of this collection is in drawing out attention to these differing vantage points.

Another theme that emerges in this volume is the importance of considering the broader contexts in which religious conversions occur, particularly given that the latter are often freighted with serving as the basis for claiming asylum. Benedikt Römer's chapter 'Contextualizing Iranian Conversions to Evangelical Christianity', for example, situates Iranian conversions to Evangelicalism in a broader context of religious and national identity transformations occurring in contemporary Iran. While Römer does not disregard the other factors that contribute to the decision to convert such as a quest for spiritual fulfilment and strategic considerations, he does caution against reductionism. Any assessment of conversions that disregards current events in Iran to focus solely on post-migratory conversion narratives runs the risk of missing a bigger picture.

The call to broaden the canvas resonates with Nadia Marzouki's study of Algerian converts to Evangelicalism, which appeared in *Middle East Law & Governance* a decade ago. Marzouki reads conversions to evangelical Christianity in Algeria through the prism of contentious Algerian state-society relations. Adapting James Scott's argument in *The Art of Not Being Governed*, she describes such conversions as 'oriented toward the detachment from state rule, as an art of statelessness' that should be understood as 'a non-oppositional practice aimed at avoiding state control while actively committing to a new set of rules'.[12] In the process she challenges the 'well-established scholarly and political narrative about Islamic conversions in which the sincerity and authenticity of Muslim converts is consistently questioned',[13] in part by drawing upon 'studies of conversions that seek to move beyond the binary opposition between reason and revelation, or religion and politics'.[14] Complicating understanding of conversion as merely a matter of choice or belief, Marzouki concludes that 'Algerian Christians' insistence on avoiding the word "conversion" ... suggests that they envision their path to Christianity as a lateral move for which they are not entirely responsible, rather than as a deliberate act of choosing a new faith'.[15]

Bringing converts and their perspectives into the conversation and moving beyond the reason/revelation binary is important. It is equally important to account for the experiences of populations and trajectories of asylum seeking beyond the Muslims and Christians that are the primary focus of this volume. Here the work of sociologist Jaeeun Kim is exemplary.[16] In her study of Korean Chinese religious asylum seekers in the United States, Kim explores 'the boundary between the church and commercial migration brokers, between sacred gift and profane exchange', demonstrating that it 'is contested, defended, and renegotiated through the interaction between the church and coethnic asylum seekers'. Kim also describes a 'migration industry' comprised of paralegals, immigration attorneys, Bible study groups and other brokers, explaining:

> [P]aralegals often provide their clients with a thick bundle of papers that pool frequently asked questions about Christianity. Some asylum-seekers would rather study these papers during their free time instead of attending the service and the Bible study group, which disrupt their demanding work schedule. One of my study participants working as a masseur at a Korean spa six and half days a week, including Sunday, proudly recalled how he created 180 index cards out of these papers and studied them day and night while diligently applying pressure to a client on a massage table.[17]

Future work in the field might also invite those who have sought asylum to offer their perspectives on the process.

The ethnographic perspectives featured in this collection would also benefit from engagement with critical analyses of the human rights infrastructure in which the right to religious asylum is lodged and from which it draws legitimacy and sustenance. If being a persecuted Christian minority grants one international protection, we are likely to see more persecuted Christian minorities. How did this set of conventions become normalized?[18] What incentive structures does it create? What limitations does it impose on vulnerable and marginalized people in need of protection who don't conform to the categories on offer? Who gets left behind?[19] What alternative protective frameworks can we imagine that would be better suited to our times, in which reasons for fleeing are as likely to have to do with environmental catastrophes and crises as any other 'push' factor?

Lastly, the religious asylum regime relies on the assumption that religious identities, reasons and actions can be cleanly distinguished from secular, material political identities and concerns. And yet as regards the treatment of Muslims and other 'suspect minorities' in North America and Europe it is often the alleged *impossibility* of establishing pure religious identities, reasons and actions as differentiable from secular political ones that legitimizes differential or discriminatory treatment. Muslim-ness is often presumed to be inseparable from, even constitutive of, one's political inclinations and allegiances, rendering an individual automatically suspect in the eyes of the authorities. Who is a persecuted religionist, a true convert, a political dissident, a witch, a terrorist or an outlaw, and (how) can one tell the difference? What is the role of scholars, judges and other experts in producing these distinctions, or, better yet, preventing them from taking hold? How does the politics of religious asylum reflect and reinforce these programmes and processes?

Reflecting on asylum-seeking in France, Didier Fassin wrote that 'the whole question to be ultimately determined is thus, for the officers, rapporteurs and magistrates, whether or not they are being told the truth'.[20] The European Union Agency for Asylum's guidelines for religious asylum interviewers insist simultaneously that 'the personal interview should never amount to a "quiz" on religion' *and* that 'if the applicant's knowledge is lacking to the point that they cannot describe the essential foundations of their new religion, a thorough exploration is needed to clarify the reasons for this'.[21] Until we sort things out, applicants will have to continue to study up for the quiz.

Perhaps historians will look back and find it curious that so many of us maintained such an enduring preoccupation with determining who has truly and sincerely converted towards or away from Christianity and other so-called world religions and non-religions, and who is merely an imposter. In the meantime, the Inquisition continues. The imposters continue to be sent away. One can only hope that the Korean Chinese masseur with the flashcards made it past the guards.

Notes

1   European Union Agency for Asylum 2022.
     The EUAA is an EU agency that supports Member States in applying EU laws governing asylum, international protection and reception conditions, known

as the Common European Asylum System. The EUAA provides practical, legal, technical, advisory and operational assistance to Member States. The Agency does not replace the national asylum or reception authorities. The aim of the EUAA's work is to reach a situation where the asylum practices in all EU+ Member States are harmonized in line with EU obligations, meaning that an application of an individual in any of the EU+ Member States will receive the same result. https://euaa.europa.eu/about-us/what-we-do. Thanks to Helge Årsheim, and to the editors, for their suggestions on this afterword.

2 There are many resources. An example from the US context is Baker et al. 2018.
3 For example: 'if the applicant's knowledge is lacking to the point that they cannot describe the essential foundations of their new religion, a thorough exploration is needed to clarify the reasons for this' (European Union Agency for Asylum 2022: 56) and 'If several discriminatory measures are mentioned by the applicant, you have to explore *each* single act and its intensity thoroughly and eventually look at the entire picture of discrimination in order to conclude whether the persecution threshold has been reached.' European Union Agency for Asylum 2022: 76 (emphasis in original).
4 'Phrasing your questions in a way that is closer to the way the applicant expresses themselves regarding their religious beliefs may result in more productive replies on the part of the applicant. A good way to do this is to formulate questions by using the applicant's own words as a starting point. For example, if the applicant mentioned that they "love Jesus", you may follow up by asking "What made you love Jesus?", rather than saying "Please explain your relation to Christianity".' European Union Agency for Asylum 2022: 33.
5 Hurd 2021.
6 Chatterjee 2010: 537. The original quote is as follows: 'state secularism does not imply the withdrawal of the state from religious matters, but on the contrary it consists of the state assuming the role of the ultimate regulator of religious affiliations and arbiter of religious claims.'
7 Göle 2010: 43.
8 Chakrabarty (2017 [2008]).
9 Agrama 2012.
10 This is the argument of my book *Beyond Religious Freedom* (Hurd 2015). This book brings global advocacy for religious rights and freedoms down to earth and into history by examining the lives of these philosophical and political ideals as they are brought to life in particular times and places, transforming the lives of those they seek to protect and reform. These efforts lead to forms of public life and politics defined by religious difference, privilege forms of religion favoured by those who write laws, control resources, govern societies (and make religious asylum decisions), and sideline other modes of believing and belonging.

11 Dressler and Mandair 2011: 18.
12 Marzouki 2012: 72, 85.
13 Marzouki 2012: 70.
14 Marzouki 2012: 89.
15 Marzouki 2012: 105.
16 Kim 2022.
17 Kim 2022: 318.
18 See Mayblin 2018.
19 See Nathalia Justo, *The Global Politics of Citizenship: Producing and Protecting the 'Deserving' Subject* (2023), for a critical analysis of national and global citizenship laws and policies with a focus on the legal production of the 'deserving subject' of rights. Justo examines how global legal norms and practices define human movement, and examines how race, gender, religion and class demarcate the boundaries of citizenship. In showing how contingent meritocratic value systems produce what are seen as 'deserving subjects' of rights through law, she offers a new understanding of how these regimes impact the stateless, trafficked and other precarious subjects.
20 Fassin 2013.
21 European Union Agency for Asylum 2022: 46, 56.

Bibliography

Agrama, Hussein Ali (2012). *Questioning Secularism: Islam, Sovereignty and the Rule of Law in Contemporary Egypt.* Chicago: University of Chicago Press.

Baker, Kelcey, Katherine Freeman, Gigi Warner and Deborah M. Weissman (2018). *Expert Witnesses in U.S. Asylum Cases: A Handbook.* Chapel Hill, NC: University of North Carolina at Chapel Hill School of Law. http://www.law.unc.edu/documents/academics/humanrights/expertwitnesshandbook.pdf

Chakrabarty, Dipesh (2017 [2008]). *Provincializing Europe: Postcolonial Thought and Historical Difference.* Princeton: Princeton University Press.

Chatterjee, Nandini (2010). 'English Law, Brahmo Marriage, and the Problem of Religious Difference: Civil Marriage Laws in Britain and India'. *Comparative Studies in Society and History*, 52 (3): 524–52.

Dressler, Markus, and Arvind-Pal S. Mandair (2011). 'Introduction: Modernity, Religion-Making, and the Postsecular'. *Secularism and Religion-Making*, Dressler and Mandair (eds.), 3–36. Oxford: Oxford University Press.

European Union Agency for Asylum (2022). 'Interviewing Applicants with Religion-Based Asylum Claims'. Publications Office of the European Union. https://euaa.europa.eu/sites/default/files/publications/2022-12/2022_Practical_Guide_Interviewing_Applicants_Religion-based_Claims.pdf

Fassin, Didier (2013). 'The Precarious Truth of Asylum'. *Public Culture*, 25 (1): 39–63.
Göle, Nilüfer (2010). 'Manifestations of the Religious-Secular Divide: Self, State and the Public Sphere'. *Comparative Secularisms in a Global Age*, Linell E. Cady and Elizabeth Shakman Hurd (eds.), 41–56. New York: Palgrave Macmillan.
Hurd, E.S. (2015). *Beyond Religious Freedom: The New Global Politics of Religion*. Princeton: Princeton University Press.
Hurd, E.S. (2021). 'Freedom, Salvation, Redemption: Theologies of political asylum'. *Migration & Society: Advances in Research*, 4: 110–23.
Justo, Nathalia (2023). *The Global Politics of Citizenship: Producing and Protecting the 'Deserving' Subject*. Ph.D. Dissertation, Political Science, Northwestern University.
Kim, Jaeeun (2022). 'Between Sacred Gift and Profane Exchange: Identity Craft and Relational Work in Asylum Claims-making on Religious Grounds'. *Theory and Society*, 51: 303–33.
Marzouki, Nadia (2012). 'Conversion as Statelessness: A Study of Contemporary Algerian Conversions to Evangelical Christianity'. *Middle East Law & Governance*, 4: 69–105.
Mayblin, Lucy (2018). *Asylum after Empire: Colonial Legacies in the Politics of Asylum Seeking*. London: Rowman & Littlefield.

Index

Afghanistan 2, 4, 20, 35, 39, 54, 62, 75, 83, 99, 125, 127, 128, 134, 139, 140, 142, 173, 174, 175, 179, 182
agency 61, 65, 81, 86, 89, 90, 91, 92, 93, 95, 96, 97, 154, 168, 176, 179
assessment 65, 174
asylum
    appeal hearing 4, 7, 9, 25, 58, 63, 105, 186
    application 2, 3, 5, 6, 20, 47, 62, 63, 64, 65, 66, 75, 79, 114, 127, 167, 169, 171, 174, 182, 183, 186, 188
    Common European Asylum System 3, 58
    decision 10, 19, 22, 30, 49, 63, 67, 69, 130, 135, 183, 192, 195
    interview 21, 22, 23, 30, 35, 104, 105, 108, 112, 113, 118, 119, 178, 194
    judge 6, 10, 58, 187
    policies 2, 4, 5, 22
    process 6, 7, 9, 11, 12, 35, 41, 45, 46, 53, 54, 55, 74, 117, 130, 175, 178
    statistics 2, 41, 45, 54, 55
asylum seeker 8, 10, 19, 42, 47, 62, 63, 64, 65, 67, 69, 70, 71, 72, 73, 75, 81, 82, 83, 84, 85, 86, 87, 89, 93, 94, 97, 98, 100, 101, 115, 130, 166, 173, 176, 178, 179, 184, 191, 192
Austria 1, 12, 61–78, 161, 168, 183
authenticity 21, 22, 25, 34, 67, 68, 91, 114, 126, 127, 128, 138, 139, 191, 193

belief *see* Christianity; sincerity

Christianity
    baptism 39, 40, 49, 70, 71, 72, 73, 85, 94, 97, 135, 140, 181
    belief 5, 11, 22, 24, 33, 34, 36, 67, 68, 70, 73, 74, 84, 94, 95, 97, 99, 105, 107, 136, 137, 155, 181, 182, 183, 189, 190, 191, 193, 195
    Bible 20, 24, 27, 28, 30, 34, 48, 71, 85, 86, 87, 88, 89, 90, 95, 97, 100, 110, 112, 125, 128, 129, 131, 135, 142, 153, 193
    Catholic 19, 21, 25, 66, 73, 74, 88, 96, 100, 159, 166
    churches
        free evangelical churches 12, 58, 130, 141
        Persian-speaking churches 151, 153, 156, 161
    congregation 6, 10, 27, 28, 29, 30, 34, 62, 68, 70, 73, 74, 85, 95, 97, 107, 113, 115, 122, 128, 130, 131, 137, 138
    evangelical 9, 19, 36, 37, 126, 130, 147, 149, 150, 151, 152, 153, 154, 156, 157, 158, 159, 162, 192, 197
    Lutheran 19, 20, 21, 26, 27, 34, 36, 37, 104, 126
    pastors 6, 40, 44, 50, 51, 128, 129, 130, 135, 142, 152, 153, 155, 156, 157, 160, 162
    Persian Christianity 159
    Protestant 11, 19, 21, 24, 61, 66, 71, 77, 78, 96, 99, 101, 135, 141, 149, 150, 152, 155, 156, 159, 162, 164, 165, 166
conversion
    fake conversions 63, 69, 73, 74
    narrative 6, 23, 24, 30, 32, 33, 62, 67, 68, 69, 71, 72, 81, 90, 91, 95, 98, 108, 109, 110, 111, 112, 119, 121, 122, 123, 125, 127, 138, 139, 143, 146, 148, 151, 153, 154, 155, 161, 162, 163, 169, 171, 173, 175, 176, 178, 179, 180, 182, 183, 185, 186, 192, 193
    process 10, 61, 69, 81, 85, 86, 88, 89, 90, 92, 93, 96, 97, 98, 113, 167, 192
    sur place 5, 21, 171

country of origin information 7, 8, 75, 192
court ethnography 41, 44, 54
credibility assessments 5, 7, 9, 11, 40, 53, 54, 55, 87, 99, 171, 186, 188
Cyrus 90, 91, 95, 96, 148, 152, 153, 154, 155, 158, 161, 163, 165

discourse 21, 22, 24, 26, 29, 33, 35, 36, 37, 65, 66, 73, 75, 91, 93, 126, 131, 135, 137, 140, 151, 154, 156, 157, 158, 172, 173, 175, 176, 177, 179, 180, 181, 182, 186

EU Asylum Agency 4
European Court of Human Rights 4
evidence 6, 20, 72, 73, 83, 84, 85, 98, 100, 139, 181

Finland 19–37, 103–122, 161, 164, 192

gender 8, 77, 78, 79, 105, 185, 186, 187, 188
Germany 2, 4, 6, 12, 39–60, 89, 101, 122, 123, 139, 151, 161, 166, 168

Hazara *see* Afghanistan

identity 5, 6, 7, 8, 9, 40, 42, 48, 49, 52, 55, 62, 63, 64, 65, 72, 86, 88, 89, 94, 95, 96, 97, 106, 110, 117, 122, 125, 128, 129, 138, 139, 140, 142, 144, 146, 147, 148, 151, 152, 155, 158, 159, 163, 164, 167, 178, 179, 181, 185, 186, 190, 192, 197
immigration officer *see* asylum decision-maker
intersectionality 167
Iran
 Iranian asylum seekers 12, 81, 87, 89, 98
 Iranian diaspora 11, 162, 164, 165
 Iranian nationalism 161, 166
 Islamic Republic of Iran 149, 150, 153, 158, 164
 Persian Christianity *see* Christianity
Iraq 20, 21, 35, 62, 154, 176
Islam
 Shia 132
 Sunni 35, 142

judgement 4, 41, 43, 44, 50, 52, 53, 54, 119, 121, 168, 169, 170, 171, 174, 176, 177, 180, 181, 182, 183

law
 guidance for decision-makers 2, 5–6
 Qualification Directive 3, 4, 5
legal system 3, 42, 43, 45, 54, 99, 170, 180
Lutheran *see* Christianity

Migration Board 171, 173, 178
Migration Court 167, 169, 172, 173, 174, 175, 176, 177, 178, 182, 183
morality
 moral discourse 29, 33
 moral proxy 105, 114, 115, 118, 120, 122
 moral tension 105, 106, 111, 112, 113, 117, 118, 119, 120

narrative *see* conversion
networks 167, 173, 174, 175, 176, 182
Norway 1, 2, 3, 4, 13, 16, 81–99, 144, 168, 192

persecution 1, 3, 4, 5, 7, 8, 13, 21, 25, 63, 142

Rambo, Louis 84, 85, 86, 87, 90, 91, 92, 94, 96, 100, 101, 168, 183, 187
recognition rate *see* asylum statistics
refugee status determination 40, 121
 refugee status 3, 20, 22, 39, 40, 41, 44, 49, 50, 53, 54, 55, 121, 171, 175, 180, 183, 184, 186
 subsidiary protection 3
religion
 definition 5, 6, 7, 19, 21, 22, 23, 34, 39, 84, 106, 168
 discursive study of religion 11, 21, 37
 material religion 10, 84, 192
 practice 5, 10, 28, 30, 36, 45, 49, 54, 93, 94, 132
 religious persecution 3, 5, 7 *see also* persecution
 sociology of religion 36

Samahon, Tuan 7, 9
sincerity 6, 7, 8, 24, 26, 34, 39, 41, 43, 44, 45, 49, 50, 51, 52, 53, 66, 74, 114, 115, 130, 189, 193
stock stories 180, 181, 182
Sweden 1, 2, 4, 7, 12, 125–146, 161, 165, 167–188

unaccompanied minors 10, 125, 128, 131, 144, 186
UNHCR 3, 5, 21, 25, 26, 37, 171, 173, 183, 184

United Kingdom 2, 7, 12, 17, 36, 121, 151, 152, 155, 161, 168, 176, 187

volunteers 104, 105, 106, 107, 109, 114, 115, 116, 117, 119, 120, 121, 135, 192

witness 12, 50, 61, 70, 71, 72, 130, 191
women 68, 107, 109, 161, 173, 175, 176, 181, 182